THE SALVATION ARMY
HANDBOOK OF DOCTRINE

THE SALVATION ARMY
HANDBOOK OF DOCTRINE

Salvation Books
The Salvation Army International Headquarters
London, United Kingdom

c 2010
The General of The Salvation Army
This edition published 2010

Publishing history

The Doctrines and Disciplines of The Salvation Army published 1881
Second edition 1883
The Doctrines of The Salvation Army 1885
Ten subsequent editions, eleventh edition 1913
Handbook of Salvation Army Doctrine 1922
Second edition 1925
Third edition, retitled *The Salvation Army Handbook of Doctrine* 1927
Fourth edition 1935
Reprints or new impressions in 1940, 1955, 1960, 1961 and 1964
New *Handbook of Doctrine* published 1969
Reprinted several times, then revised and published as *Salvation Story*
1998 with an accompanying *Study Guide* 1999
The two books amalgamated and reissued in this edition as
The Salvation Army Handbook of Doctrine 2010

ISBN 978-0-85412-822-8

Unless stated otherwise, all scriptural quotations are taken from the
New International Version

SALVATION BOOKS

Published by Salvation Books
The Salvation Army International Headquarters
101 Queen Victoria Street, London EC4V 4EH, United Kingdom

Printed by UK Territory Print & Design Unit

Contents

All biblical quotations are from the
New International Version unless otherwise indicated.

TNIV   *Today's New International Version*
KJV   *King James Version*

Foreword

I welcome warmly this re-issued, single-volume edition of *The Salvation Army Handbook of Doctrine*. We are indebted to the International Doctrine Council for most helpful work.

The very first Doctrine Book, entitled *The Doctrines and Discipline of The Salvation Army*, was prepared by General William Booth for use at the 'Training Homes' in 1881. At first it was not made available for wider use but, in response to comments that cadets were being taught from 'a secret book', a public edition went on sale in 1883. Various further editions, entitled *The Doctrines of The Salvation Army*, were published between 1885 and 1913 (which saw the 11th edition). Until 1892 these various editions were sub-titled: 'Prepared for Training Homes'. After 1900 this changed to: 'Prepared for the Use of Cadets in Training for Officership', though we should note that the use was not restricted exclusively to cadets in training. They were used by officers generally for training and study purposes in corps settings.

A new *Handbook of Salvation Army Doctrine*, prepared under the direction of General Bramwell Booth, was published in 1922. Subsequent revised editions appeared in 1925, 1927 and 1935, with reprints or new impressions appearing in 1940, 1955, 1960, 1961 and 1964.

A new *Handbook of Doctrine* was published by General Frederick Coutts in 1969 and this was reprinted several times prior to an entirely re-modelled *Handbook of Doctrine* appearing in 1998 with the title of *Salvation Story*. *Salvation Story* was swiftly followed by a related *Study Guide* in 1999.

This 2010 *Handbook of Doctrine* retains the wording of the 1998 edition except for minor clarifications and stylistic changes. The principal aim has been to maximise user-friendliness, for example by reallocating the Bible references and inserting them into the main narrative at the relevant places; renumbering the chapters to match the numbers of the Doctrines; merging the main *Handbook* with the 1999 *Study Guide* into a single volume, removing outdated material from the latter and condensing some parts of it; revising certain Appendices and introducing three new study aids by way of Appendices 5, 6 and 9.

In his Foreword to *Salvation Story,* General Paul Rader wrote: 'What Salvationists believe has never been incidental to how we live out our life in Christ as individuals, or as a global spiritual movement. Our faith, grounded in Scripture, and validated victoriously by personal experience, has been the motive force of our obedience in mission.' We can say a firm 'Amen!' to that, praying earnestly to God for the ongoing usefulness of this latest *Handbook* in reinforcing our faith and undergirding our creed as Salvationists.

Shaw Clifton
General
International Headquarters, London, England
March 2010

The Doctrines of
The Salvation Army

1. We believe that the Scriptures of the Old and New Testaments were given by inspiration of God, and that they only constitute the Divine rule of Christian faith and practice.

2. We believe that there is only one God, who is infinitely perfect, the Creator, Preserver, and Governor of all things, and who is the only proper object of religious worship.

3. We believe that there are three persons in the Godhead – the Father, the Son and the Holy Ghost, undivided in essence and co-equal in power and glory.

4. We believe that in the person of Jesus Christ the Divine and human natures are united, so that he is truly and properly God and truly and properly man.

5. We believe that our first parents were created in a state of innocency, but by their disobedience they lost their purity and happiness, and that in consequence of their fall all men have become sinners, totally depraved, and as such are justly exposed to the wrath of God.

6. We believe that the Lord Jesus Christ has by his suffering and death made an atonement for the whole world so that whosoever will may be saved.

7. We believe that repentance towards God, faith in our Lord Jesus Christ, and regeneration by the Holy Spirit, are necessary to salvation.

8. We believe that we are justified by grace through faith in our Lord Jesus Christ and that he that believeth hath the witness in himself.

9. We believe that continuance in a state of salvation depends upon continued obedient faith in Christ.

10. We believe that it is the privilege of all believers to be wholly sanctified, and that their whole spirit and soul and body may be preserved blameless unto the coming of our Lord Jesus Christ.

11. We believe in the immortality of the soul; in the resurrection of the body; in the general judgment at the end of the world; in the eternal happiness of the righteous; and in the endless punishment of the wicked.

Before you begin reading ...

For Salvationists, belief and action have always been intertwined. Our faith and practice are rooted in the Bible, personal experience and the Christian heritage. Salvation Army doctrine is part of that heritage, and it too is built upon the foundation of the biblical text as interpreted by the people of God.

This book is about Salvation Army doctrine. It explores the 11 Articles of Faith which since 1878 have been the basis of The Salvation Army's witness to the Christian gospel, showing how they are rooted in the Bible and in the tradition of the Church. It also provides opportunities to consider how they are intimately related to the personal faith of every Salvationist and the witness and fellowship of the Salvationist community.

Some people may wonder why Salvationists place such emphasis upon a written statement of faith. At the heart of Christianity is the believer's relationship with Jesus Christ, which is deeply personal and may often elude definition. Yet it is also inescapably communal and will flourish best in fellowship with other believers. Through the centuries the Church has learned to express the common experience of faith, in ways that are consistent with the biblical witness, in creeds and statements of faith.

The earliest Christians acknowledged one another in the simple confession: 'Jesus is Lord' (1 Corinthians 12:3). This was their creed. As they shared it, they grounded their personal experience in the risen Christ, verified one another's experience and called upon the world to acknowledge the Lordship of Christ. It was from these biblical beginnings that the creeds of the Church grew to be authoritative statements of the Christian faith. Three creeds dating from the early centuries of Christian faith, the Apostles' Creed, the Nicene Creed and the Athanasian Creed, have become known as the classical creeds (Appendix 1). In due course further credal statements, which often identify the doctrinal emphases of particular church groupings, have come into being. Examples of these are the Westminster Confession, which is still regarded as definitive in Presbyterian Churches, and the Augustana, which from the time of the Reformation has marked the distinctive tenets of Lutheranism.

Our Salvation Army Articles of Faith fulfil a similar function. While their origin is nowhere stated, their roots are clearly in the Wesleyan tradition. The articles bear a striking similarity in words and content to Methodist New Connexion doctrines, which can be traced back to 1838 (Appendix 2). William Booth was an ordained minister of the New Connexion, whose founders claimed their doctrines to be 'those of Methodism, as taught by Mr Wesley'. In 1865 William Booth adopted seven articles of belief for the fledgling Christian Mission. Three more were added in 1870 and the last, now number nine, in 1876. Each additional point can be traced back to the New Connexion document. With only slight editorial modifications, chiefly in punctuation, these Articles are placed as Schedule 1 of The Salvation Army Act, 1980.

Our doctrinal statement, then, derives from the teaching of John Wesley and the evangelical awakening of the 18th and 19th centuries. While there was significant correspondence between evangelicals in the mid-19th century, indicated especially in the nine-point statement of the Evangelical Alliance of 1846, the distinctives of Salvation Army doctrine came from Methodism. Our strong emphasis on regeneration and sanctification, our conviction that the gospel is for the whosoever and our concern for humanity's free will all find their roots there.

Doctrine is therefore the teaching of the Church. It is an expanded explanation of faith, founded on Scripture and developed from the creeds. The Salvation Army's 11 Articles of Faith (Doctrines) are an expression both of personal faith and a common vision. They are consistent with the classical Christian creeds and identify Salvationists as members of the body of Christ on earth.

The 11 doctrines of The Salvation Army are often taught and discussed as separate statements of faith. Rather than thinking about them one at a time, it is possible to see the genius in the doctrines by viewing them and reflecting on them in a way that identifies a pattern. The pattern is distinctively reflective of the Wesleyan theology that is at the heart of Salvationist doctrinal thinking.

Doctrines 1-4 are about God, who is the inspirer of Scripture, which provides the basis for our faith and practice; he is Creator, Governor and Preserver; and is Father, Son, and Holy Spirit, the nature or essence of the Trinity as revealed in Scripture; and is the Redeemer who is both human and divine. Doctrine 5 describes the fallen nature of humanity and its consequences, which can be redeemed only by God's gift of Jesus and his sacrifice upon the Cross (Doctrine 6). Doctrines 6, 7, 8, 9, 10 and 11 together convey the dynamic interaction of God's grace, our response and God's action in our lives as we trust in him. They explore a dynamic and interactive relationship that reflects the prevenient, justifying, sanctifying and glorifying grace of God. In other words they together reflect the *via salutis* (the way of salvation), the continuum of God's grace, the journey with Christ by those who come to faith in him. Doctrines 9 and 10 are inextricably linked, as continuance in a state of salvation leads to holiness and Christlikeness. As we consecrate ourselves (Doctrine 9), God sanctifies us (Doctrine 10). Finally, Doctrine 11 reminds us of ultimate salvation and of the consequences of our choices in this life.

The doctrines explore and define our understanding of God, humanity and the developing relationship of the Christian life, and are best understood when this pattern is kept in mind. They are unique to The Salvation Army, yet they share a common emphasis with other Christian traditions. They are the foundation of faith, providing a benchmark which helps us to interpret and judge experience in order that we might best live our faith in our own context.

Note
Each chapter is presented in two sections. The first part of each chapter contains the formal and officially approved Salvation Army exegesis of the relevant article of faith. These together constitute the official *Handbook of Doctrine.*

The second part of each chapter is entitled 'For further exploration'. These sections are intended to be a useful resource, but do not form part of the official statement of Salvation Army doctrine. There are also suggestions for reflection, discussion or an activity. These are designed to encourage and enable you to relate your knowledge of doctrinal issues to your personal spiritual experience, your life in the Christian community and your interaction with the world.

Chapter 1

Word of the Living God

The source of Christian doctrine

We believe that the Scriptures of the Old and New Testaments were given by inspiration of God, and that they only constitute the Divine rule of Christian faith and practice.

The first article of faith identifies the Bible as the source of both Christian faith and Christian practice. Our faith therefore finds its definition and defence in Scripture. The history of doctrine demonstrates the ways in which the Church has understood, interpreted and communicated biblical truth. The first article is a preliminary statement that establishes the Bible as the sourcebook for Christian doctrine.

The Bible is a book written by many writers: it is a human document. But we believe that it is also God's word (1 Thessalonians 2:13). It carries God's authority, is the revealer of truth and the guide for Christian living (2 Timothy 3:16, 17). In its pages we encounter the living God of history and from its teachings we learn to live in relationship with him.

A. A word in time

God's word has been given to us in the recorded experiences of men and women of faith over many centuries. The Bible explores the living relationship between God and his people in particular historical contexts.

1

1. The Canon

The Canon is that body of literature accepted by the Church as Holy Scripture, the revealed word of God. It is comprised of both the Old and New Testaments, and was probably first used to refer to the authoritative body of Scripture by the theologian Origen of Alexandria (c185-c254 AD). The word 'Canon' is the English equivalent of the Greek *kanon* and Hebrew *kaneh,* which means 'reed'. As a reed was sometimes used as a measuring rod, the word came to be used in that sense, and was eventually extended to refer to all kinds of rulers or means of measurement, even to rules, standards or models. Thus the Scriptures were the 'ruler' by which faith and practice were to be measured.

The first Christians accepted the Jewish sacred writings, now known as the Old Testament, as authoritative and appealed to their content to support the claims they were making for the divine mission and authority of Jesus. At the same time, they began to communicate the gospel message by the written as well as the spoken word. From very early in the Church's history, certain of these writings were recognised as possessing authority; these eventually became our New Testament.

The Old Testament originated in the experience of the Jewish people over many centuries. It records the developing, but still incomplete, revelation of God prior to the coming of his Son, Jesus Christ. Christians have always loved and respected the Old Testament while recognising that the true interpretation of its meaning and the fulfilment of its promise are found only in Jesus. Without the New, the Old Testament remains incomplete. Conversely, the New Testament is incomplete without the Old. What the New Testament announces is the fulfilment, in Jesus Christ, of the yearnings and hopes of the Old Testament.

The New Testament is the written testimony to the life, teaching and person of Jesus Christ. Its books were written to instruct believers and bring others to faith in him. When the Canon was established in the fourth century, most of the books in our New Testament were universally acknowledged by the Christian community. Those about which some reservation was expressed were included or excluded on the basis of three guidelines: authentic books were to be of apostolic origin, conform to the accepted rule of faith, and be commonly used by the churches.

By this careful process, guided by the Holy Spirit, Christians reached a consensus about the books regarded as Scripture. The authority of Scripture was not *given* by the Church; it was recognised and affirmed.

2. Testaments

The 66 books which comprise the Bible are divided into Old and New Testaments, diverse writings united by a common theme. Testament means covenant. The Jewish Scriptures witness to the covenant established by God with Israel (Exodus 34:10-28). The New Testament testifies to the new covenant, promised in the Old Testament (Jeremiah 31:31-34), established through Jesus Christ (Luke 22:20), and effective for all who trust in him.

These books, differing widely in literary form and cultural background, may be studied as individual expressions of historic cultures. Christians, however, regard them as one book – the Bible. There is one theme, the saving grace of God, demonstrated through God's dealings with his people, culminating in the saving work of God in Christ (Luke 24:25-27; 44-48; John 20:30, 31). There are two testaments and one revelation. Thus these writings stand alone as a unique witness and possess unique authority deriving from their content, theme and divine origin.

B. Revelation

1. God made known

All generations have witnessed to an awareness of divine presence, or to a conviction that the beauty and order of the universe suggest an almighty Creator (Romans 1:20). But God must always remain essentially a mystery to his creation and unaided we can make little progress in any quest to discover the saving truth about him. Since our perceptions have been affected by sin, our understanding of God is clouded and distorted (Romans1:21-32).

We believe that God, through his actions, has made known to us what we could never discover for ourselves – his loving character (Jeremiah 31:3), saving power (Psalm 68:19, 20) and eternal purpose (Isaiah 55:8-11; John 3:16). He has 'removed the veil' that shrouded his mystery. This self-revelation of God is faithfully preserved and presented in the living record of holy Scripture.

Revelation is a gift of grace, arising from God's love for humanity and the divine intention that we should come to know, love, serve and enjoy God for ever. The Bible is the record and written expression of that revelation. The insights of non-Christian religions may indicate spiritual awareness and understanding, but they do not present Jesus Christ as the Word made flesh (John 1:14-18).

The term revelation means to 'remove the veil'. In the Bible, revelation is seen to grow from the lesser to the greater and from the partial to the perfect. The self-revealing of God recorded in the Old Testament is gradual and necessarily partial, since it prepared the way for the coming of Christ, God's full and final revelation.

2. Modes of revelation

Human beings encounter God in many ways in the pages of Scripture. Through the events of their early history, the Jews were given a sense of the steadfast love of God (Isaiah 63:7-14; Hosea 11:1-4). They recognised his hand in their formation as a people, and in their ongoing history. God gave the Law to provide a pattern for living in his company (Deuteronomy 31:9-13; Psalm 119:105) and revealed the intensity and purity of his love through the prophets (Amos 5:21-24; Hosea 14:4). In the Old Testament, history, law, prophecy and other writings contribute to a deepening understanding of God's majesty, holiness and love.

All of these various modes of revelation find their focus in Jesus Christ. God, active in history, acts uniquely in Jesus to bring his salvation (Hebrews 1:1-3). The one of whom the prophets spoke is also the fulfilment of the Law (Isaiah 53:1-6; Matthew 5:17-20). The

New Testament describes Jesus' personal history and proclaims the gospel message which the Church has preached ever since. So the Bible offers what no other book can offer in the same way – the word of Life. It is a saving revelation centred upon Jesus Christ, God's living Word (John 1:1-18).

C. Given by inspiration

'All Scripture is God-breathed and is useful for teaching, rebuking, correcting and training in righteousness, so that all God's people may be thoroughly equipped for every good work.' (2 Timothy 3:16, 17 *TNIV*).

The Bible is a gift of God, not a human achievement. It results from the interaction of divine power and human response, God's enabling initiative and the free obedience of human agents. Revealed truth is communicated and preserved in written human language.

The terms 'divinely inspired' or 'given by inspiration of God' describe the ways in which the writers of the Bible, who often used many different literary sources, were so enlightened and directed by the Holy Spirit that they produced a trustworthy and enduring witness to God's saving work for humanity, centred upon the life and person of Jesus Christ (John 20:30, 31; 2 Peter 1:20, 21).

The writers enjoyed something more than the natural inspiration of an artist or author. At the same time, most Christians recognise that inspiration is not dictation, and there is nothing in Scripture to indicate that God obliterated the human personalities of the authors and turned them into copyists. Their individual styles of writing, habits of thinking, cultural background and human limitations can be seen in the biblical text.

However, the Bible cannot be explained only in human terms. The writings express not only human understanding, but also the work and word of God. An investigation into the message and claims of the Bible shows them to exceed conventional human wisdom, logic and goodness.

D. Authority

The Bible is given by inspiration and contains the saving revelation of God, therefore the authority of Scripture overshadows all other authority. The Jewish people accepted the authority of their sacred writings. Jesus concurred (Matthew 22:29-32; John 10:35b). Following the example of its Lord, the Early Church, from its inception, recognised and appealed to the Jewish Canon and saw in it the foundations of the gospel (Acts 2:16-21; 13:32-52; 28:25-27). However, it also came very quickly to recognise the inspiration and authority of writings which together came to form the New Testament. These writings are also foundational because through their message we encounter Jesus Christ as Lord and Saviour.

The Church did not give authority, but recognised it in the written word, accepting the authority of the Bible as the ultimate deciding factor on issues of true Christian belief and discipleship, and placing itself in submission to it.

History provides many examples of the Church searching the Scriptures for guidance when dealing with crises and heresies. It also records numerous occasions when the Christian community has been recalled to faith and discipleship by the Spirit through the biblical message. The content of Scripture has provided a standard for Christian life for both individuals and the whole people of God. For countless people, the Bible has proved its value as the reliable guidebook of both Christian faith and practice (2 Timothy 3:16, 17; 2 Peter 1:19-21).

E. Scripture and other authorities

1. Scripture, Spirit and Church

The Bible, then, is the major authority for the Christian. However, the Bible itself teaches that there are three pillars which provide a secure foundation for Christian faith and practice. These three are: the teaching of Scripture (2 Timothy 3:16, 17), the direct illumination of the Holy Spirit (Acts 8:29; 9:10-19; 13:1-3; 16:6-8) and the consensus of the Christian community (Acts 15:1-29; 1 Thessalonians 5:12-22). The Bible is not safely read without reference to the general understanding of the Christian community throughout history, any more than it is understood without the help of the Spirit. Each of these three foundational sources requires the authentication of the other two to ensure that gospel truth is maintained.

The New Testament authors tell of the transforming impact of a relationship with Jesus on the lives of individuals and communities. Their words remain the measuring rod for Christian experience, orthodox belief and ethical conduct, but to read them correctly we need the guidance of the Holy Spirit. He breathes through the word and brings its truth to light, interpreting God's eternal message to our contemporary situation. We also need the confirmation of the Christian community. Throughout the centuries, the witness and preaching of the gospel by the followers of Jesus has provided a key to understanding the Bible.

So the Christian has three authorities for understanding God's word and applying it: Scripture, Spirit and Church. Each authority confirms and sanctions the other two.

2. The primary authority

Within these three, however, the Bible remains the primary authority. The Spirit will make plain the biblical truth which, when properly understood, will resonate with the authentic witness of the historic Church, but history teaches that both the claimed illumination of the Spirit and the traditions of the Church, when unchallenged, can be open to abuse. Historically, the teaching of the Church has sometimes been distorted by corrupt institutional structures. At times the guidance of the Spirit has been misunderstood, misapprehended, wrongly interpreted or falsely claimed.

Scripture, however, contains the experience of the Church as well as that of individual prophets and apostles. There is an inner coherence in the message, which affirms its authenticity. By comparing Scripture with Scripture an agreement may be discerned so that the will of God is clarified. Interpretation can never be concluded, for as we search the Scriptures, we enter into dialogue with them and experience the transforming power of the message, which speaks with encouragement and correction to our own situation. Scripture is its own interpreter.

Scripture as a whole provides the final court of appeal for the Christian. Its authority supersedes all other claims, and its teaching authenticates all other spiritual truth. It is the underlying foundation upon which Christian consensus must rest, and it is the measure by which claimed illumination by the Spirit must be tested. To be accounted Christian, all other sources must conform to its essential, central teaching. In this sense, 'they (the Scriptures) only constitute the divine rule of Christian faith and practice'.

3. Pluralism

Many of us live in pluralistic societies, where other sacred writings, an amalgamation of religious ideas and humanist philosophies compete for the hearts and minds of our communities. In this setting, we continue to maintain that, for the Christian, the Bible is the only authority to define belief and direct conduct.

The sacred writings of other religions may possess insights helpful to spiritual searching, but the Bible contains the record of God's mission in the world and the nature and scope of the salvation made available in Christ. It stands alone.

Human philosophies and popular schools of thought are to be judged in the light of the timeless truths expressed in Scripture. The saving truth in the Bible cannot be reduced or revised to conform to popular attitudes or current ideologies which may deny or undermine the faith. Nevertheless, the Bible can interpret contemporary experience and inform current thinking and attitudes.

Scripture remains the only divine rule of Christian faith and practice because it presents and makes plain God's unique and unrepeatable revelation of himself in Jesus Christ, who at one particular moment in history, came as his living Word (Luke 4:16-21;

John 1:14; 1 Corinthians 1:18–2:2). To accept Jesus is to recognise the authority of the written word within which he is encountered. Jesus himself is Lord of the Scripture, and therefore the Bible is invaluable and continually relevant because it introduces us to him.

F. A word for all time

In all matters relating to Christian faith and practice, the Bible is utterly trustworthy and reliable. All that is necessary to knowledge of saving truth is found within its pages. It offers hope for the future for all who need to hear the good news of Jesus Christ. It was called into being as the living Word of God, inspired the minds of men and women, and from its pages God's living Word continues to address us with authority and power.

For further exploration 1

> 'I want to see a new translation of the Bible into the hearts and conduct of living men and women. I want an improved translation – or transference it might be called – of the commandments and promises and teachings and influences of this Book to the minds and feelings and words and activities of the men and women who hold on to it and swear by it and declare it to be an inspired Book and the only authorised rule of life.'
>
> William Booth[1]

A. Essentials of the doctrine

1. Revelation through the Bible

God is revealed through creation and human history (Hebrews 1:1; 2 Peter 1:16-21). The Bible is a record of how God works to bring about salvation through the events of history (Deuteronomy 26:5-9). We read of God making his claims, keeping his promises, pursuing us, saving us through his grace, to bring about the achievement of his purposes for humanity, including a final redemption when God establishes a new Heaven and a new earth (Isaiah 65:17-25; Revelation 21, 22).

2. Relationship in the Bible

The Bible demonstrates God's desire for a relationship with humanity. This is expressed in the Old Testament in the establishment, maintenance and fulfilment of covenants (Genesis 12:1-3; Deuteronomy 7:7-9) and in the New Testament through the incarnation of Jesus Christ. God is active in the lives of individuals, inviting them into relationship with him (Exodus 3:1-6; Isaiah 6:1-8; Jeremiah 1:4-10; Acts 9:1-9). God is ever-present and inescapable (Psalm 139), as well as one who speaks clearly at decisive or critical times in our lives, whether directly or through other people (2 Samuel 12:1-14; Galatians 1:13-24).

3. The inspiration of the Bible

The inspiration of the Bible provides a foundation for our understanding of the reliability of the divine revelation in Scripture. It is uniquely inspired in a way that is different from other writings or works of art. However, this does not mean that the Bible is infallible or inerrant, so that it is incapable of misleading and contains no human error. Whereas we believe that the overall message of the Bible is inspired and reliable, each individual passage must be read and interpreted carefully, in context and with careful reference to the whole of biblical truth.

4. The authority of the Bible

Our first doctrine establishes the Bible as definitive for Christian faith and practice. The inspiration of Scripture requires that its authority supersedes all other sources of revelation as the primary source of Christian revelation (Psalm 119:105-112). Its unique authority reveals the thoughts and actions of God.

The authority of the Bible tests all other authorities. It is therefore described as a 'sufficient authority'. Athanasius, Bishop of Alexandria (c296-c373 AD) wrote that 'the sacred and inspired Scriptures are sufficient to declare the truth'.[2] Similarly Augustine of Hippo (354-430 AD) stated 'in those things which are plainly laid down in Scripture, all things are found that concern faith and the manner of life'.[3]

Belief in the primary authority of Scripture indicates the affinity of The Salvation Army with Protestant Evangelicalism. Roman Catholic and Orthodox Christians appeal to Scripture *and* Church tradition for their authority. Other Christians, for example the Quakers, place primary value on personal experience.

The authority of the Bible is validated by the experience of believers of many races and cultures and generations who have proved the truth of its salvation and of its teaching in their lives.

5. Confirmation of the biblical witness

The Holy Spirit inspires and teaches readers of every generation, so that the words of the text become the words of God for their life and situation. In order for this to happen, the believer must be open to the Spirit's interpretation of the biblical word, which will bring vitality and relevance to the text.

There are three ways in which the biblical witness is confirmed. These are: internal verification in which one passage confirms and enlightens another; experiential verification as individuals find the truth about themselves in Scripture, encounter God and are transformed; and social verification which recognises the positive and decisive guiding role played by Scripture in the course of human events and in the lives of countless communities.

The Old Testament shows the character of God, the action of God in history and human responses to him. However, it is an incomplete revelation: a preparation (see Chapter 2). Jesus, the gift of God, completes God's saving work (John 1:1-18; 3:16; Ephesians 1:1-10; Colossians 1:15-20, Hebrews 1:1-3), which is prefigured in the Old Testament. This means that we understand Old Testament passages, for example Isaiah 53, as pointing to Christ, who gives them full meaning (see also Hebrews 5:5, 6; 10:5-7). Jesus explained his own mission in the light of the Old Testament (Luke 4:18, 19; see Isaiah 61:1, 2).

◆ *Discuss the ways in which the Old Testament points to the New, as well as how the New Testament is incomplete without the Old. Make a list of examples.*

◆ *In keeping Scripture as our primary authority, how can we avoid 'bibliolatry', or making an idol out of the Bible?*

◆ *Discuss the various ways in which God may reveal himself and how these relate to his revelation in Scripture.*

◆ *Describe the doctrine of inspiration in a way that is meaningful and helpful to you.*

B. Historical summary

1. Determining the Canon

During the first five centuries an accepted list, or canon, of authoritative writings was established under the guidance of the Holy Spirit. An understanding of the formation of the Canon shows how God has revealed himself through the process of history, inspiring the biblical writers with a true vision of his person and purpose. The basis of the Bible's authority lies in the witness of the Spirit to men and women of God throughout the ages.

a. The Canon of the Old Testament was finally agreed in 91 AD at the Council of Jamnia. The 39 books in the Hebrew Scriptures consist of books of the Law, the Prophets and the Writings.

b. The Apocrypha is also found in some translations of the Bible. These books were part of the Septuagint, the Greek translation of the Old Testament, but were not accepted at Jamnia. It is accepted by most Protestant Churches 'for edification' but should not be used alone to substantiate Christian beliefs.

c. The New Testament consists of the Gospels, the Acts of the Apostles, the Letters and Revelation. The letters of Paul and others are the earliest written testimony to Jesus Christ, they offered counsel to young churches and their leaders on matters of faith and practice – often relating to cultural issues, missional challenges or relationships within the Church. The Gospels were written to meet the need of a particular group of people for understanding the significance of the life and ministry of Jesus. The history (The Acts of the Apostles) shows how the Holy Spirit created, empowered and led the Early Church in its life and mission.

d. Some other documents became widely circulated in the Church and were collected into groups of writings. None of the original manuscripts survives but some copies date from as early as 350 AD.

e. The need to begin identifying those writings that were reliable became clear after the heretic Marcion (c85-c160 AD) issued a canon of Scripture in about 140 AD consisting of mutilated versions of Luke's Gospel and 10 letters of Paul.

f. The earliest known New Testament canon is the Muratorian Canon, a Latin translation of a Greek original, usually dated around 170-190 AD. It contains the four Gospels, the Acts and 17 of the Letters.

g. The Canon of Cyril, Bishop of Jerusalem (c315-386 AD) from 350 AD, and that of the Council of Laodicaea (363 AD), list 26 of the 27 books, with only Revelation missing.

h. The earliest known appearances of the 27-book New Testament Canon are: the Festal Letter of Athanasius (367 AD); the decisions of the Roman Synod (393 AD); the decisions of the Council of Hippo (393 AD); and the Third Council of Carthage (397 AD). Subsequent challenges to the canonicity of the 27 books were minimal.

i. Eventually Eusebius of Caesarea (c263-c339 AD), the Church historian of the early 4th century, classified all the circulated writings into three groups: the universally acknowledged, the disputed, and the spurious and heretical.

j. The present division of our Bible into chapters and verses was introduced by the 16th century. The chapter divisions are based on a scheme devised by Stephen Langton, Archbishop of Canterbury (c1227 AD). The division of the Hebrew Old Testament into verses is attributed to Rabbi Isaac Nathan (c1440 AD). This scheme was used by Robert Estienne, also known as Stephanus, who in 1555 AD divided the New Testament into standard numbered verses. Most Bible versions since the Geneva Bible (1560 AD) have used the chapter and verse divisions.

2. Criteria for inclusion in the canon

Subsequent Church Councils confirmed the selection of the New Testament Canon by the following criteria:

a. Conformity to the rule of faith (or creed) handed down in the Church.

b. Apostolic origin (written by or containing the teaching of the earliest apostles).

c. General use in the churches.

During and following the apostolic era, other writings which do not have the authority of Scripture were authored. Many were rejected as inauthentic – for example, the Gospel of Thomas, which contained some rather fantastic and dubious miracles attributed to the child Jesus.

3. New Testament manuscripts

In view of their proven spiritual value, the New Testament documents were copied and shared with other churches. Differences in the manuscripts began to appear. Hence in the years following the composition of the original letters, history or Gospels, hundreds of variant readings came into existence.

There are a number of reasons for this including:

a. Copying –
   i.   Unintended accidents – for example, miscopying a letter or a word.
   ii. Attempts to improve the grammar or style of the original or the copy.
   iii. Changes to make a sentence more understandable.
   iv. Damage to manuscripts from which copies were made.

b. Translation –
Translations varied considerably in the amount of care that was taken to maintain accuracy.

 i. 2nd and 3rd centuries: Syriac, Latin and several dialects of Coptic (used in Egypt).

 ii. 4th century onwards: Armenian, Georgian, Ethiopic, Arabic and Nubian in the East, and Gothic and Anglo-Saxon in the West.

c. Local texts –
Some communities developed local texts which contained differences from the original manuscript. They are classified under groupings usually referred to by the following designations:

 i. Alexandrian – generally considered to be the best text and most faithful to the original.

 ii. Western – traceable to the 2nd century.

 iii. Caesarean – probably an Eastern text dating from the 3rd century.

 iv. Byzantine – known also as Syrian, Antiochean, Koine or Ecclesiastical. This is a more refined text that sought to 'improve' the language. It was generally regarded as the authoritative text from the 7th until the 15th century, when the printing press was invented.

d. Accurate readings –
The process of determining the most reliable or accurate readings of a text has become a very precise science with proven criteria. These include:

 i. Earlier manuscripts tend to be more reliable.

 ii. The geographical origin of manuscripts may suggest certain 'slants' or peculiarities. But where readings from very different areas agree, that reading tends to be accurate.

 iii. Manuscripts that have been proven to be more trustworthy carry greater weight where texts diverge.

iv. Generally, more difficult readings are to be preferred because of the tendency of later copyists to 'improve' the rendering.

v. Generally, shorter readings are to be preferred, as later copyists have a tendency to elaborate rather than shorten.

vi. Where two passages agree and a third is seemingly contradictory, it is possible that the agreement could be the result of harmonisation by the copyist, and the differing texts could both accurately reflect the original manuscripts.

vii. The peculiar style, intention, and audience of the writer influences the choice of words and forms of expression.

4. Translations and paraphrases

a. The Latin version of the Bible was authoritative in the western Church. Translations in the everyday language of the people began to appear in the 14th and 15th centuries. The Byzantine text provided the basis for almost all translations of the New Testament into modern languages until the 19th century.

b. The discovery of the Dead Sea Scrolls in 1947 provided a wealth of materials for further refinement. These scrolls contain all, or parts of all, the books of the Old Testament except Esther, and have proven to be a valuable confirmation, as well as a refining corrective, to the traditional Hebrew Old Testament text.

c. During the second half of the 20th century, translations proliferated. We need to distinguish between translations that seek to be accurate interpretations of the original Greek or Hebrew texts, and paraphrases that take more liberty with the text in order to engage the reader. Both have great value, but for different purposes.

◆ *Discuss Bible translations and paraphrases that you are familiar with. List those versions of the Bible that you would consider to be more a literal translation, and those that you would consider to be more*

a paraphrase. What are the strengths and weaknesses of each?
When is it appropriate to use them and why?

C. Interpretation of Scripture

As Salvationists, we believe in the authority and primacy of Scripture in matters of faith and practice. It is therefore important that we learn to be as faithful as possible to the meaning of the text we are studying – that we learn to interpret well.

Hermeneutics is the broad discipline or practice of scriptural interpretation. Hermes was the messenger of the gods in Greek mythology. Hermeneutics, therefore, is concerned with bringing the message to the listener.

Certain factors must be taken into account:

a. The cultures, ways of thinking, and assumptions of the biblical world need to be understood if the texts are to be properly interpreted.

b. Different kinds of literature will require different methods of interpretation.

c. Each text must be interpreted in the light of other texts and in the context of the overall witness of Scripture.

Exegesis, which means literally the act of showing the way, or leading out, is the process of applying hermeneutical principles in interpreting a specific passage.

The more we are familiar with the language, the world, and the message of the Bible, the less conscious the practice of biblical interpretation needs to be. But no matter how familiar we are with the Bible and how skilled in hermeneutics, the message often still surprises – it is the word of God and therefore transcends rational explanation.

A number of hermeneutical principles are useful in the interpretation of Scripture. Some of them are used in the interpretation of any writings; others are specific to the interpretation of the biblical text.

1. General hermeneutical principles

a. Each kind of literature is interpreted according to its own genre or type. For example, poetry deals in figurative language, whereas history is more concerned with the accurate representation and interpretation of events.

b. The etymology of words (their origin, development, and present meaning) is significant. It is therefore important to gain understanding of the meaning of the words in the original biblical language as well as in translation. Similarly, the historical development of words, their use in language and their theological development are important in understanding meaning. Where there are alternative meanings the context of the text may give clues to the best translation. Similarly, comparing other uses of the word in the Bible, or comparison with synonyms and other related words, may enrich understanding.

c. It is important to apply the rules of grammar and honour the integrity of the grammatical construction. For example, to take a very minor part of a sentence and exaggerate its importance will give an unbalanced exegesis and may distort the meaning of the passage.

2. Biblical hermeneutical principles

a. There is a spiritual message to be discerned. The Bible gives an account of God's saving acts in history and invites the reader to enter into the same experience. Therefore, ultimately the meaning is not discerned solely by hermeneutical skill, but through faith in the God encountered in the text. However this does not justify 'spiritualising' texts. The 'spiritualiser' tends to find a hidden spiritual meaning behind almost every text. Good hermeneutics recognises that spiritualising is legitimate where it is clearly indicated or called for by the text itself, but when used for no reason suggested by the text is prone to private or forced interpretations.

b. The Bible has an underlying unity of purpose and message (Psalm 119:160). Therefore every text needs to be interpreted within the context of the whole witness of Scripture, and should not be interpreted in any other way. Some texts are difficult to harmonise with each other, but even the resulting dissonance usually represents contrasting aspects of the same truth or opposites that must be honoured.

c. In revealing himself to humankind, God accommodates himself to human understanding. This premise of progressive revelation suggests that over a period of time, as God interacts with his people, his will and purpose are brought into sharper focus, and gaps in understanding are closed. Progressive revelation has two important implications for hermeneutics. Where there is a strong difference, the older revelation must usually give way to the newer. It also shows that everything in the Bible is not of equal importance and value. Both these implications must be reflected in our interpretation of the text.

d. Each passage must be understood as part of the whole. To regard any text as absolute without reference to the whole context of Scripture is to open oneself to distortion and even heresy.

e. There are numerous manifestations of the supernatural in Scripture. The modern 'scientific' tendency to explain all such happenings by natural causation results in the rejection of supernatural explanations of events or experiences. However, more recently the scientific method has itself come under serious question, resulting in a renewed openness to supernatural experience. The supernatural cannot be extracted from Scripture without doing irreparable damage to the text. This is foundational to faith.

f. Revelation is contextual; the word of God is spoken in and to a particular situation. However, it remains relevant to changed contexts and circumstances, and interpretation must focus on the enduring truth contained within.

◆ *In what ways can leaders ensure that Salvationists have the necessary insight and skill to interpret the Bible appropriately as 'the divine rule of faith and practice'?*

◆ *How can you ensure that your personal reading of Scripture is faithful to the whole message of the Bible? Are you ever tempted to 'spiritualise' in inappropriate ways?*

D. Issues for Salvationists

1. Knowledge of Scripture
God's mission of salvation is made clear in the Bible. The Salvation Army, as part of the worldwide Church, is called to participate in that mission. However, the Bible can only provide 'the divine rule of faith and practice' if it is known, studied, and interpreted in order to discern God's leading. Therefore, appropriate means of biblical interpretation must be taught and modelled by leaders.

2. Recovery of scriptural authority
Obedience to the word of God is first of all obedience to the living Word, Jesus Christ. While some absolutes are evident, the Bible must not be treated as an unbending book of law controlling Christian faith and practice, otherwise it will stifle creative

discipleship. Salvationists need to learn how to read the Bible in ways that allow it to speak to both personal experience and the contemporary situation. True authority emerges from learning to understand Scripture in the light of the inspiration of the Holy Spirit and the ongoing tradition of the Church.

3. Other authorities

From the 1st century, the Church developed creeds or credal statements that summarised basic Christian beliefs as revealed in Scripture. Carrying a certain authority, these were seen as helpful guides for Christian belief (Appendix 1). Salvationists affirm the basic truth and value of the classic Christian creeds without giving them the authority of Scripture. The 11 Articles of Faith are viewed in a similar way – as helpful, but not perfect.

Movements and communities within the Church also developed guidelines and rules for their living, but these were subservient to scriptural teaching on Christian practice. The Church hierarchy became increasingly powerful, and this authority, which was concentrated in the Pope and preserved in the edicts of the Church, was viewed as binding by the Roman Catholic Church. The Protestant Reformation of the 16th century reaffirmed the authority of Scripture as primary. The Second Vatican Council (1962-65) reaffirmed its importance for life and teaching in the Roman Catholic Church.

4. Erosion of authority

In some parts of the world, the contemporary cultural climate is leading to the erosion of the influence of traditional authorities, including that of Scripture.

This has a number of consequences. Some individuals will search for a valid source of authority, but may also be susceptible to various forms of repressive and even dehumanising authority. Some people will deny the possibility of any valid authority other than individual choice. This can lead to the development of a pluralistic attitude in which every viewpoint is seen as equally valid.

In this cultural climate any claim to scriptural authority will be challenged and may be resisted. However it can be proven by the authenticity and attractiveness of the lives of those who take that claim seriously.

◆ *How far should we carry the command to obey Scripture? Are there any circumstances which might challenge this idea? What might be the reasons?*

◆ *How can we as a corps, or other group of Salvationists, ensure that we keep the word of God at the centre of our life together?*

◆ *How does seeing ourselves as 'a people of the Book' strengthen our calling to mission? What is there about the Bible and its message that helps the people of God to understand themselves as a people called to mission?*

◆ *Discuss some contemporary ethical issues which did not exist in biblical times in the same form, or at all. Indicate how other ethical teachings or general principles from the Bible can be called upon to provide needed guidance on decision-making in these matters.*

---

1 William Booth, *The War Cry* May 30 1882
2 Athanasius: Contra Gentes, I. www.ccel.org/ccel/schaff/npnf204.vi.ii.i.i.html
3 Augustine: *On Christian Doctrine* Book 2, Chapter 9.
   www.ccel.org/ccel/schaff/npnf102.v.v.ix.html.

Chapter 2

Creator of Heaven and Earth

The God we worship

We believe that there is only one God, who is infinitely perfect, the Creator, Preserver, and Governor of all things, and who is the only proper object of religious worship.

We believe that God is the Creator of the world and sustains it by his gracious purpose. The world and all that is in it was created fundamentally good because it was brought into being by a holy, wise, powerful and loving God.

A. Christian monotheism

Monotheism is the doctrine that there is only one God. This belief is not unique to Christianity; it is also held by a large section of the world's population who belong to other faiths, including Jews, Muslims and Sikhs.

However, Christian monotheism has its own particular meaning and content. Christian monotheism affirms the oneness of God (Deuteronomy 4:39, 6:4; Isaiah 44:6; Mark 12:29-31). Moreover, the one God, eternal, supreme and personal, is revealed and known as Father, Son and Holy Spirit, an eternal tri-unity. God has always been, is and always will be Father, Son and Holy Spirit (Chapter 3).

Christian monotheism does not mean that God resides in passive isolation. He is a God who is related to his creation; he is not a static being, unrelated and unmoved.

25

The great Initiator, Preserver and Governor of all things interacts with his creation. The way in which God makes himself known and meets with his people is central to the biblical record (Exodus 3:1-6, 13, 14; 34:6, 7). His desire for a holy and loving relationship with humanity is central to the message of both the Old and New Testaments (Deuteronomy 6:4, 5; 2 Kings 13:23; Jeremiah 7:23; Jonah 3:10; Ephesians 1:4, 5; 2 Timothy 1:8-12; 1 Peter 1:15).

B. The character of God

The God we meet in Scripture and in our human experience makes himself known to us as the loving God who is holy, jealous, faithful, merciful and true.

God is holy (Isaiah 6:3; Revelation 4:8; 15:4). As the one who is altogether different, the uncreated source of all being, he evokes our awe (1 Samuel 2:2). To acknowledge the holiness of God is to become aware of his utter goodness and purity.

God is jealous (Exodus 20:2-6; 34:14 Deuteronomy 4:24). A consequence of his love is the desire that we love him in return with single-hearted devotion. God cares so much for his people that he can never be indifferent to their unfaithfulness (Joshua 24:19-21; Luke 13:34, 35).

God is faithful (Deuteronomy 32:4; 1 Corinthians 1:9; 1 Thessalonians 5:23, 24). Throughout Scripture he is shown to be unswerving in his covenantal love and commitment (Psalm 89:1-37; 1 Corinthians 10:13), however much and however often we may fail him (Jeremiah 3:6-14; 2 Timothy 2:13).

God is merciful. He shows mercy to all and delights in pardoning those who turn to him (Luke 15:11-24), trusting in his love and forbearance (Psalm 51; Ephesians 2:4, 5).

God is true. He is always consistent with his character of love and righteousness. He is the source, ground and author of ultimate truth and justice (Psalm 19:7-11; 1 John 5:20; Revelation 3:7; 19:11-16).

1. Perfect in holiness

A feeling of awe in the presence of God is common to religious experience. We reach out to that which is different from ourselves, to complete purity and goodness, not simply to greater power. What we are recognising is the holiness of God. Our sense of awe is often accompanied by an awareness of guilt and unworthiness in the presence of divine holiness (Isaiah 6:1-7; 57:15).

From beginning to end, the Bible testifies to the holiness of God. From an early understanding of God's otherness that is sometimes expressed in alarming terms (Leviticus 10:1-3), the Bible moves to a profound perception of the awe-inspiring nature of his goodness and righteousness (Isaiah 5:16), which is evident in his covenantal relationship with his people (Psalm 111:9, 10). It is this holiness, this separateness, which differentiates God from us. It is this divine quality which draws us to him in worship (Matthew 6:9; Revelation 4:1-11).

2. Perfect in wisdom

While the holiness of God reminds us of his otherness, that is, his transcendence over his creation, the wisdom of God points to his engagement with us. By exercise of his wisdom, God directs all that happens towards the fulfilment of his purposes (Romans 11:33-36). God is actively involved in and with all that he has made, and his wisdom is constantly at work to bring all people to himself (Proverbs 8:6-21). God knows all things and is alongside us as the future unfolds. His knowledge is not dispassionate; he not only knows us, but he is also involved with us.

Old Testament writers saw God's wisdom at work in all his tireless activity. Wisdom was employed at creation and revealed in God's works and in the ordering of the world (Proverbs 8:22-31; Jeremiah 10:12). In his wisdom, God gave the Law to enable his people to live in right relationship with him. The teaching of Jesus expresses God's wisdom and the person of Christ fully embodies it (1 Corinthians 1:18-31; Colossians 2:2, 3).

His wise and loving understanding of us is constantly directed towards our good.

3. Perfect in power

Throughout Scripture, God's power is seen at work for our good. It is revealed in creation, in the great events of Hebrew history (Exodus 32:11; Deuteronomy 26:5-11) and is described vividly by the prophets (Isaiah 40:10, 26; Jeremiah 10:12). In the creeds, God is described as 'the Father Almighty'. By his power, God leads the world towards his own goals (Job 9:2-12). While allowing his creation a measure of freedom, God remains ultimately sovereign and works through all events towards the fulfilment of his purposes (Isaiah 40:18-31).

In the New Testament, Christ is called the power of God (1 Corinthians 1:24). The Cross reveals the deepest dimensions of God's power in the apparent weakness which disarms the powers of darkness and the agencies of evil, so accomplishing our salvation. Here God demonstrates the power of suffering love (Romans 1:16). The power of God is demonstrated as a remedy for weakness in the lives of individuals who accept this salvation (2 Corinthians 12:9; Ephesians 6:10).

4. Perfect in love

We believe in God whose love cannot be defined in terms of passing emotion, indulgence or cheap and vague benevolence.

In the Old Testament the love of God is first and foremost his steadfast burning faithfulness to his people, Israel, his covenant love (2 Chronicles 6:14; Isaiah 54:4-10; Jeremiah 31:3-5; Joel 2:13). Though constantly betrayed, God continued in loving faithfulness to lead his people towards holiness (Hosea 3:1; 11:1-11). In the New Testament, the faithfulness of God is shown in the giving of his Son Jesus Christ whose willing obedience revealed the extent of the love of God (John 3:16; Romans 5:8). In that gift, which displays the intimate relationship and complete harmony of God the Father with God the Son, we see God's perfect love (John 17:23). That love determines the nature of divine holiness, wisdom and power.

It is God's steadfast love that informs and directs his purposes and empowers his will. His love reaches out to all, whether responsive or impenitent: a covenant love, confirmed by promise and perseverance. It is an unconditional love (Isaiah 49:15, 16).

a. Love and power

Two illuminating aspects of true love are its self-communication and its self-denial.

Those who love will express love by both giving of themselves, and denying themselves, giving worth and priority to the beloved. True self-giving is rooted in an awareness of self-worth which is shared in love.

If we recognise that God is love, then we acknowledge that he must express himself in a simultaneous affirmation and denial of himself. Our own experiences of life enable us to see how God's love defines his power. To look for an unrestrained show of force fails to recognise the creative power of love. God's power, tempered by the constraints of his love, demonstrates its creativity in the gift of his Son.

Jesus' death on the Cross is the greatest demonstration of divine love, both in terms of utter self-denial (Mark 14:32-42; John 17:1-5) and entire self-affirmation (John 18:37; 19:30). God's suffering love (Isaiah 52:13-53:12; 1 Peter 2:20-24), which has transformed countless lives, is the best argument for the validity of this understanding of his power.

b. Love, power and suffering

Any affirmation of God's power and his love inevitably invites the question, 'Why does he allow suffering?' Much suffering appears cruel and pointless and no attempts at rational explanation are satisfactory. Sometimes the only real comfort comes from the assurance of the presence of a loving God who in Jesus fully entered into our present suffering. He is present in the midst of such suffering so that no-one need suffer alone (Job 36:15; Psalm 116:1-6; 130).

We may be helped by the insight that suffering is part of life in a fallen world. It is the cost of life, as growing and insight cost pain.

29

To gain maturity, wisdom and knowledge involves a measure of suffering. Pain and suffering are part of love and the cost of love is vulnerability. Christians are called to embody this vulnerable presence by standing with, and sharing the pain of, those who suffer.

On the Cross, God in Christ shared our suffering and, though no longer suffering to atone, he still shares human anguish. Such love must suffer (Luke 24:25-27). This understanding does not remove the bitterness of experience but addresses the apparent meaninglessness which makes suffering more acute (2 Corinthians 1:3-7). While no easy answers are given to the questions suffering raises, the Cross provides the most penetrating insight into the true nature of experience. It is a pointer to a plan presently hidden from understanding and a clue to the value of suffering in human lives (Romans 5:3-5; 8:17-19, 31-39).

c. A love to be shared
We best understand the love of God in relation to his revelation in Jesus Christ.

'For God so loved the world that he gave his one and only Son, that whoever believes in him shall not perish but have eternal life' (John 3:16).

'But God demonstrates his love for us in this: While we were still sinners, Christ died for us' (Romans 5:8).

This helps us to see that God's holiness, wisdom and power are defined by his eternal love. For in God holiness is an expression of pure love, wisdom is an expression of love at work, power is an expression of costly love. This love, embodied in Jesus Christ, is the love God invites us to share with the world.

'This is how we know what love is: Jesus Christ laid down his life for us. And we ought to lay down our lives for our brothers' (1 John 3:16, see also 1 John 4: 7-21).

C. Creator of Heaven and earth

1. Creation out of nothing

We believe that God created the world: 'In the beginning, God created the heavens and the earth' (Genesis 1:1). In this text, 'the beginning' does not refer to God, for he is eternal, without beginning or end. The reference is to the universe which is given birth by his will and purpose. In proclaiming that God made all things, we assert that the universe had a beginning: matter has not always existed. God brought it into being by his sovereign will expressed in his word. 'God said, "Let there be … and it was so."' Creation was out of nothing by the word of God (Psalm 33:6; John 1:1-3; Hebrews 11:3).

The universe and all it contains possesses dignity and meaning because it is not the result of chance or accident. It is the expression of divine intent and authority, which gives delight to its Creator. The creation account in the first chapter of the Bible portrays a progression from dark chaos to luminous harmony and an ordered procession of events which culminated in the creation of human beings, male and female, made in the image of God (Genesis 1:26, 27; Psalm 8; Isaiah 45:12).

God's creative power is not confined to the visible and material. All spiritual powers, even those presently opposed to God, owe their existence to him. Biblical revelation denies all suggestion that matter is inherently evil and that the physical is opposed to the spiritual. All is the creation of the one God, and the Church has rejected teaching which suggested otherwise. Such dualistic philosophies have sometimes corrupted monotheistic religions by teaching that equal opposing forces of good and evil, God and Satan, are locked in unending conflict. Christian teaching recognises the power of evil, but claims that ultimately God is sovereign and his creation good. 'God saw all that he had made, and it was very good' (Genesis 1:31).

The Christian distinguishes between God and his creation. The material world is not part of, nor does it flow from, the divine Being. God is present in all, but all is not God. We believe in the God who is both involved with his creation and distinct from it.

31

2. The problem of evil

We do not possess a logical explanation of the existence of evil in a universe created by a God of love. Both human wickedness and natural disaster pose enormous problems for Christians. There is a temptation to ascribe all such evil to the malevolence of Satan, but while referring to Satan and his angels may shed some light, it does not fully resolve the problem (Job 1). Scripture offers no explanation of the problem of irrational evil but teaches that God is in control. Ultimately, even opposing powers conform to his plans although against their will (Isaiah 45:1-24).

Evil that arises from the wickedness of human beings can be seen as a risk of our creation as free, personal beings, made in the image of God (Genesis 3; Romans 1:18-32). We were made to respond freely to the love of God, a freedom that must include the freedom to refuse. God's plan to save us from the frightening consequences of rejecting him led to the Cross (Colossians 1:19, 20). See also *Handbook of Doctrine* Chapter 6.

D. Preserver and Governor

1. God's continuing purpose

God has not ceased his creative activity. Creation is changing and the universe is developing. God is creatively sustaining his creation (Job 34:14, 15; Psalm 65:9-13; 104:24-30), bringing his world to the fullness he intends for it. The New Testament witnesses that through means both gradual and traumatic we are being prepared for a new Heaven and a new earth (Revelation 21:1-4).

In this sense, God is both Preserver and Governor of all he has made. Preservation of the created order does not mean maintenance of the status quo but rather preservation of his ongoing purpose and unfolding plan for creation. Just as all spiritual powers, even those opposed to God, owe their existence to him, so also God is ultimately Governor of all rulers and authorities, even though for the present they may appear to be operating outside the boundaries of his control (John 19:11). The redemption brought about by the

Cross will ultimately reconcile the whole creation to God (Romans 8:21; Colossians 1:17-19, see also *Handbook of Doctrine* Chapter 11).

The purposes of God are the final reference point for all human activity. In our planning, our designs for the future, we are all accountable to God. This is a source of confidence and hope. We can be secure in God's loving care, even in the presence of so much that seeks to harm us. In the face of unexplainable evil or suffering, we know that we are firmly in the hands of a loving creator God.

2. Caring for God's world

God's authority over the created order does not mean rigid and overbearing control but rather a caring, dynamic, interactive relationship with his creation. He works in co-operation with his creation to fulfil his purposes for it. He is in control, but invites us to share responsibility for his world (Genesis 1:28-31).

The relationship of God to his creation is one of loving care and concern. Humanity's stewardship of the earth is a reflection of that care, as human beings are made in the image of God. Our Creator has given us responsibility to care for his creation (Psalm 8). We have the freedom to take the raw materials of the universe and work them into good for present and future generations. That freedom should not be abused. Our challenge is to treat the earth well in the light of increasing population and diminishing resources.

The world was made to praise God and reveal his glory (Psalm 19:1-6); our stewardship of it furthers that end.

3. The glory of God

When we meet this God, we meet one who transcends our human limitations, both our finite human nature and the sinfulness that inclines us to idolatry. We meet a God who is exalted above powers and philosophies, over space and time, and yet whose awesome presence can be apprehended by those who love him. In the Old Testament the glory of God is evident in his encounters with individuals and groups (Exodus 24:15-18; Ezekiel 1:25-28), but ultimately the glory of God is seen most clearly in Jesus Christ and is experienced in the life and worship of the redeemed community, the Church (John 1:14; 17:1-5; 2 Corinthians 4:6).

E. The human response: worship

1. Responding to God

It is this God whom alone we worship. In worship we recognise and give worth to what is central in our lives. We express where our full allegiance lies. As Christians we declare our complete allegiance to the triune God. This declaration is foundational to our faith and unalterably identifies the God who is worshipped (1 Chronicles 29:10-13; Psalm 96:1-3).

Christian worship is our wholehearted response to the God who is eternally in community (Chapter 3), living and acting, relating to his creation, known by his works and revealed by his saving activity: Father, Son and Holy Spirit.

Worship begins when God makes himself known to us through his presence and his word, and by so doing makes possible the community of faith. It is completed when we express our gratitude, respond in faith, enter into spiritual fellowship and live the life of God in mission in the world.

The Lord Jesus confirmed the centrality of worship by his own practice and teaching. This was seen in his attendance at synagogue and in his personal prayer life (Mark 1:35; Luke 4:16-21), in his assertion that the Father seeks true worshippers (John 4:21-24), and in the way he linked worship with obedience to God's will. The apostle Paul also taught that the principle of worship was to be expressed in the consecration of our entire lives to God (Romans12:1, 2).

In worship we respond to who God is.
● The glory of God evokes our adoration.
● The holiness of God evokes our awe.
● The jealousy of God evokes our exclusive devotion.
● The love of God evokes our sense of worth.
In worship we respond to what God does.

- The saving action of God evokes our response in gratitude.
- The seeking God evokes our response in prayer.
- The sanctifying God evokes our response in consecration.
- The merciful God evokes our response in penitence.
- The community-making God evokes our response in fellowship.
- The loving God evokes our response in compassionate evangelism and service.

Worship is life-changing. It helps worshippers move from fear to love, guilt to forgiveness, weakness to power, irresponsibility to stewardship, insecurity to trust, spiritual hunger to fullness of joy, sorrow to comfort, confusion to direction.

2. The danger of idolatry

Idolatry is worship offered or allegiance shown to false deities, demonic powers or material objects or values.

In the Bible, idolatry is forbidden by the second commandment and is continually condemned in both the Old Testament and the New (Exodus 20:4-6; 1 Corinthians 10:14). It was the target both of Old Testament prophets (Hosea 14:8, 9), and of Christian preachers when they moved into the pagan world of the Roman Empire (Colossians 3:5; 1 John 5:21).

Today idolatry remains a persistent and pernicious enemy of true religion. It sometimes takes the form of traditional ways of worshipping objects and images. It is also seen in more subtle ways, in the worship of the state, of wealth, of status, race, other individuals, or other concepts.

It is an ever-present danger to the Christian who must never divert to religious movements or to leaders the worship and adoration that is due to God alone.

To guard against idolatry, we must focus on Jesus. By doing this we will be reminded of the glory of the Father who is revealed in the Son. The Holy Spirit will help us to resist all temptation to give to any other person or power that ultimate devotion which is due to God alone.

F. A God to make known

As it is in the nature of God to make himself known, it is the calling of Christians to share that revelation. God is the source of all love; he is the foundation upon which all longings for true human community are built. To be found by him is to know oneself loved by the one, true, merciful and faithful God. To find him is to be aware of his glory and moved to worship and praise. It is this God who calls us to share in his mission.

For further exploration 2

> 'It is mind-boggling to contemplate the beauty and majesty of God's creation. Our world is one of extravagant beauty and marvellous design. We live under star-strewn skies, are greeted each day with the grand spectacle of a sunrise, walk among the exquisite beauty of flowers and songs of birds and know the restless tides of oceans and the towering grandeur of mountains. These and countless wonders all about us render us fabulously wealthy with the endowments of our Creator.'
>
> Henry Gariepy[1]

A. Essentials of the doctrine

1. One God

Monotheism means belief in one supreme God. It is contrasted with polytheism, which is belief in more than one god, and with atheism, which denies the existence of any god.

In different parts of The Old Testament the existence of other gods is either implied (Exodus 22:20) or denied (Deuteronomy 4:35, 39; 2 Samuel 7:22; Isaiah 44:6-8), indicating that there is an element of the progressive revelation embedded in the biblical text (Chapter 1). However, the concept of one God who is significant for Israel is foundational to biblical understanding (Exodus 6:6, 7; Isaiah 47:4; Jeremiah 31:31-34). Thus Israel is commanded to worship only one God (Exodus 20:3-6, Deuteronomy 6:4-9; Joshua 24:14, 15). This can be described as monolatry.

In the Gospels, Jesus affirms the *Shema*, the Jewish proclamation to love and obey the one God (Matthew 22:37-39; Mark 12:29, 30; see Deuteronomy 6:4). The New Testament history and letters record the development of the earliest church in a pagan environment, including teaching which challenges the worship of non-existent idol-gods (1 Corinthians 8:1-6; 10:14-20).

The Christian concept of the Trinity affirms the oneness of God (Chapter 3).

2. Infinitely perfect

The perfections of God are seen in his revealed attributes. Some attributes are sometimes described as incommunicable, that is, having no analogy in humanity. An example would be God's self-existence. In contrast, communicable attributes are reflected in human characteristics. These include love and justice.

Attributes of God as a divine person
- God is Spirit – he is not limited by time and space (John 4:24),
- God is eternal (Psalm 90:2),
- God is self-existent (Genesis 1:1; Acts 17:25),
- God is unchanging – this is the immutability of God (Malachi 3:6; James 1:17).

Attributes of power
- God is omnipresent (Jeremiah 23:23, 24; Psalm 139:7-12),
- God is omniscient – he is all knowing (Psalm 147:5 Hebrews 4:13),
- God is omnipotent (Genesis 17:1; Luke 1:37).

Attributes concerned with God's nature
- God is holy – God is utterly pure and perfect. Related terms include righteousness, justice, wrath, goodness (Leviticus 11:44; Joshua 24:19; Isaiah 6:3; 57:15; 1 Peter 1:15, 16),
- God is love – includes the Old Testament concept of God as showing *hesed* which is steadfast faithfulness to his covenant (Hosea 3:1) and the New Testament *agape*, characterised by God's loving gift of Jesus as 'an atoning sacrifice for our sins' (1 John 4:10).

3. Creator, Preserver and Governor

Creation is not the consequence of a mindless accident but a planned work which is being shaped by a loving God to achieve his ultimate will. God, as Preserver, is also committed to the maintenance and care of creation. This is sometimes described as God's providence. Humanity has a role in the management of the created order (Genesis 1:28-30). God, as Governor, has ongoing creative strategies and an ultimate purpose for creation (Genesis 45:5; 50:19-21; Romans 8:18-25)

Humanity is a special part of God's good creation. Therefore we must learn to value the worth of all human beings as having been made in the image of God (Genesis 1:26, 27; Psalm 8:5). God will hold us accountable for how we live: in community, in relationship to all living creatures as well as to the whole of our natural environment. This knowledge will shape our moral choices and our stewardship of creation.

God is the guarantor of life and the rewarder of those who, even in the midst of suffering, by their cooperative participation in his work, fulfil his life-enriching purpose (Section C).

4. Only proper object of worship

To worship is to acknowledge and celebrate the supreme worth of God, who alone is worthy (Psalm 96:4, 8; Matthew 4:10). Worship 'represents the most obvious way in which the Church fulfils its purpose of bringing honour to God'.[2] Two significant terms indicate the principles of Old Testament worship. It is described as 'bowing down' (Genesis 24:52; 2 Chronicles 7:3; 29:29), that is recognising the greatness of God and human unworthiness, and as the service of the servants of God, who acknowledge a privileged relationship with God in joyful obedience (Psalm 89:3, 20). Formal worship in the New Testament is marked by prayer (Acts 1:14; 4:23-26; 12:12; 13:1-3; 2 Corinthians 1:11) and praise (Luke 1:47, 68; Acts 2:47; Hebrews 13:15). Paul, writing to the Romans, notes that true worship is found in the whole and self-sacrificial response of the believer to God (Romans 12:1).

◆ *'There is only one God.' What opportunities and challenges does this belief bring in your cultural context?*

♦ 'Reflect upon the list of attributes of God given above. How can we ensure that our personal understanding of God encompasses all that we can know and experience of all that he is? Are we ever guilty of concentrating too much upon one, or several, of God's attributes and so distorting our experience of him?

♦ 'Discuss how your observation of God's creation enriches your understanding of the Creator.

♦　　I'm not outside thy providential care,
　　I'll trust in thee!
　　I'll work by faith thy chosen cross to bear,
　　I'll trust in thee!
　　Thy will and wish I know are for the best,
　　This gives to me abundant peace and rest.[3]
Reflect on this verse, relating it to your own life experiences.

♦ Read Job 38:1-42:6. How does this passage help you to understand and appreciate Doctrine 2?

♦ 'The heavens declare the glory of God' (Psalm 19:1). This is sometimes described as the perfect worship of the universe. What is important when we offer a 'sacrifice of praise' (Hebrews 13:15) to God?

B. Creation and science

1. Interpretations of Creation

Christians believe that God created everything out of nothing (this is sometimes described as creation *ex nihilo*) for his glory (Genesis 1-2; Psalm 8; Isaiah 43:7) and that he continues to work out his purposes for the universe. However, there is sometimes unnecessary conflict between Christians who adhere to different explanations as to the 'how' of creation.

Richard T. Wright gives helpful guidance: 'Our study of Genesis 1 will point up some differences between Christians in approaches, interpretations and conclusions. We must recognise that these are differences between believers, between people who are sincerely trying to understand biblical teaching. However strongly we support a given view, we must not be tempted to judge opposing viewpoints as being non-Christian. These matters have been debated for many centuries, and still the differences persist. So we must accept as a starting premise that the issues surrounding Genesis 1 are sufficiently cloudy that no one view can be considered *the* Christian view.'[4]

With this in mind, while affirming God as 'Creator, Preserver and Governor of all things' the following issues must be carefully considered:

2. A theological account

a. To treat the Bible as if it were a scientific text book is not helpful to either theology or science. The authors of the biblical creation narratives are telling a story about a God of grace and power who is bringing the universe to be out of nothing. Their stories complement the scientific experience of unity and order in the universe. They tell of the human condition, of the unique status of humanity and of our relationship to our creator God and to the world. However, the writers are not suggesting that this story is a scientific account of the origins of the universe.

b. The creation accounts speak of God viewing his creation as 'good' and ultimately, 'very good' (Genesis 1:4, 10, 18, 21, 31). The work of God is 'complete' (Genesis 2:1), but this completeness does not suggest that there cannot be development and change within the boundaries established at creation.

c. The universe has not remained static; well documented changes in flora and fauna suggest that creation is an ongoing project. Some Christians find it helpful to accept some of the broad principles of evolutionary science and to suggest that there is reason to celebrate a creator God who is able to conceptualise and bring into being a system that continues to be formed, to develop and to achieve his purposes. So that *creatio originalis* is supplemented by *creatio continua* – the continual creation of God in our world.

d. As theological accounts, the creation stories do not provide us with information in the sense of scientific data, but they are important to our formation as the people of God. They help us to understand that our place in creation as unique, rational, self-aware beings requires that, however we define the 'image of God', we must act responsibly to the world in which we live because ultimately it has been created by God, is sustained by him and through Christ he has provided for its redemption – *nova creatio.*

3. Seeking for truth

Essentially, the truth of creation is that God is Creator, Sustainer and Redeemer of the universe in which we are created beings. Those who are comfortable with the straightforward record of Scripture as satisfying all we need to know of God's creative work will guard against closing their minds to observable facts about creation's history and mechanisms. Those who are at ease with widely accepted scientific theories of the day concerning the 'how' of creation will guard against failing to see God's initiative, providence and purpose in a creation revealing his sovereignty and glory. For all of us there needs to be a care for truth. We should also respect our God-given ability for reflection, debate and the constant restructuring of ideas in order to approach a clearer understanding of reality.

◆ *Discuss the arguments set out in this section. How would you explain the relationship between creation and science to a new Christian?*

C. The problem of suffering

Suffering is both an intellectual problem and an experiential challenge to faith. 'How can a loving God allow evil and suffering?' is the primary question of theodicy. Theodicy is concerned with how it is possible to maintain, in the face of innocent suffering, that an all-powerful God is a God of love.

1. Old Testament interpretations of suffering

a. In Genesis 1-3 we see that the world was intended to be a good place. Disobedience resulted in pain and suffering and, in consequence, all humanity is vulnerable to it.

b. There is a cause-and-effect relationship built into creation. The cycle of sin is perpetuated from generation to generation (Exodus 34:6, 7; Numbers 14:18; Deuteronomy 5:9, 10).

c. The prophets of the pre-exilic period (Amos, Hosea, Isaiah, Micah, Jeremiah and Ezekiel) identified the injustice and idolatry of their society. They made a connection between the sins of the people, especially the leaders of the people, and the national disaster which was coming. God is active in the world to execute justice, even to the extent that he uses enemies to torment the disobedient (Amos 3:11-15). There is no escape for the pious or the righteous. All suffer.

d. In Deuteronomy the consequence of choosing to keep the Law will be prosperity and long life (Deuteronomy 30:15-20). The Deuteronomic understanding of God's part in human suffering keeps a balance between God's power and justice.

e. During and after the exile the doctrine of retribution moves away from a strictly corporate understanding. Individuals make their own decisions and determine their own future, emphasising personal accountability in contrast to c. above (Ezekiel 18:4; Jeremiah 31:29, 30).

f. Isaiah (40-55) did not deny that the suffering of the people was punishment for sin, but added that it should not be defined only in negative terms. Suffering is part of God's work in the world. The people are the witnesses of God (43:9, 10), called to be a 'light to the nations' (42:6; 49:6). God will work some greater good for others out of the suffering of the faithful. This is the concept of a group or one individual suffering for others – vicarious suffering (53:4-6).

g. The book of Job examines in great detail answers that earlier traditions had to offer in order to find meaning in suffering. It is clear that Job is a case of innocent suffering. He does not deserve his fate and protests that he is a victim of injustice. God answers with a 'no answer'. The wonders of creation point to the presence and care of God in the world even when we cannot clearly see God's activity either in our personal or corporate history (38:1 – 42:6). Job is content to live with the mystery (42:3) and leave the unknown in the hands of God whom he can trust. This is an attempt to be willing not to push the logic of theodicy to the point where we must blame humans in order to protect God's justice and power, or doubt God's justice in order to protect our integrity (42:1, 2). This attitude can also be seen in the Psalms of Lament, in which continued trust in God is important, even in times of suffering (Psalm 88).

h. Only rarely is the demonic mentioned as a contributor to suffering. Three passages point to the relationship between the problem of evil and the problem of suffering (Job 1-2; 1 Chronicles 21; Zechariah 3).

i. In Apocalyptic writings, for example the book of Daniel, the distant future is seen as the time when justice will be finally achieved. Suffering is to be expected in the present age which is judged to be under the dominion of evil powers.

2. New Testament interpretations of suffering

For the early Christians the big questions were how to make sense of the suffering of Jesus and how to understand the suffering they themselves experienced. The New Testament deals with these dilemmas.

a. The disciples persistently failed to understand the coming suffering of Christ and his redemptive mission (Matthew 16:21-23), but after the Resurrection they were taught the necessity for his atoning suffering (Luke 24:13-35). This became a focal point of the preaching of the apostles (Acts 2:23; 17:3; 26:22, 23) and in the letters of Paul (2 Corinthians 5:15; Ephesians 5:2).

b. The suffering of Jesus was for a greater good – the salvation of humanity (John 3:16). The followers of Jesus should be willing to suffer for the sake of spreading the gospel (John15:18-21). This could be interpreted as suffering for others.

c. Even though Christians share the experience of suffering with all humanity, they can respond differently as their experience of God gives it meaning (Hebrews 12:5-13). Christians are not saved from suffering, but saved in suffering and sustained by the fact that Christ suffers with them.

d. The New Testament clearly rejects the doctrine of retribution which connects sin with punishment, either individual or corporate (John 9:1-3). In a corrupt world, it seems that the ones who appear to have success may be the evil ones who have come unjustly to their reward (Luke 6:20-26). Suffering may be a sign that you are one of the faithful, rather than being the consequence of a sinful life (Acts 14:22, 1 Peter 4:12-19).

e. In the midst of suffering there is the promise of resurrection and the day of judgment. Justice will finally be done. There is an assurance that God can work for ultimate good (Romans 8:28-39). Paul said that we can rejoice in our suffering (Colossians

1:24). It is possible in retrospect to realise that lessons have been learned and to understand that God's presence has been with us even in the depths of suffering.

f. The Gospels relate some suffering to the demonic. In Matthew, Mark and Luke the casting out of demons was a significant and powerful aspect of Jesus' ministry which indicated the arrival of the Kingdom of God. The working of evil spirits was believed to cause violently insane behaviour (Matthew 8:28; Mark 5:1-5), the inability to speak (Matthew 9:32) or to hear (Mark 9:25), blindness (Matthew 12:22), characteristics of epilepsy (Luke 9:39) and apparent tendencies to self-destruction (Matthew 17:15). It is not that all illness is attributed to the presence of evil spirits, rather that all three Gospels describe those people whose illness is attributed to the demonic in different ways from those suffering with other diseases (Matthew 4:24; Mark 1:32; Luke 7:21). Mark especially differentiated between the two and never uses the word 'heal' in connection with demons. There are no references to the casting out of demons in the Gospel of John. In the rest of the New Testament references to demons focus on moral and spiritual opposition to believers rather than on physical affliction.

3. Suffering in Christian theology – Does God suffer?

a. Due to Hellenistic (Greek) influence in the early Christian environment, the classic pagan idea of the impassibility of God, in which God is beyond all human emotions and pain, came into Christian theology. It was argued that God cannot be affected by anything outside himself because this would suggest that God can change and therefore that he is not perfect, or would not be perfect once the change had taken place. Anselm of Canterbury (c1033-1109 AD) argued that God is compassionate, in terms of our experience, because we experience the effect of compassion. God is not compassionate, in terms of his own being, because he does not experience the feeling (*affectus*) of compassion.[5]

b. In contrast, Martin Luther's (1483-1546 AD) theology of the Cross contrasted two ways of thinking about God: 'the theology of glory', that is knowledge of God through his works in creation and history, and 'the theology of the Cross,' or knowledge of God through his sufferings and Jesus' death on the Cross.[6] He used a phrase from the mysticism of the Middle Ages 'the crucified God', to speak of the way in which God shares in the suffering of the crucified Christ.

c. In the 1920s, reflection upon the horrors of the First World War made a deep impact on Christian theology, resulting in renewed interest in this concept. In the Second World War, German theologian Dietrich Bonhoeffer (1906-1945 AD) contrasted Christianity with other religions, arguing that human beings look for the power of God in the world, but the Bible directs us to God's powerlessness and suffering. 'Only the suffering God can help.'[7]

d. Kazoh Kitamori (1916-1998 AD), also drawing on Luther's theology of the Cross, argued that true love was rooted in pain. God's own pain and suffering enables him to give meaning and dignity to the human experience and heals our pain.[8]

e. Jürgen Moltmann (1926-) argues that a God who cannot suffer is a deficient, imperfect God who also cannot love. God cannot be forced to change or undergo suffering, but his suffering is a direct consequence of the divine willingness to suffer. The Cross provides the foundation for Christian theology, as the Son suffers dying and the Father suffers the death of the Son in order to bring about human redemption. The Father suffers the loss of the Son, whom he has given, to suffering pain and death. The Father and the Son are deeply separated by the forsakenness of the Son and yet also one in their willingness to suffer.[9]

f. The problem of human suffering continues to be explored in the work of authors, including theologians, poets and novelists.

Theodicy remains one of the most challenging aspects of Christian doctrine, which, even if not explored intellectually, affects the experience of every person.

◆ *In* The Problem of Pain, *C. S. Lewis (1898-1963 AD) deals with pain seen in the light of God's love. His conclusion is that God inserts pain into our lives in order to awaken us: 'But pain insists upon being attended to. God whispers to us in our pleasures, speaks in our conscience, but shouts in our pain: it is his megaphone to rouse a deaf world.'[10] However, at a later date Lewis was to discover that his personal experience of grief resulted in a sense of forsakenness and absence of God followed by a growing acknowledgement of our limited understanding, but a certainty of God's presence. Ultimately, pain teaches us to love and to be loved.[11] To what extent does Lewis's conclusion resonate with your own experience?*

◆ *How would you respond to a friend who is struggling with the experience of suffering and asks you, as a Christian, to give an explanation of why God lets this happen?*

D. Issues for Salvationists

1. Worship
Doctrine 2 reminds us that we worship a God who is the infinitely perfect Creator and Sustainer of creation. Salvationists need to ensure that our worship acknowledges and celebrates all the attributes of God and not just those which resonate most closely with our own experience of him.

2. Accountability
It has sometimes been suggested that human beings have exceeded the sacred trust given at creation (Genesis 1:29, 30) and in 'ruling over' the world they have abused it rather than been a steward of its resources. The Salvation Army, and individual Salvationists, have a responsibility to care for the created world. This is not always easy

in parts of the world where resources for humanity are scarce and life is precarious. Nevertheless, we need to develop a sense of accountability for our life in the world and our behaviour towards our own and future generations.

3. Human worth

The Salvation Army's international mission statement affirms that 'its mission is to preach the gospel of Jesus Christ and meet human needs in his name without discrimination'. This statement implies the worth and dignity of all of humanity as made in the image of God (Genesis 1:26, 27).

The compassion of the Army's social action depends upon an understanding that God is Father of all without discrimination or partiality. In particular, we recognise in Scripture a divine emphasis on the pressing needs of the poor and underprivileged. This 'bias to the poor' gives a priority to the mission of the Christian Church and has been recognised and acted upon by the Army since its founding days.

The establishment of the International Social Justice Commission has provided a major impetus and a point of international coordination for social justice issues. As 'The Salvation Army's strategic voice to advocate for human dignity and social justice with the world's poor and oppressed'[12] it speaks on behalf of the powerless in the international public arena, particularly the United Nations, and works to address social injustice in a manner which is consistent with Salvation Army principles and purposes. In addition it encourages and offers guidance to territories throughout the world in addressing social justice issues in the local context.

◆ *'We call Salvationists worldwide to worship and proclaim the living God, and to seek in every meeting a vital encounter with the Lord of life, using relevant cultural forms and languages.'*[13] *What factors must be considered? How does your own cultural context affect your answer?*

49

◆ *What practical things can The Salvation Army do to ensure that it is a wise steward of the earth's resources?*

◆ *Read Luke 4:18, 19. What can you do to live out the mission of Jesus? Make a plan of action.*

---

[1] Henry Gariepy, *Wisdom To Live By,* quoted in Henry Gariepy 2000 *A Salvationist Treasury* Alexandria: Crest Books :220

[2] Bruce Milne, 1982 *Know the Truth.* Leicester: IVP: 221

[3] John Lawley, *The Song Book of The Salvation Army* 761:2

[4] Richard T. Wright, 2003 *Biology Through the Eyes of Faith* Harper & Son:80-81

[5] *Anselm, Proslogion 8 http://www.ccel.org/ccel/anselm/basic_works.iii.ix.html*

[6] Martin Luther, *Heidelberg Disputation* 1518, Clause 21
http://bookofconcord.org/heidelberg.php

[7] John de Gruchy, ed. 1987 *Dietrich Bonhoeffer: Witness to Jesus Christ. Selected Writings.*

[8] Kazoh Kitamori, 1965 *A Theology of the Pain of God.* Richmond VA: John Knox Press

[9] Jürgen Moltmann, 1974 *The Crucified God.* London: SCM: 251

[10] C. S Lewis, 1940 *The Problem of Pain* London: Fontana: 81

[11] C. S Lewis, 1961, *A Grief Observed.* London: Faber and Faber: 7-8, 56-58

[12] International Social Justice Commission: *Singing the Songs of Justice*

[13] International Spiritual Life Commission Report: *Call to Worship* see Appendix 4

Chapter 3

The God who is never alone

We believe that there are three persons in the Godhead – the Father, the Son and the Holy Ghost, undivided in essence and co-equal in power and glory.

We believe in one God who is at the same time three.

Christians worship this one God as Father, Son and Holy Spirit. This is the doctrine of the Trinity, which is essential to an understanding of God as revealed in the Bible, and is basic to the Christian faith.

A. A God in fellowship

God is never alone. Within himself he enjoys perfect and full fellowship. Although God is always three, he is not three individuals who could be in competition or opposition. He is three persons, always united in being, attitude and action, a threefold God of love.

God is a communion, a community of being, whose three persons share in intimate fellowship with one another. He is always Father, Son and Holy Spirit, each one always in fellowship with the others.

Father, Son and Holy Spirit represent a dynamic circulation of life among equal persons without any authority or superiority of one over another. The persons are distinct, but united; different but not separate from one another. Any attempt to develop a false hierarchy of power and glory within the Trinity is to weaken the integrity of the Godhead and to undermine the complete unity of the persons.

51

The three-in-one definition attempts to describe a God who as Father creates, governs and sustains; as Son redeems, befriends and disciples; and as Holy Spirit sanctifies, counsels and empowers. In persons and work he is three: in personality, love and intention he is one.

The three persons of the Trinity are continually revealing one another to us. The New Testament tells us that the Spirit bears witness to Jesus (John 15:26), Jesus Christ reveals the Father (Matthew 11:25-27; John 14:8-14) and testifies to the Spirit (John 14:16, 26), the Father testifies to the Son (Matthew 3:17).

God created humanity because love expressed in community is the very essence of his nature, not because of any incompleteness within himself. As human beings, we are created in the image of God with a natural capacity to relate to one another. We reach our fulfilment only when we are in community with him and with one another. Without him and without each other, we lack wholeness and the possibility of gaining maturity through developing relationships.

God, then, is always in fellowship within himself and with us (2 Corinthians 13:14). The Bible witnesses to this truth, which is the foundation of the Christian doctrine of salvation and of Christian experience itself. An understanding of the Trinity helps us identify, and so avoid, many heresies.

When we speak of the triune God as one, it is in the sense of his wholeness and togetherness, and when we speak of God as three, it is in the sense of his threefold nature.

B. God the Father

The picture of God as a father can be found in the Old Testament (Deuteronomy 32:6; Isaiah 63:16; Malachi 2:10), but it is in the New Testament that God's Fatherhood is given prominence through the teaching of Jesus (Matthew 6:5-15). He taught that God is Father and his own relationship with God is described in his use of the intimate phrase, 'Abba, Father' (Mark 14:36). God the Father is the one with whom Jesus enjoyed unimpaired fellowship and to whom he offered complete loving obedience. He is the Father in whom Jesus trusted when tempted in Gethsemane, and to whom he could surrender his spirit when dying on the Cross (Luke 23:46). The Son was raised from death through the glory of the Father (Romans 6:4). Through Jesus Christ, he is our Father, too.

Like Jesus, therefore, we now have a relationship with God similar to that of a child with his father. The writings of Paul and others endorse the intimate words of the Lord Jesus. As Paul says: 'You received the Spirit of sonship. And by him we cry, 'Abba, Father' (Romans 8:15).

There are some challenges associated with this image. For example, it is possible to focus unduly on the maleness of the Father. The scriptural description of God as Father does not mean that God is male, but rather that he acts towards us as a loving father would. The Bible also describes God as loving us with the tenderness and loving care associated with motherhood (Isaiah 49:15; 66:13).

Another difficulty is that human fatherhood is too often a travesty of true paternity. Even when faithful and loving, it is imperfect. There is evidence that Jesus was aware of this difficulty but believed that it could be overcome, for he said that though human fathers were faulty they still gave good gifts to their children, and pointed to a perfect divine Fatherhood that would give to those who asked in faith (Luke 11:5-13).

Jesus' own life and character defines his meaning, for he tells us that to have seen him is to have seen the Father (John 14:9). To worship God through Jesus is to know the fatherly relationship of compassion and care for which human beings long. The almighty Creator, the eternal God revealed in the Old Testament, is the 'Abba, Father' to whom we come through Jesus Christ.

God is our Father because he is the Father of Jesus Christ, who is our Lord. Though the whole creation, including all humanity, issues from God, this fatherly relationship is the special inheritance of Christian believers (Galatians 3:26–4:7).

C. God the Son

1. A God who makes himself known

God discloses his person and purposes as Father, Son and Holy Spirit in the unfolding revelation of Scripture and in his saving encounters with us.

Though God reveals himself in many ways, in the Bible he discloses himself through relationships and critical events. He reveals himself in his relationships with individuals (Genesis 18:1-3; Exodus 3:1-6) and with Israel. He makes himself known through critical events, such as the Exodus (Psalm 136, Hosea 11:1-4), the rise and fall of the Hebrew kingdoms (Luke 1:67-75), and the Exile and return (Psalm 126), recorded in the Old Testament. In the New Testament, he makes himself known uniquely and supremely in the Advent, life, Crucifixion and Resurrection of Jesus (John 3:16; Galatians 4:4-5, Philippians 2:5-11).

In human interaction, individuals experience mutual self-disclosure as they enter and honour relationships and share critical events. In the same way, God, who is personal and respects human personality, discloses his nature and his love for us.

We speak of God's self-disclosure because it is the nature of God to make himself known. God is love, and it is the characteristic of love to seek to be known to the loved one.

2. A God involved with us

When we meet God we meet him in his completeness. The triune God is of one undivided essence or being.

We believe that God is not distant from us but is involved with us. This is seen in the history of the people of Israel as recorded in the Old Testament (Exodus 34:1-10; Nehemiah 9:9-17; Psalm 103:1-14; 137) and most powerfully in the Incarnation, the coming of God as a human being, Jesus of Nazareth (Luke 1: 30-33, 46-55; Chapter 4).

God's involvement and initiative are further expressed in the gracious work of the Holy Spirit in regeneration and sanctification, which transforms our lives (Titus 3:4-7; Chapters 7 and 10.) God is not indifferent. He is involved in human experience and is concerned to nurture human life.

3. A God who saves

God is a saving God. The Old Testament records God's gracious action to save his people through human history (Deuteronomy 7:7-9; Psalm 106; 126), and their failure to respond appropriately (Judges 3:7; 12; 4:1; Nehemiah 9:5-37; Jeremiah 7:4-7; Hosea 11:1-11). The Incarnation of Jesus, who from the beginning was named as Saviour (Matthew 1:21; Luke 2:11), led to the 'once for all' sacrifice for sin (Hebrews 10:10) and the possibility of human redemption.

> 'You see, at just the right time, when we were still powerless, Christ died for the ungodly. Very rarely will anyone die for a righteous man, though for a good man someone might possibly dare to die. But God demonstrates his own love for us in this: while we were still sinners, Christ died for us. Since we have now been justified by his blood, how much more shall we be saved from God's wrath through him! For if, when we were God's enemies, we were reconciled to him through the death of his Son, how much more, having been reconciled, shall we be saved through his life! Not only is this so, but we also rejoice in God through our Lord Jesus Christ, through whom we have now received reconciliation' (Romans 5:6-11).

In the atonement for sin brought about by Jesus Christ in obedience to the Father, we see God crossing barriers to save the lost (Luke 4:18, 19; 19:10; 2 Corinthians 5:19). This atonement makes possible the restoration of our relationship with God. The whole of the Trinity is active in this work of redemption (Chapters 6, 7).

D. God the Holy Spirit

To the Christian, the Holy Spirit is both a tender, intimate presence and a mystery beyond full understanding. He brings God near to us and directs our attention to Jesus. Although the Nicene Creed speaks of him as 'the Lord and Giver of life' the historic creeds are generally brief and reserved in their descriptions of his status and function. Nevertheless, a true understanding of the triune God requires a description of the third person of the Trinity and his work.

1. The Holy Spirit is the Spirit of Christ

The Holy Spirit glorifies the living Christ and presents him to us. Through his abiding presence and continuing ministry, we are made aware of the reality of the risen life of Jesus and are united in our relationship with him (John 14:16-18; 26; 16:12-15). He is the guarantor that Jesus is with us to the end of the age. Through the Spirit we stand alongside Jesus and cry, 'Abba, Father'. In this way the Spirit gives us our identity as brothers and sisters of Christ, confirms our relationship with the Father (Romans 8:15-17; Galatians 4:6) and enables us to enter fully into the new life that redemption offers (Acts 1:8).

2. The Holy Spirit is Lord

Study of Scripture reveals that the Holy Spirit is the Spirit of God. He shares the divine attributes and activities and is given the title properly applied to God – the Lord (2 Corinthians 3:17, 18). He is one with the Father and the Son, distinctive in person, yet one in essence.

For centuries Christians have searched for ways in which to describe the person of the Holy Spirit and the extension of his presence from the inner life of the Godhead to the experienced life of the Church. Most Christian churches affirm that the Holy Spirit proceeds from the Father and the Son, to emphasise the mutual relationship among the three persons in the Trinity (John 14:26; 15:26; 20:22, 23). Eastern Orthodox churches have held that the Spirit proceeds only from the Father, to emphasise the role of the Father as the cause of all things, and to underline the distinctiveness of the Holy Spirit's person and role within the Godhead. All Christians uphold the co-equality of the three persons, however this may be expressed. Spirit, Son and Father are together as triune God.

3. The Holy Spirit is free and powerful

In Scripture the presence of the Spirit is sometimes made known by such manifestations as wind, fire, or the form of a dove (Genesis 1:1, 2; Matthew 3:16; Acts 2:1-4). The language of Scripture suggests an element of mystery and sovereign freedom. The presence of the Spirit is both tangible and intangible, invisible yet powerful.

Jesus taught that the Holy Spirit is not to be commanded or contained by individuals or structures. His illustration was that as the wind has liberty to blow wherever it wills with its source and destination unknown, so the Holy Spirit achieves his will in unexpected and unpredictable ways (John 3:1-8; Acts 8:39). He is free of human manipulation or control.

Although the Holy Spirit is active in the Christian community, the Bible teaches that his activity is not confined to the life of the Church. No human group, whether defined by race, class or culture, is beyond his reach (Acts 10:34-38; 11:15).

4. The Holy Spirit is the giver of life

a. In creation

The Creator acts by the movement of the Spirit. With energy like the wind, yet able to impose form and order, the Spirit effects and sustains the living process and brings creation towards the fulfilment of God's purposes (Genesis 1:1-2; Job 33:4). The Spirit remains creatively active in the world (Psalm 104:29, 30; Romans 8:18-25).

b. In re-creation

The Holy Spirit is also the agent in the re-creation of God's people. This is the witness of the entire Bible, which is itself inspired by the Spirit. This is evident throughout the Old Testament but is most clearly seen in the New Testament witness to the life, ministry, death and resurrection of Jesus and the story of the Early Church (Chapter 7).

The Holy Spirit is always contemporary. He is God acting for us today, giving us confidence in the Christian mission and enabling us to look forward with hope to the ultimate fulfilment of God's purposes. By pointing back to the work of Christ for us, he points ever forward to the Father's ultimate creative purpose of uniting all things in him (Ephesians 1:13, 14).

E. A God who is three and one

God is three persons; God the Father, God the Son and God the Holy Spirit are distinct and different, but not divided or separate. God is also one. In this trinity we see modelled a perfect fellowship, mutually affirming and life-giving, with no false hierarchy or unequal distribution of power and glory.

The biblical record shows that God, as Father, Son and Spirit, is at work in creation, redemption and re-creation as he brings the whole universe towards his ultimate purpose of reconciliation to himself.

For further exploration 3

'There is no richer diversity than is manifest by the Trinity,
yet no diversity is more completely a unity,
with the Father, Son and Holy Spirit sharing every
act of thought, will and feeling.'

Frederick Coutts.[1]

A. Essentials of the doctrine

1. Dynamic, loving creativity

The doctrine of the Trinity helps us to understand something of the dynamic creativity of God. Within a mutual, loving relationship, God is always creating, interacting and sharing, and is neither static nor remote from his creation.

2. Three persons, one God

The three persons of the Trinity are distinct, yet not divided (*distincti non divisi* – Tertullian). The entire work of creation and redemption comes from the one, true God. Nevertheless each person is referred to in distinctive ways.

- We refer to God the Father as the first person in the Trinity, because he is associated particularly with creation and the origin of all things.

- We refer to the Son as the second person in the Trinity because he came 'in the fullness of time' to fulfil the Father's plan of redemption.

- The Holy Spirit is described as the third person in the Trinity who has been poured out upon humanity in a new way since the first Pentecost.

Belief in a Trinitarian God is distinctive to Christianity among the monotheistic faiths. The way that the doctrine is described is not significant, so long as the oneness and the threeness of God are not compromised.

3. Co-equal in power and glory
There is no superiority or inferiority within the Godhead. It is important to resist any idea that the Trinity is a hierarchy of persons, with God the Father superior to the Son and the Spirit.

4. A trinity of love
The Persons of the Trinity relate to one another in mutual love. They share a common inner life and purpose, and demonstrate the true nature of love. We cannot love on our own; true love is about relationship and sharing. Creation and redemption are the actions of the relational God whose nature is love. This inter-relationship is often expressed using the Greek term *perichoresis*, which allows for both individuality and mutual sharing in the life of the other two persons. The Trinity is a 'community of being'. Humanity is created in the image of God and is therefore made for relationship, to live and share in community, thus reflecting the love of the Trinity.

◆ *How would you explain the doctrine of the Trinity to a Jewish or Muslim friend? (This could take the form of a role play)*

◆ *What can the image of the Trinity as a community of being teach us about our relationships with other Christians?*

B. Historical summary

The doctrine of the Trinity emerged in the early centuries of Christianity as believers began to understand and interpret the biblical witness in the light of their experience of God. It cannot fully describe the nature of God, yet provides a means by which all who call themselves Christian can be identified.

1. The Old Testament

The Bible is the record of the self-revelation of God through his actions in human history. Although the word Trinity does not appear in Scripture, this doctrine is built on firm biblical foundations. The Old Testament description of the one God who is both Creator and Redeemer cannot adequately be contained within the confines of simple monotheism. At times God acts or speaks through his Wisdom or his Word, almost giving them a personal identity (Proverbs 1:20-33; Psalm 33:6). There are also hints of the presence of God's Spirit in personal form (Psalm 139:7). Such personifications offer hints of Trinitarian revelation and prepare the way for the new revelation of God that is shown in Jesus.

2. The New Testament

a. Following the Resurrection, the early Christians began to worship Jesus as Lord with no sense that they were being inconsistent or denying their understanding of God as one (Philippians 2:6-11). They also began to describe the indwelling Spirit as Lord (2 Corinthians 3:17, 18). A new understanding of the nature of God was beginning to emerge as the disciples began to interpret the events of Jesus' life, ministry, death and Resurrection and the experience of the emerging Church.

b. Writers of the New Testament saw new meaning in the Old Testament writings. They identified Jesus Christ with the concepts of Wisdom and Word (John 1:1-18; 1 Corinthians 1:23, 24). They stressed the inter-relatedness of Father, Son and Spirit in the great work of salvation (Matthew 28:19; John 14:26; 15:26; 2 Corinthians 1:21, 22; 13:14; 1 Peter 1:2).

3. The Early Church

a. The Early Church was influenced by both Jewish and Hellenistic thought forms as the doctrine developed. Hellenistic understanding suggested that matter is inherently evil and therefore could not be created by a supreme being who was pure spirit, remote and unknowable, untouched by direct contact with the world. Therefore lesser deities were believed to have created, and continued to sustain, the material world. A number of spiritual beings controlled the universe, some more divine than others.

b. Arius (c250-c336 AD), an Egyptian Christian priest, took these ideas to a logical, and finally untenable, conclusion. He taught that Jesus was the first created being, through whom God then created the world. This led to an understanding of a 'graded' Trinity, where the Son was a lesser God than the Father, and the Spirit was subordinate to the Son. His bishop, Alexander, strongly disagreed and as a result the Church Council of Nicea was held in 325 AD.

c. Arius was opposed by Athanasius who argued that only God can save, yet the Bible and the tradition of the Church regard Jesus as Saviour. Similarly, Christians worshipped Jesus Christ, but their monotheistic faith would not allow the worship of a created being or a second God. Therefore Jesus must be God incarnate. Athanasius defended the unity of God by using the word *homoousios* (which means 'of one substance') to describe the relationship between God the Father and God the Son. This challenged the idea of a graded Trinity. The teaching of Arius and his followers was ultimately judged as heretical.

d. Two other ecumenical councils debated the issue: Constantinople (381 AD) and Chalcedon (451 AD), where the wording of the Nicene Creed was finally decided and, with the exception of the *filioque* controversy (j below), it has remained the same ever since. The Nicene Creed is still regarded by Christians of all traditions, including Salvationists, as a definitive statement of orthodox belief. The creed proclaims the Father, the Son and the Spirit as worthy of worship and carefully describes the relationship between the three Persons (Appendix 1).

e. As early as the second century, Tertullian (c160-c225 AD) used the Latin word *substantia* (which means 'substance') to describe the unity between the Father, Son and Spirit. However diverse the roles of Father, Son and Spirit, the three persons are identical in substance. The word *persona,* which literally describes the mask which is worn by an actor to represent their role, was used to describe their distinctiveness. Despite their different roles, the persons of the Trinity have a basic unity of life and purpose. It is from these Latin foundations that the credal description of the Trinity as three persons of one substance is derived. Our Salvation Army doctrine similarly describes 'three persons ... undivided in essence'.

f. Augustine's teaching on the Trinity emphasised the unity of the Godhead and the equality of Father, Son and Holy Spirit throughout eternity. He identified God the Father with the Creator, God the Son with wisdom, and God the Holy Spirit with love, through which God binds people to himself. He used the interior life of human beings, who are the height of God's creation, as his analogy for the relationship between the three persons. Just as a human being recognises within himself a triad of mind, knowledge and love (or memory, understanding and will), so God the Creator is one-in-three, a Trinity of Father, Son and Spirit.

g. Augustine was so eager to emphasise the unity of the Godhead that it is not as easy to see the Son and the Spirit as separate persons within the Trinity. In particular, the Holy Spirit is seen almost as a quality, binding people to God and the persons of the Trinity together. However, Augustine's choice to use the interior life of a single human being, rather than three human beings, as his analogy for the Godhead emphasises the deep, inner unity that he saw between Father, Son and Spirit.

h. The Eastern Orthodox tradition places greatest emphasis on the uniqueness and lordship of each of the three persons in the

Trinity. Much less precise than Latin, the Greek language allowed early thinkers a measure of flexibility in working through the divine relationship. While careful to maintain an understanding of the divine unity through the use of *homoousios*, instead of using the Greek equivalent of *persona*, which is *prosopon*, Greek thinkers used *hypostasis*, a word that implies a being of actual substance. The notion of *hypostasis*, or hypostatic union, is particularly significant in describing the humanity and divinity of Jesus (for further exploration 4C2). The primary theologians in this tradition were the Cappadocian Fathers, Basil of Caesarea (c330-379 AD), Gregory of Nazianzus (c329-389 AD) and Gregory of Nyssa (c330-c395 AD).

i. Since the 4th century, Eastern Christianity, following the influence of the Cappadocian Fathers, has emphasised the distinctiveness of the three persons of the Trinity. Western Christianity, following Augustine, has concentrated on the deep inner unity of the Godhead and the complex inner relationship between Father, Son and Holy Spirit.

j. By the ninth century a further dispute developed over the Nicene Creed. Western Christians began to recite that the Holy Spirit 'proceeds from the Father and the Son' using the Latin term *filioque* (which literally means 'and from the Son'), an addition not present in the original creed. The aim was to emphasise the divine unity, but in the minds of eastern Christians it failed to give due weight to the Father, who alone is the cause of all things including the Son and the Spirit. This difference of understanding has persisted until the present time, and is thought to have contributed to the eventual split between Eastern and Western Christianity around 1054 AD.

4. The Reformation

During the Reformation John Calvin (1509-1564 AD) emphasised the doctrine of the Trinity. He recognised that it was essential to the doctrine of redemption, because of its witness to the divinity of Jesus Christ and to the salvation he provided.

5. The 20th and 21st centuries

a. In the 20th century the Trinity once again came to the forefront of Christian theological debate. This can largely be attributed to the work of Karl Barth (1886-1968 AD), who believed that everything we know about God comes to us by revelation – the saving revelation of Jesus. God reveals himself as Trinity. He is the revealer (the Father), the form in which that revelation is given to us (the Son) and the one who enables us to receive the revelation (the Holy Spirit). This definition makes the Trinity the basis for the whole saving activity of God. It emphasises the unity of God, as essentially the one who reveals himself, and so follows the western understanding developed from Augustine.

b. Other approaches to the doctrine have emphasised the significance of the three persons of the Godhead. The development of ideas stressing the social character of the Trinity and the inter-relationship betweens persons provides a model for human relationships, where unity and diversity are affirmed, and provide a basis for right living before God and with each other.[2] Phrases such as 'a community of being', 'community of love' and 'social model' are used by theologians seeking to relate Christian truth to contemporary concerns for a just and fair society[3]. Miroslav Volf agues that the relationships between the persons and community of the Trinity provide a model for relationships in the Church, which should reflect the image of the Triune God.[4]

When we think of God as Father, Son and Holy Spirit, we are facing mystery. But it is a mystery that speaks to us and draws from us the response of our heart. In our worship, we contemplate the mercy of the one who is Creator, Redeemer and Life-giver, eternally one and eternally three. In our ministry, we reflect the love of the one who loved us into existence, loved us to the point of death and who loves us continually. In our fellowship, we acknowledge our diversity as we care for one another, while safeguarding the unity upon which our faith is built.

◆ *'Undivided in essence and co-equal in power and glory.' Discuss the significance of this phrase for Salvation Army worship.*

◆ *Andrei Rublev's (1370-1430) icon of the Trinity shows the triune God as three angels sitting at a table with a cup at the centre (see Genesis 18). In the icon the figure in the centre (Christ) and the one to the right (the Holy Spirit) look attentively to the person at the left (God the Father). There is an atmosphere of unity and closeness, yet each figure is different. The Father-Creator wears a luminous, ethereal robe and holds the staff of authority, the Son wears the brown of earth with a gold stripe, signifying Kingship and the Spirit wears green for new life. Spend some time looking at the picture. How does it help you understand the unity and diversity of the Trinity?*

C. Trinitarian heresies

Historically, attempts to clarify and explain the doctrine of the Trinity have sometimes led to heresy. Most trinitarian heresies can be classified under one of the following three types:

1. Modalism
The belief that the one God projects himself in three ways or modes. This is caused by the impulse to avoid the idea of three gods but results in the loss of the relationship between three distinct persons.

2. Tritheism
The belief that the three persons have different characteristics, desires and objectives. This arises from the impulse to protect the integrity and identity of the three persons but results in the loss of the oneness of God's attitude and action.

3. Subordinationism
The belief that the Father is eternally superior to the Son and the Spirit. Causes of this may include a projection of a society's hierarchical structure, or a desire to equate the Father with other monotheistic deities.

Other heresies include:

1. Polytheism

Belief in many gods. This is refuted by the unmistakable scriptural command to have no other gods.

2. Deism

The belief that God is a remote First Cause who brought the universe into being but left it to run as a machine. This is contrary to the scriptural doctrine of God's involvement with his creation.

3. Pantheism

The belief that God and creation are one without distinction. Pantheistic teachings are prevalent in many New Age movements, whose subtlety and diversity can cause confusion.

4. New Age

An umbrella name for many forms of neo-paganism that combine the mysticism and spiritism of some eastern religions and ancient mythologies, with belief in the unlimited potential of human beings to determine their own destiny. Its techniques are designed to increase self-awareness, leading to 'divinity'. New Age recognises no distinction in kind between God and humanity; the spiritual facility in all human beings, fully exploited, is thought to be sufficient to bring in a new age of peace and love. This approach is characteristic of tendencies to dilute Christian truth by combining it with other philosophies and religions.

◆ *To what extent are these heresies evident in society today, either within or outside the Christian Church?*

D. God the Father

1. The Old Testament

a. Israel understood the Fatherhood of God in relation to his covenant relationship with the nation. This understanding developed through the Old Testament, especially in the teaching of the 8th century BC prophets and the Psalms, towards the full revelation brought by Jesus. The prophecy of Hosea is particularly significant (Hosea 11:1-11).

b. The Psalms show the personal care of a loving father for individuals and for those who are most vulnerable (Psalm 68:5). Although God is wholly other, almighty and unfailingly righteous, the very frailty and humanity of his people evokes tender longsuffering and a readiness to forgive those who respond to him with respect and a willingness to obey. 'As a father has compassion on his children, so the Lord has compassion on those who fear him' (Psalm 103:13).

2. The New Testament

a. The understanding of God the Father in Christian doctrine is exemplified by Jesus' relationship as Son, as revealed in the New Testament. The particular focus of Jesus was that of the intimate, trusting relationship between a growing child and a revered, adored parent. The Gospels show Jesus as trusting, obeying and learning from his Father God. The supreme example of both his trust and obedience is seen in his willingness to accept the Cross (Mark 14:36; John 12:27, 28; 18:11). The uniqueness of the relationship, and the way in which the Son reveals the Father is especially evident in John's Gospel (John 1:18; 10:30; 14:13, 31).

b. As Christians receive, by a gift of the Holy Spirit, the privilege of adoption as children of God (Romans 8:15; John 1:12), so they experience and develop a child/parent relationship with God. This defines Christian experience, character and conduct as we become more like Jesus the Son. Like Jesus we can enjoy intimate prayer with, joyous obedience to, and restful trust in, God our Father.

c. This new intimacy was communicated by the Holy Spirit to those who put their faith in Jesus. It marked the Christians' understanding of the Creator and Lord of all, the God and Father of the Lord Jesus Christ, as source, sustainer and fulfiller of their new life in Christ.

♦ *Jesus taught us to see God as Father: how is this image helpful to you personally? Does this present any difficulties for you? How might you address them?*

♦ *Plan a Bible study which shows how the teaching and life of Jesus transforms the biblical concept of God as Father.*

♦ *Read Mark 14:32-42. Is it possible for human beings to obey fully the will of the Father?*

E. God the Holy Spirit

1. The Old Testament

a. The use of different genders in different languages seems to safeguard the unlimited freedom of the Spirit to be as the Spirit wills, while also attempting to give definition. In Latin *spiritus* is masculine as in German *geist* and Russian *dukh*. In Hebrew *ruach* is feminine, and in Greek *pneuma* is neuter.

b. The word 'spirit' has the basic meaning of air in movement as, for example, wind, breeze or breath. Thus images of the Spirit signify the dynamic energy of God. The image of the Spirit as wind or the storm could alternatively evoke the destructive power of God as judge (Psalm 103:15-18; Jeremiah 4:11, 12), or the refreshment brought by coolness and rain (Hosea 6:3). The image of breath is connected with creation and the giving of life (Genesis 1:2; 2:7; Psalm 33:6; 104:29, 30). Similarly, the vision of the valley with the dry bones in Ezekiel 37:1-10 reflects the breath of God bringing new life into what is dead. The Spirit is God's power in action shaping creation and giving life (Job 33:4). Verbs which are sometimes used in connection with the work of the Spirit indicate a substance in a liquid form (Isaiah 32:15; 44:3; Ezekiel 39:29; Joel 2:28, 29).

c. Individuals who were filled with the Spirit were able to reveal God's message to his people through prophecy (Isaiah 61:1-4, Micah 3:8). By the Spirit, leaders were chosen and equipped for strong and effective leadership (Isaiah 63:11, 12). Others were given wisdom (Deuteronomy 34:9-12) and skills for creative work (Exodus 31:1-11). The Spirit taught the people how to be faithful, righteous and fruitful and he called them to faith, repentance, obedience, praise and prayer (Psalm 51).

d. The combination of 'holy' and 'spirit' is quite rare in the Old Testament as it occurs only in Isaiah 63:10, 11 and Psalm 51:11. Even though the phrase is widely used in the New Testament, even there 'Spirit' alone appears more often than 'Holy Spirit'.

2. The New Testament

a. In the New Testament the Holy Spirit is identified as the Old Testament Spirit of God, giving life and dynamic power, and as the creative power of God (Acts 2:16-21). The action of the Holy Spirit is evident in the birth and ministry of Jesus (Matthew 1:18; Luke 1:35; 4:18, 19; Acts 2:32, 33) and in the birth of the Church (Acts 1:8; Acts 2).

b. Luke could be called the theologian of the Holy Spirit. In his Gospel it is evident that the ministry of Jesus is marked by the power of the Holy Spirit (Luke 3:22; 4:1-2, 18-19). In the Acts of the Apostles the Spirit empowers the disciples and the new Christians for witness (Acts 1:8), service (Acts 6: 1-7) and mission (Acts 13:2).

c. In the Gospel of John the Spirit is portrayed as a distinct person. He is the Spirit of Truth and the Paraclete, which means the one who comes alongside (John 14:15-17; 15:26, 27; 16:7-11).

Following the death of Jesus, the Spirit will be counsellor and teacher who will testify to Jesus, bringing to mind his words. He will also convict the world in regard to sin, righteousness and judgment. After the Resurrection Jesus gives the Spirit to the disciples (John 20:19-23). Here the gift of the Spirit is significantly linked to the authority to forgive sins.

d. The letters of Paul stress that the Spirit enables believers to live as God requires (Romans 8:1-11) and that only those who have the Spirit belong to Christ (Romans 8:9). The Spirit prays effectively in and for believers, and enables a close and intimate fellowship with God (Romans 8:1-17). The Holy Spirit is called the Spirit of holiness (Romans 1:4) and the gift of the Holy Spirit is related to the goal of sanctification (1 Thessalonians 4:7, 8; Chapter 10).

e. The relationship of the Holy Spirit with the Father and the Son is highlighted in Matthew 28:19 and in 2 Corinthians 13:14.

3. The Early Church
a. Irenaeus (c130-c200 AD) described God's Word and Wisdom (Christ and the Holy Spirit) as the two hands of God. However, during the first 300 years of Christianity there was little exploration of the theology of the Holy Spirit as theologians struggled with the problem of how to explain the mystery of Christ and how to transmit the Christian gospel to a pagan world. Gregory of Nazianzus gave the following explanation:

> The Old Testament preached the Father openly and the Son more obscurely. The New Testament revealed the Son, and hinted at the divinity of the Holy Spirit. Now the Spirit dwells in us, and is revealed more clearly to us. It was not proper to preach the Son openly, while the divinity of the Father had not yet been admitted. Nor was it proper to accept the Holy Spirit before [the divinity of] the Son had been acknowledged

... Instead, by gradual advances and ... partial ascents, we should move forward and increase in clarity, so that the light of the Trinity should shine.[5]

b. Subsequently the doctrine of the Holy Spirit became a significant question on the theological agenda. Gregory of Nazianzus stressed that Scripture applied all the titles of God to the Spirit. He argued that divine holiness did not come from a source outside the Spirit, but was the consequence of the Spirit's nature. The Spirit is the one who sanctifies, rather than the one who requires sanctification. Similarly, Basil of Caesarea stated that the Holy Spirit performed functions which were specific to God and therefore shared in the divine nature. He is the one who sanctifies, refreshing the believers and enabling them to pursue their true purpose in life.

c. Augustine, basing his argument on 1 John 4, describes the Spirit as the Spirit of both Father and Son binding them together in a bond of love. The Holy Spirit is the God who is love, who is also the bond of unity between God and the believer, and between believers. The same Spirit who unites the Father and the Son in the Godhead also unites believers in the unity of the Church.

d. Cyril of Alexandria (c378-444 AD) saw the Spirit as guaranteeing unity between believers:

All of us who have received the one and the same Spirit, that is, the Holy Spirit, are in a sense merged together with one another and with God ... He binds together the spirit of each and every one of us ... and makes us all appear as one in him.[6]

e. The classical creeds acknowledge the dependence of the Church on the Holy Spirit. This has sometimes been misinterpreted as suggesting either that the Church and the Spirit are identical or that the Spirit is bound to the Church and cannot be found elsewhere. This is not so, but nor can the Church be the true Church without the presence and power of the Holy Spirit. When the Church has gone astray, the Holy Spirit has renewed and revived it.

4. The 20ᵗʰ and 21ˢᵗ centuries

a. Throughout Church history there has seldom been a focus on the theology of the Holy Spirit in the Church, except in the personal experiences of mystics and visionaries and in some dissenting groups. However, since the inception and growth of the Pentecostal/Charismatic movement in the early 20ᵗʰ century there has been new interest in the theology of the Trinity and in the role of the Holy Spirit in personal experience in all parts of the Church.

b. It might be suggested that Church history is more a history of division than of unity. A growing consciousness of the sinfulness of this condition led to the inauguration of the Ecumenical Movement in the 20th century. This has kept a dynamic dialogue alive between different denominations worldwide, leading to a growing understanding and acceptance between Christian traditions which have different theology and practices. The presence of the Holy Spirit in the Church creates the genuine unity for which Jesus prayed (John 17:20, 21). Thus the 20th century could be called the century of the Holy Spirit, as different movements have worked to bridge the gaps of understanding among Christians and create a deeper fellowship across church boundaries. This search for unity is continuing into the 21st century. Whenever unity is realised it is a glimpse of the coming Kingdom. The full unity or oneness with which we are challenged in the prayer of Jesus is an eschatological concept which belongs to the Kingdom of God. This unity is integral to our Christian hope. It will only be fully realised when the Kingdom breaks through in all its fullness.

- Listen to a recording of the sounds of a storm, wind and a gentle breeze, of gentle rain, of a burning fire, and reflect upon the Holy Spirit as revealed in Scripture. What does this teach you?

- Are there any contemporary images which would help describe the doctrine of the Holy Spirit to someone who is not yet a Christian?

- Read again Gregory of Nazianzus's rationale for why the doctrine of the Spirit was not often discussed in the early years of the Christian Church (Section E, 3a). What does this suggest about the nature of revelation?

F. Issues for Salvationists

1. The greatness of God

The doctrine of the Trinity challenges us to recognise the greatness of God, his majesty and perfection, and to explore ways of worshipping him that honour his greatness. In making us aware of the divinity of Father, Son and Holy Spirit, the doctrine teaches us to honour God in his threefold nature: the Father who gives us life and reveals himself to us; the Son who redeems us by his own self-offering; the Holy Spirit who comes alongside us with sustaining grace. Salvationist worship should always endeavour to reflect fully this understanding.

2. An inclusive community

The doctrine describes a God-in-community who reaches out to create community. It is the very basis of the inclusive gospel. From its beginning, The Salvation Army has consistently proclaimed this gospel, calling people of all nations to respond to the love of God. We seek to include and welcome into the family of God those who feel themselves to be excluded from society. In so doing, we have created communities which reflect the inclusiveness, genuine acceptance and mutual love of the triune God. The challenge for us today is to retain that genuine inclusiveness, resisting developments in our corps and centres that may lead people to feel alienated.

3. The loving Father
This intimacy which we can have with God as Father can speak with great power and meaning today in a world in which the concept and role of fatherhood is often devalued or absent. However, it can also be a source of distress if an individual's experience of human fatherhood is painful or absent. This image must always be used with care and sensitivity, and may need re-interpretation in some circumstances.

4. The Spirit and mission
As mission is the very essence of Salvationism, the connection between the Holy Spirit and mission and the Spirit's empowerment for this must always be affirmed and lived out. The Holy Spirit must also direct the mission, setting the pace and identifying the context. Salvationists must be open to his leading. This eases the burden of commitment to mission and service because we are not doing these on our own.

5. Unity in Christ
Salvationists need to be aware of the prayer of Jesus in John 17:20, 21. A proper understanding of the Trinity will help to define and describe the experience that Christian unity should model to the world. Salvationists need actively to seek unity; in their corps, in the Army and with the wider Christian community.

◆ *How do you picture God in your mind when you pray to him? Do you address him in prayer as Father, Son or Spirit? How important do you think this is?*

◆ *How do you create worship that truly honours the triune God and that succeeds in making everyone feel welcomed into his loving community?*

◆ Make a list of ways in which it is possible to create community in a Christian fellowship. Choose two or three that may be suitable for your own worshipping community and plan how you could put them into action. If possible, do so.

◆ Read John 17:20, 21 This prayer has been a constant challenge for Christian fellowship, because we fall short of it and therefore the very essence of the fellowship is hurt by strife and division. What challenges Christian unity in your situation?

◆ How can we ensure that we allow The Holy Spirit to direct our mission? What might hinder this process?

---

[1] Frederick Coutts, 1978 *The Salvation Army in Relation to the Church*. London: International Headquarters

[2] Colin Gunton, 1991 *The Promise of Trinitarian Theology*. Edinburgh: T. & T. Clark

[3] Jurgen Moltmann, 1981 *The Trinity and the Kingdom of God*. London: SCM Leonardo Boff 2000 *Holy Trinity: Perfect Community*. Maryknoll NY: Orbis; 2005 Trinity and Society. Eugene Oregon: Wipf & Stock Publishers

[4] Miroslav Volf, 1998 *After Our likeness: The Church as the Image of the Trinity*. Grand Rapids, Michigan: Eerdrmans

[5] quoted in Alister E. McGrath, 2007 *The Christian Theology Reader 3rd edn*. Oxford: Blackwell: 192

[6] quoted in Alister E. McGrath, 2007 *The Christian Theology Reader 3rd edn*. Oxford: Blackwell: 205

Chapter 4

God's eternal Son

The doctrine of Jesus Christ

We believe that in the person of Jesus Christ the Divine and human natures are united, so that he is truly and properly God and truly and properly man.

Faith in Jesus Christ as Lord and Saviour is central to Christian experience and witness (Romans 10:9-13). We believe in Jesus Christ who reigns with God the Father and with God the Holy Spirit. God sent Jesus to rescue our fallen world. We recognise God's perfect will and purpose in his birth, life, death and Resurrection, his Ascension and his second coming. In him we hear God's living word and we see God's glory (John 17:1-5; 1 Timothy 3:16).

A. Jesus the man

Our doctrine speaks of Jesus as 'truly and properly God and truly and properly man'. As we explore this mystery, we look first at Jesus of Nazareth, who was truly human, and whose story is recorded for us in the Gospels.

1. A historical figure

Jesus lived 2,000 years ago, and the Gospels as well as other sources tell us about him. He was a Jew living in Palestine when it was a province of the Roman Empire. The account of his birth is linked to events in the time of Caesar Augustus (Luke 2:1-7). His life and his death on the Cross are referred to in other ancient manuscripts. His whole life and ministry must be seen in the context of Jewish religious life and history. Though his universal message and ministry broke the boundaries of Judaism, he belonged to the Jewish/Roman world of the first century AD.

We believe that Jesus was a historical person. In him, God has revealed himself and acted in history for us. If Jesus did not live, he did not die for our salvation, nor was he raised by God. Without the Jesus of history, there is no Christ of faith.

2. A real human being

We believe that Jesus' true humanity is clearly revealed in the Bible. The Gospels describe how Jesus possessed normal human faculties. He felt hunger and thirst and weariness (Mark 11:12; John 4:6), experienced delight, anger and grief (John 11:35), affection and compassion (Mark 1:41). He developed from childhood to adulthood (Luke 2:52). He learned facts by observation and could be surprised and horrified. He bled and died. In addition, the Gospels witness to the significance of his prayer life, the reality of his temptations (Matthew 4:1-11; Luke 4:1-13), the importance he gave to Scripture and the role of community and religious tradition in his growth and development. He was fully human.

His love for God, compassion for all people, personal freedom and moral integrity reveal to us the kind of life that God intended for all human beings. He is the true man.

3. A unique human being

In the human life of Jesus we are confronted with the biblical witness to his perfection. He is the true image of God for, alone among all human beings, Jesus lived without sin (Hebrews 4:15). This must be understood in the context of his unique relationship with God the Father (John 10:30; 14:6-14, 31). The very closeness of that relationship exposed him more intensely to all the realities of temptation, to real conflict with the powers of darkness, to suffering, isolation and death (Mark 14:32-42). In that loving relationship he was able to resist temptation and remain sinless, even to the point of death on the Cross (1 Peter 2:21-25).

B. Jesus, God's Son

1. The Incarnation

Jesus Christ was not only truly man, but 'truly and properly God'. 'He was with God in the beginning. Through him all things were made' (John 1:2, 3). The character and being of God were fully present in the life of the man Jesus, who said 'He who has seen me has seen the Father' (John 14:9). The early Christians adopted the word 'Incarnation' to describe this truth. The word is not strictly a biblical term, but literally means 'embodiment' or 'in the flesh'. The doctrine of the Incarnation declares that our God became one of us, though without sin.

This truth is expressed in different ways by the New Testament writers. In the Gospel of John we read that 'the Word became flesh and lived for a while among us' (John 1:14). In Philippians Paul expresses this truth when he describes Christ as 'being in very nature God' and yet 'taking the very nature of a servant' (Philippians 2:6, 7). In Colossians Jesus is 'the image of the invisible God' through whom 'all things hold together' and through whom God provided reconciliation 'through his blood, shed on the cross' (Colossians 1:15-20). In Hebrews Jesus Christ is referred to as 'the radiance of God's glory and exact representation of his being' (Hebrews 1:3). A number of names and titles taken from the language of the Old Testament and from the first-century world are brought to the aid of those seeking to express in relevant language the inexpressible mystery of the fullness of God present in Jesus Christ (for further exploration 4 B).

The doctrine of the Incarnation was formally developed in the Early Church as Christians pondered the record of the New Testament, experienced the presence of Christ in their worship and found it necessary to respond to doctrinal errors. At the Council of Chalcedon in 451 a statement was formulated which embraced the twin truths that Jesus Christ is one integrated person, with a divine and a human nature, 'without confusion, without change, without division, without separation ... at once complete in Godhead and complete in manhood, truly God and truly man' (for further exploration 4 C2c). In the person of Jesus we see humanity fully open to divine grace and we see God revealed to us.

2. The Virgin Birth

In the Gospels of Matthew and Luke we read about the conception of Jesus by the Holy Spirit (Matthew 1:18; Luke 1:35). Like all human beings, Jesus was born of a woman, Mary, whose obedience to God opened the way for his outpouring of grace in the person of Jesus (Luke 1:35-38). But Jesus' person, life and character cannot be explained solely in terms of human heredity. God was at work in Jesus from the moment of conception. This conviction is bound up with his conception by the Holy Spirit and his birth to Mary, usually referred to as the doctrine of the Virgin Birth.

This illuminates our understanding of the nature of the Lord Jesus Christ. It asserts his divinity as well as his advent in time as a man, made in the image of God. It reminds us that Jesus is both like us and unlike us.

C. Jesus Christ our Lord

'Jesus is Lord' is the earliest credal statement found in the New Testament (Philippians 2:11). It testifies to the deity of Jesus Christ, that he is one with the Father, sharing the Father's very being and fulfilling the Father's mission (Matthew 3:17, 17:5; Luke 5:1-11). The disciples recognised in their risen and ascended Lord the true image, presence and power of God (John 20:26-28). Through their experience they realised that worship given to him was as given to God. The confession that Jesus is Lord is the mark of the true

Christian believer, for 'everyone who calls upon the name of the Lord will be saved' (Romans 10:13; cf Joel 2:32).

D. Salvation through Jesus

Christianity is a historical faith. The New Testament, especially the four Gospels, tells the history of Jesus. The major creeds also provide an outline of his life. To tell the story of Jesus is to preach the gospel, for the Christian faith is based upon what actually happened in the life, death and Resurrection of Jesus Christ.

The public ministry of Jesus followed his baptism in the River Jordan. Filled with the Holy Spirit, Jesus set out to teach and to preach the good news of the Kingdom (Mark 1:14). He taught that the time had come for God's reign to be established: his very coming had brought the Kingdom near. All people, especially the poor and the marginalised, were invited to share in the celebrations (Luke 4:16-21). With great authority, he called disciples to follow him (Mark 1:16-20; Mark 2:13-17). He healed the sick and oppressed (Matthew 4:23-25; Mark 1:29-34). He challenged and defeated the power of evil as a sign of the coming Kingdom (Mark 1:21-28; Luke 11:14-23). But Jesus' actions also challenged the religious authorities of his day, who sought to kill him (Mark 2:23–3:6). Jesus believed that his suffering and death were within the will and purposes of God and did not yield to the temptation to avoid their bitterness (Mark 14:32-42; John 12:27, 28).

Thus, the death of Jesus was no accident or tragic mistake. Jesus did not give up his life as a victim suffering for a cause. He died on the Cross fully trusting that through his death, and by his obedience, the purposes of God would be fulfilled (Matthew 16:21-23; Mark 8:31-33; Luke 9:22). His arrest and trial by the religious authorities, the death sentence imposed by the Roman government, the terrible crucifixion he endured, his death and burial in a borrowed grave – these were not the meaningless events they appeared to be at the time to his followers (Matthew 26:47–27:56;

Mark 14:43-15:41; Luke 22:47-23:49; John 18:1-19:37). Though they were due to the actions of sinful people, it became evident that God was at work through Jesus in all that happened, and the offering of his life was God's gift to the world (John 10:17, 18; 11:49-52; Acts 2:22, 23; Romans 5:15-19).

The death of Jesus was not the end of the story. The whole New Testament resounds with the proclamation that God raised Jesus from the dead (Matthew 28:5, 6; Mark 16:1-7; Luke 24:1-9; John 20:1-18; Acts 2:32; 1 Corinthians 15:3, 4). The Resurrection of our Lord Jesus Christ in bodily form turned apparent failure into triumph and confirmed the power of self-giving love over evil and death. God's transforming presence brought life out of death: Jesus is exalted as Lord and Christ (Acts 2:36).

The New Testament presents the Resurrection as the fulfilment of prophecy (Luke 24:46). The empty tomb and post-resurrection encounters with the believers give witness to its truth. In the Resurrection, the Kingdom of God bursts through by the power of the Holy Spirit. It is also our assurance of life to come in all the fullness that God wills for us.

No satisfactory explanation of the birth of Christianity can be given without taking seriously the conviction born in the disciples that their Lord was risen from the dead. The existence of the Church, Christ's living Body on earth, is evidence of his risen life.

The Ascension of the Lord Jesus signified the end of the post-resurrection appearances recorded in the Gospels, and the return of the Son to the glory eternally shared with the Father and the Holy Spirit (Luke 24:50-52; Acts 1:9-11). It also prepared for the Church's understanding of Christ's continuing ministry as intercessor in Heaven.

The return of Christ is an integral part of the gospel as proclaimed in the New Testament (Matthew 25:31-46; 26:64). Jesus himself warned against speculation about dates and times, but we look forward expectantly to Christ's ultimate triumph; we pray for his return and prepare ourselves for the consummation of God's purposes through the return of his Son (Matthew 6:10;

1 Corinthians 15:23, 24; Colossians 3:4; 1 Thessalonians 4:13-18;
2 Thessalonians 2:1-4; Revelation 22:7, 20; Chapter 11).

E. Our salvation, our mission

The life, death and Resurrection of Jesus proclaim the reality of our redemption.

Jesus' whole life centred on his relationship with God the Father. He lived in the joy of God's presence and trusted him so completely that his life was fully open to those around him. He loved God wholeheartedly and was completely obedient to his will, even to the point of suffering and death. It is this kind of self-forgetfulness that is the real measure of human wholeness. In the example of Jesus we see our pattern for living (John 13:12-17).

The loving obedience of Jesus was the means through which God reconciled the world to himself (Romans 5:10, 11; 2 Corinthians 5:18, 19; Colossians 1:20). We are part of that world. Salvation is to accept that gift of reconciliation, so that, associated with, and transformed by, his death and risen life, we may share the fruits of his self-giving (John 3:16).

Our mission is to share in the mission of God; to tell the story of Jesus and the reconciliation he offers with compelling passion so that other people recognise within it the source of their own salvation.

Jesus Christ, God's eternal Son, was conceived by Mary through the Holy Spirit. In him humanity and deity are united. He lived a perfect life, died an atoning death, rose from the dead and lives at the right hand of the Father; he intercedes for his people and will return in power and glory.

For further exploration 4

The area of doctrine which is concerned with the nature of the person of Jesus Christ, who is both human and also the second person in the Trinity, is generally described as Christology.

A. Essentials of the doctrine

1. The divine and human natures
In the person of Jesus Christ the two natures are fully and indivisibly united. Jesus in his divine nature is one with God the Father and in his human nature is one with us. Jesus reveals God to us (John 14:9).

2. God and our salvation
In Jesus, God himself has come to us with the offer of reconciliation and new life. Jesus' death on the Cross can only have atoning value as we recognise that, in Jesus, God has offered himself for our salvation. Only the one who has created us has the power to re-create us by a fundamental reconciliation and cleansing from sin (2 Corinthians 5:19).

3. Jesus our example
Jesus is the believer's true example of a godly life, revealing in himself the likeness to God that is the mark of authentic humanity (Hebrews 2:11). More than that, through his reconciling work he makes it possible for us to live a truly human life in real obedience to God (2 Corinthians 5:21; 1 John 3:24).

4. Jesus our Saviour

Jesus lived a complete, fully human life at a particular time in history, died a real death on a cross, and was raised to life. The response to questions raised by his life, death and Resurrection marks the historical starting point for Christian belief. Continuing reflection on these questions is foundational to Christian doctrine, life and mission.

5. The human response – worship

The first disciples were drawn to worship and praise their risen Lord and from there they began to understand his divine nature. Worship in the name of Jesus focuses our hearts and minds on God and expands our understanding of his grace towards us (Matthew 28:16-20; Luke 24:50-53).

◆ *Using Hebrews 4:14-16, reflect on Christ as high priest, who can be approached with confidence because of our common humanity. In what ways is this significant in your own experience of God?*

◆ *List the attributes of God we see most powerfully demonstrated in Jesus, giving reasons for your answer.*

B. The names and titles of Jesus

The New Testament speaks of Jesus Christ in a language of awe and wonder at the majesty and humility of God who has made himself known through him. Its writers searched for models from Scripture and from their own world of meaning to describe Jesus, whom they had discovered to be central to their new understanding of God and of life. The following are some examples of titles given to Jesus.

1. Lord

This title indicates that Jesus shares authority with God the Father, exercising sovereign power and deserving complete obedience. He is the Lord of all, bringing salvation to those who believe he is the risen Saviour (Psalm 110:1; cf Acts 2:36; Luke 2:11; Romans 10:9).

2. Christ

This is the Greek translation of the Hebrew 'Messiah', meaning 'anointed one'. This term links the gospel to its Jewish beginnings: the Messiah was to inaugurate God's Kingdom on earth. Jesus transformed the concept while fulfilling the promise. After the Resurrection, the followers of Jesus identified him as the Messiah, the Christ, to such a degree that the title came to be regarded as a personal name of Jesus (Mark 1:1; 8:29; Luke 2:11; John 20:31).

3. Son of God

Jesus is the eternal Son of his Father God, in a loving relationship of obedience and trust, and in perfect unity with the Father and the Holy Spirit (Mark 1:1; Romans 8:32).

4. Son of Man

This is Jesus' own self-description. It could simply be a description of Jesus' humanity but may also refer to the coming of a 'Son of Man' at the end of history (Daniel 7:13, 14). It is thought to be linked in Jesus' thinking with the concept of the Messiah and the suffering servant. Through the suffering, death and triumph of the Son of Man, the glory of God will be revealed for salvation (Mark 10:33, 34, 45; 14:61, 62).

5. Saviour

God has given us Jesus to be the means of our salvation. The name 'Jesus' means 'one who saves'. This deliverance from the dominion of evil and death was achieved by him on behalf of all and is effective for the salvation of those who believe (Matthew 1:21; Luke 2:11).

6. Servant

Jesus is God's servant who is perfectly obedient, and our servant who willingly suffers with and for us. He described himself as the one who serves, and the Church saw him as the fulfilment of the prophecy of the suffering servant of Isaiah (Isaiah 52:13–53:12; Mark 10:45; Philippians 2:7).

7. The Word
Jesus is the meaningful expression of God in creation and re-creation – the *Logos,* which is translated Word. As the Word made flesh, he embodies the reality of God in human history (John 1:1-5, 14).

8. King
Jesus' message declared the coming of the Kingdom of God. Jesus reigns with the Father over the Kingdom of God. His rule comprises a radical reversal of the values by which secular kingdoms operate (Mark 1:14; Luke 4:18-21; John 18:36, 37).

9. Judge
Jesus will return to judge the living and the dead, but also his costly love is a present judgment upon us and the supreme challenge to obedient faith (John 9:39; 2 Corinthians 5:10).

10. High Priest
Jesus is the one who sympathises with our weaknesses and who effectively intercedes for us with the Father. He is able to do this because of the atoning value of his outpoured life (Hebrews 4:14-16; 7:23-28).

11. Last Adam
Jesus is the one by whose obedience the consequences of the first Adam's disobedience are overthrown and the will of the Creator for humanity is both vindicated and fulfilled (Romans 5:12-21; 1 Corinthians 15:45).

12. Head of the Body
Jesus Christ is the Governor of the Church of which he is both the origin and completion (Ephesians 1:22, 23; 4:15; Colossians 1:18).

◆ *Which title of Jesus is most significant for you? Why?*

◆ *How is it possible to ensure that Christians understand the full implications of the titles given to Jesus? Devise creative ways in which you can facilitate this (drama, art, music etc).*

C. Historical summary

Although belief in both the humanity and the divinity of Jesus is central to the Christian faith it has been the subject of considerable debate throughout the centuries.

There are two key questions:

- If Jesus was God come to earth, can he have been truly human?

- Alternatively, if Jesus was a real human being, in what sense can he be considered to be God?

1. Biblical background

a. There is clear New Testament witness to Jesus' true humanity as well as to his historical existence. But the New Testament record of the life, teaching, death and Resurrection of Jesus of Nazareth also 'sets these events in the light of eternity, proclaiming the Lord Jesus Christ as incarnate Son of God'.[2] Each of the Gospels, while reflecting on the mission of the human Jesus, tells the gospel story through the eyes of his faith in Jesus Christ as risen Lord. For example, the Gospel of Mark, while emphasising Jesus' true humanity, commences with the words: 'The beginning of the gospel about Jesus Christ, the Son of God' (Mark 1:1).

b. In addition to proclaiming Jesus' mission, the gospel writers also draw attention to Jesus' origin. In his teaching ministry, Jesus felt no need to defer to others, as was usual for the rabbis of his day. He spoke with his own unique authority (Mark 1:21-28; Matthew 5:21, 22). He called people to follow him, he did not wait for disciples to seek him out (Mark 1:16-20). He performed miracles that provoked speculation about him (Mark 4:35- 41). He forgave sins, which was something only God could do (Mark 2:1-12).

c. The Gospels point to Jesus' special relationship with God, whom he called Abba, Father (Mark 14:36; Luke 2:48-50). He was utterly dependent on the Father (John 5:19, 30). He identified himself utterly with the purpose and the character of God (John 10:30). He was completely obedient to his Father (John 8:28). The ultimate, crucial test of Jesus' obedience to God lay in his complete self-offering on the Cross (Mark 14:36; John 10:17-18). In the crucifixion of Jesus, in addition to the obedience of the Son, we recognise the love of God himself (1 John 4:10), a love vindicated by Jesus' Resurrection.

d. The early Christians proclaimed that Jesus was the man whom God raised to life and who is 'exalted to the right hand of God' (Acts 2:33). A new understanding of Jesus' person began to emerge. Paul speaks of Jesus 'who through the Spirit of holiness was declared with power to be the Son of God' (Romans 1:4).

2. The Early Church fathers

a. The Early Church did not find it difficult to accept the divinity of Jesus and the coming of the divine in human form. However, this was often at the cost of accepting his true humanity. Eventually it was acknowledged that defending the true humanity of Jesus is vital to our salvation. Salvation is only possible because God has taken on our humanity in order to redeem it, therefore our total redemption depends on Christ's total humanity.

b. Two main schools of theology developed, at Antioch and at Alexandria, with two ways of understanding the Incarnation.

● The Antioch school defended Christ's full humanity and particularly emphasised his moral example.

- The Alexandrian school were particularly concerned with the divinity of Jesus, interpreting it in terms of John 1:14 'the Word became flesh.' Jesus took upon himself human nature and came into the world in order to redeem it.

c. After centuries of debate, which sometimes led to heresy, the development of the Chalcedonian definition (451AD) effectively settled the question of the understanding of Christ's person until modern times.

> Following the holy Fathers we teach with one voice that the Son [of God] and our Lord Jesus Christ is to be confessed as one and the same [Person], that he is perfect in Godhead and perfect in manhood, very God and very man, of a reasonable soul and [human] body consisting, consubstantial with the Father as touching his Godhead, and consubstantial with us as touching his manhood; made in all things like unto us, sin only excepted; This one and the same Jesus Christ, the only-begotten Son [of God] must be confessed to be in two natures, unconfusedly, immutably, indivisibly, inseparably [united], and that without the distinction of natures being taken away by such union, but rather the peculiar property of each nature being preserved and being united in one Person and subsistence, not separated or divided into two persons, but one and the same Son and only-begotten, God the Word, our Lord Jesus Christ, as the Prophets of old time have spoken concerning him, and as the Lord Jesus Christ hath taught us, and as the Creed of the Fathers hath delivered to us.[3]

This is described in theological terms as hypostatic union – from the Greek *hypostasis* which means 'person'. So it is a union of persons. The two natures can be distinguished, but not separated, because they exist in perfect unity.

It provides a form of words that helps Christians hold on to the mystery of Jesus Christ and avoid falling into fundamental error. Jesus is both human and divine.

3. The Reformation

During the Protestant Reformation (16th century), the reformers studied the human life of Jesus, especially his suffering on the Cross, thus linking Christological issues closely to the doctrine of salvation. Luther developed a 'theology of the Cross', which emphasised the humiliation of the man Jesus as he accepted his Father's will. But Jesus suffered not only as man, but as God. Luther used the phrase 'the crucified God' (Chapter 2 for further exploration C3), a startling phrase in a society that still thought of the divine as beyond the reach of suffering. In Luther's understanding, the divinity and the humanity of Christ were so intermingled that it is possible to speak of a suffering God and an exalted Saviour.

4. The modern world

Since the 18th century, in the West, the understanding of the person of Jesus has been fundamentally influenced by the Enlightenment. This philosophical movement emphasised the importance of reason, encouraged the development of scientific enquiry, believed in universal progress and rejected the authority of traditional belief. Religious belief became the subject for rational enquiry and there was widespread scepticism about the supernatural. In this cultural atmosphere, belief in the divinity of Jesus has been questioned. The concern is not so much how God can become man, but how a man can be considered God. This has led to a fascination with the human life of Jesus and numerous attempts to understand his life in terms of the divine.

a. Among the many attempts to respond to this question are those which have focused on the personality of Jesus. He has been presented on one hand as the greatest moral teacher and perfect example and on the other as a mysterious, apocalyptic prophet.

93

In such cases it is the power of Jesus' personality that is the catalyst for worship.

b. A more orthodox approach has been found in Kenotic theory (from the Greek *kenosis,* which means 'emptying'), which argues that Jesus was indeed God who became man for us – one who voluntarily surrendered, or emptied himself of divine attributes in order to become one with humanity (Philippians 2:5-11, especially verse 7). In effect, taken to its logical conclusion, this suggests that he was no longer God. This negates the full indwelling of God in the person of Jesus, and endangers the whole of belief. If God is not God, then he no longer has the qualities that make him worthy of worship and that sustain creation. Other scholars have suggested that the 'emptying' described by Paul (Philippians 2:7) applies to divine prerogatives – glory and privileges – rather than to divine attributes.

c. Alternatively, others have argued for a man so devoted to God, and so perfectly filled with his grace, that the fullness of God could be perfectly seen in him (Colossians 1:19).

◆ *How would you respond to the statement: 'If Jesus was truly human, he could not have been divine'?*

◆ He left his Father's throne above,
So free, so infinite his grace,
Emptied himself of all but love
And bled for Adam's helpless race.[4]
In the light of this study, how do you understand this verse?

D. Contemporary debate

1. The Jesus of history
In spite of the supposed secularisation of many of our societies today, there is no lack of interest in the subject of Jesus Christ. At

the present time, some of the major questions that are being asked about Jesus are as follows:

- How much evidence is there for the existence of Jesus?

- Is the New Testament a reliable record of his life and work?

- What evidence is there in the ancient writings to corroborate its story?

There has been rigorous scrutiny of historical sources over many years and much has been discovered that confirms the Gospel accounts.

a. Almost everything we know about Jesus comes from the New Testament. Other ancient writings also refer to him, but are of limited reliability and historical value.

i. Pliny the Younger (c61-c112 AD) wrote to Emperor Trajan concerning how to deal with Christians who refused to worship the emperor and instead worshipped Christ.[5]

ii. The Roman historian, Tacitus (c56-c117 AD), writing in 115 AD, says of the Christians: 'Christus, from whom the name had its origin, suffered the extreme penalty during the reign of Tiberius at the hands of one of our procurators, Pontius Pilatus ...'[6]

iii. Suetonius (c69-c130 AD) refers, if obliquely, to Jesus and the movement he founded. 'He banished from Rome all the Jews, who were continually making disturbances at the instigation of one Chrestus.'[7]

iv. The most notable ancient historian to speak of Jesus was the Jew, Flavius Josephus (c37-c100 AD), whose history of his own people includes the time of John the Baptist and Jesus and the early Christians. He writes of Jesus:

'Now, there was about this time Jesus, a wise man, if it be lawful to call him a man, for he was a doer of wonderful works – a teacher of such men as receive the truth with pleasure. He drew over to him both many of the Jews, and many of the Gentiles. He was [the] Christ, and when Pilate, at the suggestion of the principal men amongst us, had him condemned to the cross, those that loved him at the first did not forsake him, for he appeared to them alive again the third day, as the divine prophets had foretold these and ten thousand other wonderful things concerning him; and the tribe of Christians, so named from him, are not extinct at this day'.[8]

b. There are good reasons for accepting the New Testament as a reliable source for knowledge of Jesus. Much of the text dates from the 1st century AD, with manuscripts dating from 350AD. The New Testament is the most dependable ancient document in existence.

c. During the past 200 years, some scholars have questioned the historical reliability of the New Testament record, arguing that the New Testament is not so much a historical record as an expression of the faith of the Early Church. They argue that the writers were only secondarily interested in providing reliable information about the real man who lived and died in Palestine. Therefore the accounts of Jesus' earthly life have been so coloured by the staggering claim of his Resurrection that the real person has been lost to us.

d. The New Testament was written by the Early Church and its purpose is to call people to faith, but this does not mean that it is not a valid source of historical information. Compiled from the older oral tradition that initially preserved the stories of Jesus, the Gospels vividly portray real incidents and sayings of the man Jesus. The stories, sayings and style are similar to others found in the writings of Jewish teachers of the time.

e. The Dead Sea Scrolls are almost certainly the ancient remains of the library of the Qumran community which flourished near the Dead Sea in the 1st century. While there is no reference to Jesus in the library, the writings reveal something of the thought world of ancient Palestine and confirm the general context of the New Testament writings.

f. The New Testament reveals the identity of a complex individual and gives various interpretations of the way he understood his mission. For example, in Mark's Gospel, at times Jesus appears unwilling to reveal his true identity, while in John's Gospel, he speaks openly about it.

g. Several different approaches to understanding Jesus' historical identity have therefore emerged in an attempt to place Jesus of Nazareth into an authentic context that makes historical sense and also makes sense of the New Testament witness to his unique relationship with God. This has become known as the *Quest of the Historical Jesus*, following the title of a book written by Albert Schweitzer (1906). The aim was to separate the simple religious teacher from the 'Christ of faith' and so to arrive at a more credible version of Christianity. The quest has taken on a number of different forms and has resulted in significant movements in theological studies. These include

i. Jesus is viewed as an apocalyptic prophet of the end time, declaring the Kingdom of God. His expectations were not fulfilled.[9]

ii. William Wrede (1859-1906 AD) argued that it is impossible to strip away the theological interpretations of the New

Testament writers to establish a historical foundation for the 'real' Jesus of history.[10]

iii. Rudolf Bultmann (1884-1976 AD) argued that history is not of fundamental importance; the gospel proclamation of the death and resurrection of Jesus (or *kerygma*) determines faith.[11]

iv. Arguing against Bultmann in his inaugural lecture as Professor in Göttingen, Ernst Käsemann (1953) maintained that it is necessary to consider both the historical narrative and the gospel preaching stressing the continuity between them (this is sometimes described as the new quest of the historical Jesus).

v. Most recent developments – sometimes called 'the third quest' – focus on the Jewish context of Jesus as providing a foundation to his own understanding of his mission. Scholars include E. P. Sanders (1937-) and N. T. Wright (1948-)

'Jesus of Nazareth was conscious of vocation, a vocation given him by the one he knew as "Father," to enact in himself what, in Israel's Scriptures, Israel's God had promised to accomplish. He would be the pillar of cloud for the people of the new Exodus. He would embody in himself the returning and redeeming action of the covenant God.'[12]

This modern scholarship affirms that the Gospels reveal an authentic person, who lived and taught, performed miracles and died on a cross. His message of the imminent coming of God's Kingdom was realised through his death and Resurrection. The Church that resulted preached Jesus the Christ, and faith in him as the way into that Kingdom. There is continuity between the man who lived and the Christ who reigns.

2. The divinity of Jesus

The Bible witnesses to the unique character of Jesus during his earthly life – his exceptional spiritual authority, forgiveness of sins, his miracles and his unique relationship with God the Father. It also testifies clearly to his Crucifixion and Resurrection, seeing them as of eternal significance for the whole of humanity. How has contemporary New Testament scholarship understood Jesus' divinity in the light of the biblical evidence?

a. Bultmann answered the challenge of Jesus' divinity by severing the connection between the man Jesus and the Christ who is the object of faith. For him, questions about Jesus the man were meaningless. We simply cannot know anything about him, for the stories in the New Testament were largely the products of the churches that grew up in response to the gospel message. The Christ who is present in the *kerygma* brings us salvation.

b. In contrast, Karl Barth (1886-1968) placed great emphasis on the historical Jesus and on the Gospel accounts of his life and teaching. He is the distinctive, God-given revelation who alone brings salvation. The gospel, rooted in history, is not open to historical enquiry or contemporary speculation: it is God speaking his word, to be accepted or rejected. This uncompromising approach reinforced orthodox teaching: 'Alongside the statement that Jesus Christ is the eternal Son of the eternal Father one may thus put the statement that he is the eternal Word of the eternal Father who speaks from all eternity.'[13]

c. Donald M. Baillie (1887-1954) argued that the Incarnation of Jesus does not concern two 'natures' held in tension with each other. The divinity of Jesus is best understood through the exceptional humility which the Gospels reveal in Jesus' relationship with his Father. Rather than present his own claims, Jesus is supremely 'God-conscious', so open to God that the Spirit of God totally possesses him: in a 'paradox of grace' the

99

glory of Jesus was seen in his humility as he allowed the work of God to be fulfilled through him.[14]

d. J. I. Packer (1926-) writes: 'The really staggering Christian claim is that Jesus of Nazareth was God made man – that the second person of the Godhead became "the second man" (1 Corinthians 15:47), determining human destiny, the second representative head of the race, and that he took humanity without loss of deity, so that Jesus of Nazareth was as truly and fully divine as he was human.'[15] If we understand the Incarnation rightly we can appreciate the significance of Jesus' death and the possibility of his Resurrection.

3. What is the evidence from his Resurrection?
The Resurrection of Jesus, as it is recorded in the Gospels, is the greatest challenge of all to scepticism about Jesus' divinity.

a. According to Bultmann, the Resurrection was not a historical event, but an experiential event in the lives of the disciples who were transformed by their encounter with Christ. In other words, it was something that happened to the disciples and not something that happened to Jesus himself.

b. While he sympathised with Bultmann's approach to the call to faith, Karl Barth disagreed profoundly with him about the historicity of the Resurrection. Barth argued that the Resurrection was an historical event and the empty tomb witnesses to it. We have no right to question it on historical grounds, but must accept it by faith as God intends.

c. Wolfhart Pannenberg (1928-) bases his thinking about the divinity of Jesus on an historical Resurrection. The Resurrection of Jesus is the precursor to the whole purpose of God in history – that is, the resurrection of the dead and the creation of a new Heaven and a new earth. Jesus rose from death to demonstrate

God's purposes. Therefore Jesus must be, as the Bible maintains, uniquely related to God, divine as well as human.

d. N. T. Wright argues that, both historically and theologically, the only way to make sense of the Resurrection is to affirm the belief of the disciples that Jesus had been bodily raised from the dead.[16]

Salvationist doctrine affirms belief in an historical resurrection as foundational to belief and practice.

4. Who, then, is Jesus Christ?

Many in the Western world today would say that the period of Enlightenment thinking is giving way to a new, postmodern age, where spirituality is once more valued and the supernatural more easily accepted. This movement has not yet led many to return to faith in Jesus Christ, so much as to a new paganism (for further exploration 3 C7). The person of Jesus, the only Son of the Father and the way to salvation, still presents a tremendous challenge in a world strongly influenced by pantheistic thinking. Christian responses to this cultural shift are needed in the 21st century.

Our personal salvation does not depend ultimately on how we understand the New Testament or the relation between Jesus' humanity and his divinity. What we are called to do is to commit ourselves in faith to the risen Christ and to accept the reconciliation he offered through the Cross. With this, most modern Christian theology would agree.

This commitment comes about through an encounter with Christ which is the bedrock of our salvation experience. Christian doctrine traditionally maintains that in this encounter we meet the one who, as Jesus of Nazareth, lived and died, as well as rose again, for us. If Jesus was not a real human being who died a real death, his Atonement was of no significance and our salvation is not secure.

In Christ we meet with one who stands with us in his humanity and reigns over us in his divinity.

◆ *Describe the essential qualities of Jesus and his ministry as recorded in each of the four Gospels. How do the individual accounts help you to understand his life and mission?*

◆ *Is it important that we cannot know the actual historical facts of Jesus' life? Why?*

E. Christological debate and heresies

From the earliest times, distorted pictures of the person of Jesus Christ have emerged in the Church. Sometimes the pictures have over-emphasised the divinity of Christ, sometimes his humanity. The result has always been to undermine or destroy the person of Jesus that the Bible reveals. Many modern heresies have their origins in the ancient debates that were resolved at the Council of Chalcedon.

1. Ebionitism
The term Ebionitism derives from the Hebrew, meaning 'the poor', and was originally a term of honour in the early Palestinian churches. It also referred to an early Christian heresy. This primarily Jewish sect saw Jesus as a purely human figure, although recognising that he was endowed with particular charismatic gifts which distinguished him from other humans.

2. Docetism
However, in general, the Early Church did not find it difficult to accept the divinity of Jesus and the coming of the divine in human form, but this was often at the cost of accepting his true humanity. Often it was suggested that Jesus was not actually human, but was God come to earth, having the appearance of a human being. This is the heresy of docetism (from the Greek *dokeo* which means 'to

seem'). It refuses to acknowledge the reality of Jesus' true humanity. If Jesus only appeared to be human he did not really die on the Cross, and no sacrifice was made for sin. Docetism has appeared in various forms throughout the history of the Church.

3. Gnosticism

Docetism is a feature of Gnosticism, one of the most persistent heretical sets of belief that came to the fore in the first and second centuries. Most Gnostics held a dualistic view which divided reality into matter and spirit, and saw matter as the realm of evil and spirit as the realm of good. They made a distinction between the unknowable true God and a lesser deity who created the world. They believed that human beings, who were created of matter, nevertheless possessed a spark of the divine imprisoned within the outward covering of the body. To gain redemption individuals must escape from the earthly prison and be reunited with God. This was achieved through knowledge (Greek *gnosis*). Knowledge once awakened, possibly through a heavenly redeemer, enabled the divine spark, or soul, to ascend through various steps towards its heavenly goal. Some of these ideas reflected the thinking of the Hellenistic world, others were corruptions of the teaching of the early Christians.

So-called 'Christian Gnostics' denied the real humanity and actual death of Jesus, since such humanity and death could not be reconciled with deity and immortality. The Gnostic heretic, Cerinthus (c100 AD), for example, said that Christ was not truly 'in' the flesh, but only came 'into' the flesh temporarily. He appeared temporarily in the form of a man, but all the time was in essence a heavenly being, not one of flesh and blood. In the New Testament, the First Letter of John particularly seeks to correct this heretical tendency (1 John 1:1; 1 John 4:2).

4. Arianism

Arianism dating from the fourth century taught that Jesus, though in some sense divine, was the first created being. Arius argued that the scriptural titles attributed to Jesus which appeared to point to his divinity were courtesy titles which were intended as metaphors. He was not 'one with the Father' as the New Testament proclaims (John 10:30; 14:9; 17:20, 21). This heresy leads to the conclusion that only God can save, therefore Jesus, as a created being, cannot bring about salvation.

5. Apollinarianism
Apollinarius (c310-c390 AD), a follower of Athanasius, taught that Jesus possessed the body of a man but the mind, or rational being, of God, so that he was 'a miraculous mixture'. Apollinarianism was docetic in its attempt to disengage the soul or spirit of Jesus from his human body, suggesting that in Jesus Christ the Word (the *Logos*) took the place of the human soul, and that at his Incarnation Jesus Christ took residence in the body of a 'soul-less being'. The consequence was that since such a being could not possess a full human nature, Jesus Christ did not become fully man.

6. Adoptionism
This belief maintained that Jesus was 'adopted' at some time in his human life as Son of God. It arose from a misinterpretation of Jesus' baptism experience. It is a denial of his pre-existence as declared in the New Testament.

7. Nestorianism
Nestorius (c386-c451 AD) strongly defended Jesus' true humanity as well as his divinity, but in attempting to separate the divine and human natures Nestoriansism effectively questioned the possibility of the unity of God and man in one person.

8. Eutychianism
Eutyches (c380-c456 AD), an opponent of Nestorius, confused the divine and human natures so completely that Jesus became neither God nor man, but a composite, third order, of being.

A helpful reminder:
There is no adequate theory of the Incarnation that can fully explain the mystery 'God was in Christ reconciling the world unto himself' (2 Corinthians 5:19, *KJV*). The fullness of God was present in the man Jesus and thus the way was secured whereby all humanity could be united to God.

◆ *Chose two of these heresies and describe how they might be encountered in the contemporary world. What arguments would you use to oppose them?*

◆ *Does the presentation of the Incarnation and the Crucifixion in art and music fully express both the humanity and divinity of Jesus?*

F. Issues for Salvationists

1. A foundation for spiritual life, worship and mission
It is important that Salvationists have a securely grounded and comprehensive understanding of the nature of Jesus. This will give depth and substance to personal spiritual experience as well as provide a strong foundation for worship and praise.

An understanding of the person of Jesus Christ is necessary to a proper understanding of mission. Central to Salvationism is the task of calling people to new life in Jesus Christ. We need to know the one we are proclaiming.

2. An example for living; a call to obedience
Recognising that Jesus was fully human, Salvationists can draw upon his example, as one who resisted temptation and as a moral teacher, in order to challenge and develop their own life. The doctrine inspires radical discipleship in obedience to Christ. As Jesus' intimate relationship with his Heavenly Father was marked by unquestioning obedience, the true disciple seeks to follow Christ without reservation, to grow in his likeness and to participate in his mission.

3. A model of compassion

To call on Christ is to call on one who knows the human situation – who looks with compassion on the sinful and the suffering, and who cares about injustice and evil. When we come alongside others for Christ's sake we bring the powerful and loving presence of Christ to the centre of human need.

◆ *The humanity of Christ has implications for our own humanity, for we are made in the image of God. As humans we have a potential for the grace of God to fill our lives. In the light of this understanding, how would you understand the promise of Jesus: 'Anyone who has faith in me will do what I have been doing. He will do even greater things than these, because I am going to the Father' (John 14:12)?*

◆ *In what ways can Christians celebrate and share God's gift of Jesus in a multi-faith society or in a society where people are strongly influenced by New Age ideas?*

◆ *In what ways can my personal life and ministry to others reflect the true nature of Christ?*

◆ *Are there ways in which we can share the celebration of Christian festivals (for example, Easter, Christmas, Pentecost) with our friends and neighbours, so that the significance of Jesus' life, death and Resurrection becomes clearer to them?*

---

[1] Harry Dean, 2009 *What and Why We Believe*. London: Salvation Books: 11
[2] *The Salvation Army Handbook of Doctrine*, 1969: 49
[3] *The Definition of Faith of the Council of Chalcedon.*
http://www.ccel.org/ccel/schaff/npnf214.xi.xiii.html
[4] Charles Wesley, *The Song Book of the Salvation Army* 283:2
[5] Pliny *Book 10 Letter 96*: http://www.vroma.org/ ~ hwalker/Pliny/PlinyNumbers.html
[6] Tacitus *Annals* 15: http://classics.mit.edu/Tacitus/annals.11.xv.html

[7] Suetonius: *The Lives of the Twelve Caesars* Tiberius Claudius 25: http://www.globusz.com/ebooks/TwelveCaesars/00000016.htm

[8] William Whiston, (trans), 1998 Josephus, Flavius: *Antiquities* Book 18 Chapter 3.3 Nashville: Thomas Nelson: 576

[9] Johannes Weiss, (1863-1914) *Jesus' Proclamation of the Kingdom of God* 1892; Albert Schweitzer, t (1875-1965) *The Quest of the Historical Jesus.* German 1906, English 1910.

[10] William Wrede, 1971 *The Messianic Secret*

[11] Rudolf Bultmann, 1953 *Kerygma and Myth* London: SPCK

[12] N. T. Wright, *The Historical Jesus and Christian Theology* www.ntwrightpage.com/Wright_Historical_Jesus.htm see also Sanders, E. P., 1985 Jesus and Judaism 1985 SCM Press

[13] G. W. Bromiley, (trans), 1975 Karl Barth, *Church Dogmatics* Volume 1.1. 2nd Edn. Edinburgh: T. & T. Clark: 436

[14] D. M. Baillie, 1961 *God Was in Christ.* Faber and Faber

[15] J. I. Packer 1975 edn. *Knowing God* London: Hodder and Stoughton: 53

[16] N. T. Wright, *The Historical Jesus and Christian Theology* www.ntwrightpage.com/Wright_Historical_Jesus.htm see also N. T. Wright, 2003 *The Resurrection of the Son of God.* London: SPCK

Chapter 5

Distorted image

The doctrine of humanity

We believe that our first parents were created in a state of innocency, but by their disobedience they lost their purity and happiness, and that in consequence of their fall all men have become sinners, totally depraved, and as such are justly exposed to the wrath of God.

Christians believe that the arrival of human beings on the earth did not happen accidentally, but according to the deliberate purpose of God. Human life is sacred because we have been created as the crown of God's creative activity, to love, worship, serve and enjoy him for ever.

However, to speak of the nobility of our creation is also to be made aware of the shameful reality of our sinfulness. From the Bible we learn that human beings were created by God in his own image (Genesis 1:26, 27). God's intention was that we would live in a state of love and harmony with him, with one another, and with the rest of creation. He also made us free, wanting us to love him voluntarily, not as puppets. That freedom was, and is, misused, which accounts for the pain and paradox of our condition (Genesis 2, 3). The universal experience of human sin has brought estrangement from God (Isaiah 59:2) and disharmony within God's created world. We therefore live in a state of confusion and distress and are unable to fulfil the high purpose for which God created us, a situation which the Bible describes as a bondage to sin, resulting in spiritual death (Romans 3:23; 6:16-23; Ephesians 2:1).

A. Creation and Fall: the biblical witness

This revelation, that we are both specially created and wilfully fallen, is discerned throughout Scripture. However, the first four chapters of Genesis are a key to understanding our human situation and God's provision for salvation which subsequently unfolds. Much of what follows will be a commentary on these chapters.

In these chapters, we find the following truths which are reflected throughout the Bible.

- Humanity is created in the image of God (Genesis 1:26, 27).

- God's intention is the harmony of humanity with himself and all creation (Genesis 1, 2).

- We have been terribly scarred by sin arising from human disobedience (Genesis 3, 4; Jeremiah 2:20, 21; John 3:19-21).

- The consequence of sin is separation from God (Genesis 3:23; Isaiah 43:27, 28; Matthew 15:8; cf Isaiah 29:13).

- This is our universal human condition (Romans 5:12-14; 1 John 1:8).

B. Created in the image of God

This phrase summarises all that Christians believe about humanity's significant resemblance and relationship to the Creator. Male and female, we are made in God's image, and can therefore enter into full fellowship with him and with one another.

God is free, personal spirit and this is mirrored in the gift of human personality. We are living beings with individuality, autonomy and reason. At the same time we long for deep spiritual communion with God (Psalm 42:1; John 4:24).

Our capacity for human relationships reflects the nature of the Trinity and the steadfast love of God. This capacity finds an important expression in the family, and in the Church, when loving and responsible relationships are based on the making and keeping of covenants.

God has also gifted us with the potential for creativity and the ability to appreciate beauty. The image of God is reflected in the working of conscience (Romans 2:14, 15), and is expressed in the possibility of holiness of character through God's sanctifying work in our lives (Matthew 5:48; 1 Thessalonians 5:23).

God's intention for all who are created in his image has been realised in Jesus Christ. In him we see the full human expression of God's holiness and love. He is the one true image of God, the one through whom we find our hope of fulfilling God's intention (2 Corinthians 3:18; Colossians 1:15; Hebrews 1:3).

We were created to live in harmony with God and the rest of creation, and 'in the beginning' did enjoy this innocence and purity. We were created to love, serve and enjoy God; to stand in a unique position within creation and before God as his stewards, responsible to him. We were created to mould, develop and care for all that God has made on earth (Genesis 1:26-31).

C. Fallen humanity

Humanity has fallen very far from God's intention. Though made in God's image, we are marred and flawed by sin (Psalm 14:1-3). This has caused disharmony throughout the whole created order. Not only are we ill at ease throughout the whole of our human personality, but we are also out of harmony with the created universe. We are at war with ourselves and with each other, and among races and cultures. Aware of inner strife and fearful of judgment, we turn away from God. This evil that troubles us is found not only in individual lives but is also built into the very structure of society (Romans1:18-32). We are caught in its trap.

D. The origin of sin

Sin is an intrusion into human life. It was not originally present in human nature. Our slavery to sin originated in human disobedience to God's command (Genesis 2:17; 3:1-7; Romans 1:18-20). In consequence, because sin had been committed, evil was known; and because the good had been lost it was recognised and longed for.

Adam and Eve were tempted to usurp God's Lordship. Their sin resulted from their wilful choice to disobey God and submit to temptation. The role of Satan indicates the pervasiveness and power of evil in our world, but does not absolve us from our responsibility for sin.

The nature of sin

Sin is failure to believe and trust in God, and to desire to be independent of him. God gives commands and establishes moral laws for our good. In the Genesis account, the serpent at first undermined belief in God's commands, so preparing Adam and Eve for disobedience (Genesis 3:4, 5). It is sin to act, as they did, in unbelief and to fail to trust God's goodness. To do so is to base our lives on a lie.

Sin is idolatry. The serpent assured Adam and Eve that rebellion would elevate them to a position of equality with God. Such rebellion represents a presumptuous attempt to place ourselves and our own will in the place of God. It is an attempt to attain abundant life by following the path of self-will. The result is that, far from rising into a state of godlike independence, we decline into a condition of spiritual slavery and moral destitution (Genesis 6:5; Deuteronomy 4:25-31).

Sin is failure to live according to the high standard of love for God and one another that true humanity demands. Because our desires are corrupted by self-centredness, we miss the mark. We grieve God, a truth made starkly evident in the Cross of Christ. We fail one another not only by breaking rules but also by violating the wholeness of persons and communities (Mark 7:21-23; Isaiah 59:2-15).

The definition of sin as anything contrary to the known will of God can serve as a practical guide. Sin impairs our sense of what is right and our ability to discern God's will, though it rarely destroys it completely (Romans 8:15-25). Repeated acts of disobedience, together with the influence of a godless society and the blind acceptance of peer-group norms, may drastically deaden the conscience. This can result in a moral insensitivity that the New Testament describes as being 'dead in your transgressions and sins' (Ephesians 2:1 see also James 1:13-15). Only by the renewing power of the gospel can we hope to recover an awareness of God's will and the desire to do it (Romans 8:13).

Guilt feelings make us conscious of having sinned. Sometimes these feelings are excessive, brought about by pressure from others or problems of background or temperament. Genuine guilt is the result of conscious transgression and consequent blame: it arises from what we do (Psalm 32:5; 38:1-4).

However, sin relates to more than what we do. It arises from what we are. The doctrines of original sin and depravity address this truth.

1. Original Sin

The term 'original sin' emphasises the origin and radical consequences of the Fall. It reminds us that, although originally an intrusion, sin is inborn. Our tendency is to sin. In that sense, we are 'born in sin' (Psalm 51:5). This does not refer to the physical aspects of procreation. Human instincts are morally neutral and can be used either creatively or destructively. The phrase 'born in sin' rather refers to our condition under the power of sin.

2. Depravity

The terms 'original sin' and 'depravity' are often used to mean the same thing, but the latter refers more specifically to the moral condition of fallen humanity, rather than to the beginnings of sin.

In statements of doctrine, depravity is often called total depravity. This does not mean that every person is as bad as he or she can be, but rather that the depravity which sin has produced in human nature extends to the total personality. It is not concerned with the depth of sin but rather about the breadth of the influence of sin in human life. No area of human nature remains unaffected.

We are sinful in disposition so that even attempts at righteousness are tainted with sin. Human freedom to respond to God and to make moral choices is therefore impaired (Romans 7:14-25).

F. The consequence of sin

1. Separation from God

The universal consequence of sin is separation from God and loss of fellowship with him (Genesis 3:23, 24; Isaiah 59:2). In the story of the Fall, Adam and Eve disobey the command of God and give in to the temptation to sin. They seek to evade the Lord's presence, hiding from him among the trees of the garden. He calls out to them but their response to his seeking is fear (Genesis 3:8-13).

Though God seeks us, and we are sometimes aware of his presence, there remains a separation caused by our disobedience, with resulting guilt and fear. Separated from God, the source of community, our relationships are threatened. Isolation and fragmentation destroy the fragile communion we have with one another and with the created world. This profound sense of isolation may stimulate a search for truth about the meaning of life. But only a desire to turn to him will result in an encounter with the living God (Deuteronomy 4:29-31; Jeremiah 29:13, 14; Hebrews 11:6).

For God's part, the consequence of sin is the punishment of the disobedient. In the Genesis narrative, Adam and Eve are banished from the garden where they have enjoyed God's presence and companionship. They experience the reality of the wrath of God (Genesis 3:14-24).

2. The wrath of God

Divine wrath is evidence of the faithfulness of God, who is righteous and true to himself. It is not a way of describing extreme or uncontrolled anger in God, but is a powerful expression of his love and holiness. In his wrath, God judges, condemns and is unable to tolerate sin, while in his love he seeks to bring us to repentance (Isaiah 48:9-11; John 3:36). In the book of Revelation, for example, it is the Lamb, embodying the saving love of God in Christ, who also expresses God's enduring wrath towards the impenitent (Revelation 5:6-10; 6:15-17). It is our own sin that brings the wrath of God upon us (Romans 2:5-11).

The wrath of God is purposeful and disciplinary at present, designed to lead us toward repentance. But although restrained now, in the final consummation that wrath will be complete when God's righteous judgment will be revealed to the ultimately unrepentant (John 5: 28, 29).

The Bible links our sinful state, our separation from God, and the wrath of God, with the sting or anguish of death. It also warns of the dreadful possibility of spiritual death resulting in final separation from God. To reject God's mercy is to risk becoming unable to respond to divine love. The consequence is that we die in sin (John 8:24; Ephesians 2:1-3).

G. Salvation through the grace of God

Scriptural revelation and our personal experience confirm the powerlessness of human nature to achieve moral reformation. Our only hope is in the grace of God which issues from God's will to overcome the separation caused by sin (Jeremiah 29:12, 13; 31:31-33; 1 Thessalonians 5:9).

Because the divine image has been marred through sin, because humanity now lives under the compulsion of sin, and because sin has caused separation from God, unaided human nature has been rendered powerless to achieve righteousness on its own. A saving relationship with God is not earned by good works. But what we cannot do for ourselves God has done for us as a work of divine grace (Mark 10:45; 2 Corinthians 5:18, 19; Ephesians 2:1-10).

'At just the right time, when we were still powerless, Christ died for the ungodly' (Romans 5:6).

'For it is by grace you have been saved, through faith – and this is not from yourselves, it is the gift of God' (Ephesians 2:8).

Humanity is not only disfigured by sin but is also ready for hope. The gospel story is infused with hope. It moves from the despair of sin to the triumph of grace. In mission, we are called to invite people to experience hope, receive grace and rejoice in a renewed relationship with God.

We were created in the image of God to live in harmony with God and creation, a state which was broken by disobedience and sin and, as a result, we live under the compulsion of sin, separated from God and unable to save ourselves.

For further exploration 5

A. Essentials of the doctrine

1. The image of God

Humanity was created in the image and likeness of God (Genesis 1:26, 27). The Latin phrase *imago dei*, which means 'image of God', is often used to describe the original dignity which this suggests, although there are a number of different approaches which suggest how the image and likeness are evident in human nature (Section B).

2. Stewards of creation

God intended us to be stewards on earth (Genesis 1:28, 29; 2:15). Sometimes the notion of dominion (Genesis 1:28 *KJV*) has been practically understood as 'domination', and human beings have abused the trust they have been given to use responsibly and wisely, protect and care for, creation's resources.

3. Human disobedience

Human disobedience resulted in a fall from the ideal state, and in separation from God (Genesis 3:23). The doctrine focuses on the reality of evil, and the need for God's initiative to deal with it both individually and culturally. We should avoid speculating over the origin of evil or blaming others, either human or demonic. Excuses, denials and shifting responsibility for sin are dishonest and finally futile. All human beings are affected by this disobedience, and sin, which separates us from God, affects the whole of human nature.

117

4. The wrath of God

God's response is shown in his wrath, his righteous anger; that quality of God which shows his revulsion against anything which is in opposition to his holy nature. Without God's wrath, his love would become sentimentality. It is not arbitrary or subject to emotion but is a natural consequence of sin, which is seen working itself out in history and in human society as well as in the lives of individuals (Hosea 5:10; John 3:36; Romans 1:18-32; Ephesians 2:3).

5. God's redemptive plan

The aim of God's redemptive plan is to restore us to a state of harmony and perfect fellowship with him. The Creator is also the Redeemer who offers hope to a rebellious world, individually, relationally and in the structures of society.

◆ *Create an artwork in any medium which expresses your understanding of this doctrine.*

◆ *God's love is incomplete without God's wrath. Discuss this statement in the light of patterns of Salvationist worship in your territory.*

◆ *Consider a time when you either made excuses for your behaviour or tried to shift the blame for your rebellion against God onto other people. What were the consequences? How can you avoid this tendency in the future?*

B. Historical summary

1. The image and likeness of God

a. In the biblical account of creation, only humanity is said to be created in the image and likeness of God. This has been interpreted in various ways which include the human capacity for knowledge, moral awareness, original moral perfection, immortality and the ability to share in fellowship with God.

b. During the patristic period a distinction was often made between the image and the likeness of God, particularly in relation to how these were affected by the Fall. For example, Tertullian argued that although after the Fall the image of God was retained, the likeness of God could be restored only through the renewal of the Holy Spirit.[2] But for Origen, the image of God referred to humanity from creation and after the Fall, but the likeness of God would be fulfilled only at the final consummation of God's Kingdom (1 John 3:2).[3]

c. Luther, acknowledging Genesis 1:26 as an instance of Hebrew parallelism in which the two lines of text are directly related, concluded that 'image' and 'likeness' were synonyms, and that both therefore were lost at the Fall and could be restored only through the Holy Spirit.

d. However, the Bible does not imply a total loss of the image of God (Genesis 9:6; 1 Corinthians 11:7; James 3:9). Calvin suggests that through the grace of God individuals retain some goodness, gifts and creativity despite the all-pervading consequences of the Fall.[4]

e. The Bible concludes that through the grace of God in Jesus Christ, who is the image of God (2 Corinthians 4:4; Colossians 1:15), the restoration of the *imago dei* will be effected in the lives of believers (Colossians 3:10).

◆ *'He (Jesus) is the image of the invisible God' (Colossians 1:15). Romans 8:29 speaks of being 'conformed to the likeness of his Son'. In the light of these statements, what qualities of God's image are lacking in your life?*

2. The universal reality of sin
We are made in the image of God and are intended to reflect his glory both in our individual lives, in our relationships and in society.

Yet this we fail to do. The Bible describes and interprets the vast difference between our intended nature and its flawed reality.

Genesis 1-3 speaks of the origins of human separation from God but also looks forward to a way out, by teaching that the alienation between the Creator, his creation and his creature, is not total (Genesis 3:21).

a. In the covenant between God and Abraham (Genesis 12:1-3) the Creator promised blessing, and initiated and provided the redemptive sacrifice (Genesis 22:13). The covenant with the people of Israel, which was inaugurated by the Passover (Exodus 12-13:16), included rituals given by God which allowed the relationship between God and his covenant people to be continually renewed. The sacrifices 'purged' the sins of the nation and re-established the well-being of the people despite their continual rebellion.

b. Later, Israel's prophets realised that suffering, especially innocent suffering, in some way deals with the alienation between God and his people (Isaiah 53). At the same time, both political and natural disasters were firmly identified with the nation's failure to live by God's will and laws (Isaiah 9:8-21; Jeremiah 6:1-8). Moral failure always begins with a rejection of God's sovereignty and ends in oppression by corrupt, self-seeking hierarchies or powerful élites. Nevertheless, the Lord not only judges and punishes this sin, but he also is the Redeemer who will re-enable right living (Zephaniah 3:1-13).

c. In the New Testament, Jesus is the Saviour. 'God was reconciling the world to himself in Christ' (2 Corinthians 5:19). Jesus not only taught and lived the perfect human life but also, through the gift of himself in love upon the Cross, rekindled the desire for the renewal of God's image in humanity.

d. Paul saw that the whole creation will be revitalised in consequence (Romans 8:18-25). Creation itself is made new in the vision of God's Kingdom come (Revelation 21:1-4), thus completing the mighty purpose of God and answering the deep need we have of salvation.

3. Original sin and total depravity

This need for salvation derives from a combination of factors. Any teaching about sin needs to take account of:

- Our experience of personal moral failure;

- Our observation that bad consequences arise from moral failure;

- The assumption that there is 'right' behaviour which promotes well-being. Right behaviour can be determined by our God-given conscience, or externally by family, tribe or nation and especially by the 'professional' guardians of morals – rulers or religious leaders – and in certain societies by a media-promoted culture.

Possibly the most significant historical debate took place between Pelagius and Augustine.

a. Pelagius (c354-c420 AD) taught that God has given us the gift of free will and therefore we are morally responsible before God for choices we make.

> 'When God created the world he was acting freely; no other force compelled God to create the world. Thus by creating human beings in his image, he had to give them freedom. A person who could only do good and never do evil would be in chains; a person who can choose good or evil shares the freedom of God.'[5]

b. In contrast, Augustine argued that we are no longer capable of choosing good (Romans 7:12-24) and wrote of the 'bond' of original sin by which 'we all die in Adam' (1 Corinthians 15:22).[6]

c. The controversy between Pelagius and Augustine hinged on the interpretation each placed on the account of the Fall in Genesis. Pelagius emphasised freedom and responsibility.

> 'When Adam and Eve ate from the tree of knowledge they were exercising their freedom of choice; and as a consequence of the choice they made, they were no longer able to live in Eden. ... Before eating the fruit they did not know the difference between good and evil; thus they did not possess the knowledge which enables human beings to exercise freedom of choice. By eating the fruit they acquired this knowledge, and from that moment onwards they were free. Thus the story of their banishment from Eden is in truth the story of how the human race gained its freedom by eating fruit from the tree of knowledge. Adam and Eve became mature human beings, responsible to God for their actions.'[7]

d. But Augustine understood the variety of limitations on that freedom of choice, including the effects of human history, peer-group pressures and our indecisive will. For example, as a youth Augustine stole pears: all done for a laugh but 'alone I had never done'.[8] He was conscious of being linked to Adam by nature, 'borne down by custom'.[9]

e. Both had valuable insights to contribute, but their arguments were also flawed. Pelagius did not acknowledge genetic or cultural (including family, race, peer etc) transmission of wrong strategies for moral living. Augustine did not allow sufficiently for personal autonomy or free will, assuming the inevitable powerlessness of the individual.

f. The Church has generally followed Augustine's position as far as its official teaching is concerned. But in practice it has accommodated the Pelagian view to some considerable degree, for example in Wesleyan theology.

g. John Wesley (1703-1791 AD) has been criticised for not being sufficiently realistic in admitting the tendency of human nature for failure. But in his teaching on original sin and its consequence, which is described in Doctrine 5 as 'total depravity', Wesley is clear that human nature, unaided by God, is 'wretched, and poor, and miserable, and blind, and naked ... He has a deep sense of the loathsome leprosy of sin, which he brought with him from his mother's womb, which over-spreads his whole soul, and totally corrupts every power and faculty thereof.'[10]

h The common experience of humanity is that sin is at the centre of one's being, and that it affects the total person – body, mind and spirit. This does not mean that humankind is completely evil and incapable of any response to good. The depravity of the sinner is, however, 'total' in the sense that every part of the being is affected by the corruption of sin. Wesley spoke of this as 'a threefold cord against Heaven, not easily broken, a blind mind, a perverse will, disordered affections'.[11]

i. However, alongside this, Wesley's theology included a distinctively optimistic understanding of the workings of God's grace before one is born again, that which theologians term 'prevenient' grace. He could not agree with the pessimistic view he found in Augustine and Calvin – that fallen man is nothing but evil desire, that only the elect can be saved, that they are saved by God's irresistible grace, and that grace for salvation is available to them alone. Neither could he agree with the opposite, unrealistically optimistic Pelagian view of human nature, that humankind is born with a natural capacity for choosing good or evil.

j. Wesley held that because of their fallen nature, humans are powerless to choose good or evil solely on their own. However, all humans benefit from God's prevenient grace. The term 'prevenient' comes from the Latin, *pre* – before, *venient* – coming to. Thus, grace available before coming to Christ. Through this grace humans are enabled to choose good, and ultimately by faith to accept God's saving grace. Salvation by grace through faith begins then with preventing –or prevenient or enabling – grace, grace which can be resisted by free will, but if accepted, becomes the beginning of the path to salvation.

k. The question of original sin remains a live, contemporary issue. It is not only a topic for scholarly debate but a vital matter for every individual. The contemporary debate centres on reluctance, both inside and outside the Church, to accept the doctrine of original sin. This does not necessarily deny the influences that lead to sin, but does suggest that sinfulness is not an inborn trait. This notion necessarily brings challenges for Christian witness and discipleship.

Nevertheless, the biblical perspective (Romans 5:12-19) supports the notions of original sin and total depravity. We are always, in New Testament language, sinners in need of forgiveness and grace.

♦ *Read again the arguments of Pelagius and Augustine. Which of them do you believe to be most convincing in contemporary society? What are your reasons for your choice?*

♦ *How does your understanding of yourself either reflect or seem to be at variance with the doctrines of 'original sin' and 'total depravity' (Romans 7:14–8:2)?*

♦ *Do you agree that a doctrine of original sin should take into account the way that poor environments and heredity affect our ability to live in a way that respects others and brings glory to God? Why, or why not?*

♦ *Write a modern parable which illustrates the doctrine of total depravity for a friend who is not a Christian.*

C. Issues for Salvationists

1. Human worth

Humanity was created in the image and likeness of God. This gives dignity and worth to every individual whatever their personal, cultural, religious or socio-economic circumstances. The ethos, history and present practice of The Salvation Army affirm this fact. Both individual Salvationists and the whole body of the Army must guard against any teaching, policies or practices which are not in harmony with this belief.

2. Sin in human life

It is essential that we recognise our potential for rebellion against God and tendency to sin. Sound teaching, which acknowledges potential for sin, its nature and its effects, is vital. The doctrine challenges any thinking that might suggest that sin can be restricted to one part of a life or personality. It encourages a holistic notion of the human condition. In the same way that the whole of a life is affected by sin, so the whole life can also be redeemed and made holy.

3. Sin in society

Sin is not only personal, but, as a consequence of the Fall, is also embedded in the structures of society. Salvationists need to be willing to challenge the practices of their culture that are not in harmony with the ongoing creative purposes of God.

4. Integrity and Responsibility

Individual Salvationists need to be clear about the responsibility of all people for the ethical integrity of their lives, their accountability for the same to God, to creation generally and to their fellows.

◆ *Research the work of the Salvation Army International Social Justice Commission and write an account of the ways in which it is seeking to challenge the cultural and structural effects of human disobedience to God.*

125

◆ *How can you ensure that your relationships with individuals and groups reflect the truth that all of humanity is created in God's image?*

◆ *Reflect on the wisdom of James 1:13-15. What does this teach you about personal responsibility for sinning and the tendencies of our sinful nature?*

---

[1] *The Song Book of The Salvation Army* 1986 38:4

[2] Tertullian quoted in Alister E. McGrath, ed., *The Christian Theology Reader 3rd Edition*. Oxford Blackwell: 407

[3] Origen quoted in Alister E. McGrath. ed., *The Christian Theology Reader 3rd Edition*. Oxford Blackwell: 408

[4] John Calvin, *Institutes of the Christian Religion* Chapter 2. http://www.ccel.org/ccel/calvin/institutes.iv.iii.html

[5] Pelagius: *Letter of Pelagius to Demetrias*. www.pelagius.net/demetrias.htm

[6] Augustine: *Confessions* Book 5 Chapter 9. http://www.ccel.org/ccel/augustine/confess.vi.ix.html

[7] Pelagius: *Letter of Pelagius to Demetrias*. www.pelagius.net/demetrias.htm

[8] Augustine: *Confessions* Book 2 Chapter 9. http://www.ccel.org/ccel/augustine/confess.iii.ix.html

[9] Augustine: *Confessions* Book 8 Chapter 9. http://www.ccel.org/ccel/augustine/confess.ix.ix.html

[10] John Wesley, 1986 *The Works of John Wesley*. Peabody, Massachusetts: Hendrickson Publishing House: Volume 5:253

[11] John Wesley, 1986 *The Works of John Wesley*. Peabody, Massachusetts: Hendrickson Publishing House: Volume 9:457

Chapter 6

Atonement through Christ

God's provision for our salvation

We believe that the Lord Jesus Christ has by his suffering and death made an atonement for the whole world so that whosoever will may be saved.

The Cross of Jesus Christ stands at the very heart of the Christian faith. It is the greatest revelation of the love of God. Through the Cross, God overcame the separation caused by sin. Once and for all, Jesus' death and resurrection opened the way for humanity to be reconciled to a loving God. This reconciliation is called the Atonement, literally making at one, or 'at-one-ment'.

God has taken the initiative in providing the way. It remains with us to respond to the divine provision in repentance and faith in order to experience the personal benefit of reconciliation to God and fellowship with him.

A. The means of Atonement

1. The Atonement foreshadowed
The writings of the Old Testament are the first powerful witness that God is the originator of our salvation. He is the God who saves. From the beginning, this theme is woven into the story of his relationship with his people. If the story of the Fall describes the separation from God caused by sin, the Old Testament moves very swiftly to offer hope through God's gracious intervention (Genesis 3:21; Exodus 6:6-8).

127

In the book of Genesis, the rescue of Noah from the flood provided an example of God's saving activity (Genesis 6:5–9:17). The call of Abraham signalled the making of a people committed to God by covenant and promise (Genesis 12:1-3). Exodus describes the release of God's people from slavery in Egypt by the mighty act of God. By his covenant, the holy God provided a means of reconciliation for his sinful people. In spite of their sin, they could come to him. Through the system of sacrificial offerings that God had himself ordained, the covenant relationship was maintained (Psalm 50:5).

The Old Testament revelation comes to a climax in the messages of the prophets. Many of them spoke clearly of a coming day when God would act definitively to deal with sin and bring peace to his people (Isaiah 35:3-4; Jeremiah 33:14-16). They spoke of the transformation of the heart through a new, inward relationship and a new, redeemed community (Jeremiah 31:31-34). Some began to look forward to the coming of God's Messiah who would inaugurate a new age of peace and justice.

The New Testament records that Jesus fulfilled his mission as Saviour and Messiah that was both prophesied and defined in the Scriptures of the Old Testament (Isaiah 9:6, 7; 53:4-6). He taught his disciples to find in Hebrew prophecy the key to unlocking the meaning of his death (Luke 24:25-27). Consequently the first Christians used texts from the Old Testament to confirm the validity of their message that the risen Jesus was both Lord and Christ (Acts 8:32-35).

2. The Atonement completed

The reconciliation prophesied in the Old Testament was fulfilled in Christ. Through the incarnation of Jesus, God took the initiative leading to our salvation.

This found its complete expression in the self-offering of Jesus Christ on the Cross of Calvary. Fully open to God in life, he was fully obedient in death and laid down his life for others (Matthew 26:42; John 10:17, 18). By dying on the Cross, Jesus made the Atonement. The Father's gift and the Son's loving response bridged the separation between us and God. We are reconciled to God in Christ and our sins are forgiven.

B. Understanding the Atonement

There is no single comprehensive way to interpret the Atonement through the sacrifice of Christ. But in the New Testament, helpful analogies and images, when taken together, provide insight into its meaning.

1. Ransom
Jesus himself indicated that he had come as a redeemer to give his life as a ransom (Mark 10:45; 1 Timothy 2:6). The term 'ransom' was used in the slave markets of the ancient world where a slave was set free through the payment, by another person, of a redemptive price. This picture illustrates our captivity to sin and shows there is a price to be paid if we are to be set free. Our redemption is costly.

2. The law courts
Another concept was borrowed from the law courts: anyone who breaks the law, which is given for our good, deserves punishment. In God's morally ordered world sin has consequences. Jesus paid the penalty and bore the cost of sin on our behalf: 'He was pierced for our transgressions, he was crushed for our iniquities' (Isaiah 53:5). Christ voluntarily accepted punishment as a substitute for us (John 10:11-18; 15:13).

3. Redemptive sacrifice
Another New Testament picture of the Atonement emphasises that Christ became the once-for-all sacrifice which buys our salvation (Hebrews 10:10-14). He gave himself for our sin and so fulfilled the purpose of the great sacrifices of the Hebrew faith, to restore the fellowship between God and human beings (Matthew 26:28). The death of Christ provides a way by which all people can be reconciled

to God (Ephesians 1:7). His was a vicarious sacrifice, that is to say a sacrifice made on behalf of others. It was not made for his own sin, for he was sinless: it was made for us – on behalf of humanity (Romans 3:25, 26; 2 Corinthians 5:21).

4. Victory over sin

The New Testament describes Christ's sacrifice as a victory over sin and over the powers of evil which imprison humanity. By our faith in what he has done for us we participate in the achievement of Christ's sacrifice. The Cross, the place of seeming defeat, is actually the place of triumph. Christ's victory on the Cross becomes our victory (Colossians 2:13-15).

5. Self-giving love

The Cross of Jesus is at the heart of the reconciling work of God. It is also the most effective picture of self-giving love (Romans 5:8). We can be drawn to it or repelled by it, but, when acknowledged, few can remain indifferent to the God it reveals. It is a call to be reconciled to the God of the Cross, and to love as he loved us (2 Corinthians 5:18, 19).

Our atonement is made possible at the great cost of the sacrifice of Christ.

> 'God so loved the world that he gave his one and only Son, that whoever believes in him shall not perish but have eternal life' (John 3:16).

Christ did for us what we could not do for ourselves. He embraced our sin that we might share in his righteousness (see Romans 5:18, 19).

C. Our crucified and risen Lord

It is through the death of Jesus that our sins are forgiven and we are reconciled to God. The resurrection of Jesus Christ from death is the ultimate confirmation of God's work of salvation through him

(1 Corinthians 15:3, 4). The Resurrection is God's great life-affirming act which transcends the boundary between life and death. God's creative power at work here reveals his glory and greatness. In his resurrection Jesus Christ passed through death to a new life in which he reigns with God the Father in Heaven (Ephesians 1:19b-21). By the Resurrection his people are led to worship him as Lord and follow him into eternal life (Acts 2:32-36).

For that reason the Resurrection provides the triumphant climax to the gospel proclamation of the earliest Christians. The obedient self-giving of Jesus has opened the way to his exaltation and to our salvation (Philippians 2: 6-11).

D. Death and life for all believers

By the death and resurrection of Jesus, Christians enter into the new relationship with God that is described as 'a new creation' (2 Corinthians 5:17). New life begins when we participate in spirit in this great act of God. To turn away from our sinful life and to come to Christ in repentance and faith is to experience a kind of death (Romans 6:1-11; Colossians 3:3). We are called to the same obedience to God and letting go of self that led Jesus to the Cross (Luke 14:27).

When we put our faith in Christ we come into new life by receiving the Holy Spirit (Acts 2:38). Resurrection is not only something that happened to Jesus Christ, it is also, very powerfully, something that happens to his followers (Ephesians 2:4-7). In Christ, all of us can experience power over the twin enemies of sin and death. We will all die physically, but that ultimate death, which is the consequence of sin, has no more power over us (Hebrews 2:14-16). When we turn to Christ we begin immediately to be part of the new humanity that has been brought into being through his death and Resurrection (1 Corinthians 15:14-22). Because of our fallen human condition, the new life cannot be experienced in its entirety now, but the risen Christ is our hope for the future, guaranteed by the living presence of the Holy Spirit in us (1 John 3:2).

E. Grace and free will

The Atonement is God's act of unconditional love for all people everywhere (John 12:32; Romans 10:9-13). All who receive Christ in faith, all who bear witness to Jesus Christ as Lord, pass from death into life and enter into a new relationship with God through his grace (2 Corinthians 5:14, 15). The doctrine of the Atonement clearly reveals that God's grace is fundamental to our salvation (Luke 15:11-31).

God is constantly at work by his grace to draw all people to himself. And yet response to God's grace is an act of free will; we can accept or reject the new life that is offered to us.

Grace and free will are not easily harmonised, and this has led some Christians to emphasise the grace and sovereignty of God to the extent that they teach a doctrine of predestination that disallows free will. This implies that God alone determines who will be saved without the need for any co-operative response from us. Free will is therefore undermined. Alternatively, it is possible to forget that our God-given free will is flawed by sin. It cannot operate in true freedom without the grace of God.

We believe that God saves all who believe in Jesus Christ (John 3:14-16; 5:24; Romans 10:9; 1 Timothy 2:3–6; 2 Peter 3:9). Without the grace and mercy of God, we have no hope. But it is possible for grace to be resisted or abandoned. The grace of God does not compromise the freedom God himself has given.

The love of God is such that, with profound sorrow, he allows us to reject him (Mark 10:17-27).

F. A gospel to be proclaimed

The love and mercy of God are mysteries beyond human comprehension. Jesus Christ suffered and died to save the whole world and was raised by the Father. In the Atonement we recognise the astounding generosity of God's love towards all people. We realise the depth and gravity of our sin and, by turning in repentance to God, discover the joy of our salvation in Christ.

The Church's mission is to share the message of this generosity, to declare its power, to proclaim its inclusiveness and live its truth, so that the atoning power of the Cross becomes a reality in the lives of all who choose to respond.

For further exploration 6

A. Essentials of the doctrine

1. The Atonement is central to Christian life and ministry

The Cross is fundamental to the Church's understanding of Christ as
Saviour (1 Corinthians 1:23, 24; Philippians 2:6-11). Without the
atoning work of Jesus, Christianity would not exist.

Theories of the Atonement (Section B3) however valuable, never
exhaust its truth; it is fundamentally a divine mystery and a divine
gift.

2. A unique and single event

The 'once for all' nature of the death of Jesus to reconcile humanity
to God means that there is no longer any need for repeated sacrifices
of atonement (Hebrews 9:26; 10:10-12). The benefits can be
experienced by all people in all generations.

3. A real and costly death

Jesus' death was a real death on a real cross (for further exploration
4 C2). The Atonement was a costly gift from a loving God in order
to bring about human redemption (John 3:16; for further exploration
2 C3).

4. A resurrected Lord

The resurrection completes the work of reconciliation and
redemption (Acts 2:32; Romans 6:4).

5. A universal invitation to a personal experience

Although differing Church traditions vary concerning the value placed on personal experience, it might be argued that the Atonement was first understood in the Church through the experience of being redeemed. The Salvation Army believes that this experience is open to all people who freely choose to accept the gift that is offered (Romans 5:6-11; 10:9-13).

◆ *The importance of the Atonement to Christian faith is evident in the architectural and artistic symbolism in Christian churches. The Cross is displayed as the sign of the atoning grace of God through the death of Christ for the sins of the world. In what ways is this symbolism present in Salvation Army life and culture? How might symbols of the Atonement be used in teaching, preaching and worship?*

◆ *'The love of God is such that, with profound sorrow, he allows us to reject him' (chapter 4 E). Discuss the inter-relationship of mission, grace and free will in the process of salvation.*

◆ *Read 1 Corinthians 2:2. To what extent is the Cross central to your life and faith?*

B. Historical summary

The word 'atonement' can be traced back to the translation of the New Testament into English (1526) when there was no English word which meant 'reconciliation'. William Tyndale (c1494-1536 AD) invented the term, which came to mean the benefits to believers through Jesus' work on the Cross. However, it is not often used in contemporary theology, which tends to refer to the doctrine of the work of Christ, or to soteriology (from the Greek *soter* which means saviour) – the doctrine of salvation.

1. Old Testament teaching

a. The Hebrew words translated as 'atonement' in the Old Testament mean 'cover' or 'coverings' or 'to cover'. The sacrificial system outlined in the Pentateuch, the five Old Testament books of the Law, established the need for daily sacrifices as sin offerings (Exodus 29:36). The people of God recognised their sinfulness, their unrighteousness, their inability to keep the law of God, and their need for 'covering' for their sins. The sacrifice provided a covering for sin, a screen to shield God from it, a release from the burden, and the power to leave it behind.

b. The smoke of the sacrifice is described as producing an 'aroma pleasing to the Lord', an indication of the restoration of the sinner's relationship with God (Leviticus 1:17). As sins were blotted out, sinners could come before a holy God.

c. The annual Day of Atonement was a special observance made for all the sins of the Israelites (Leviticus 16:34). The sacrifice of Atonement took place at the initiative of God, who provided for the sacrifice (Leviticus 17:11). The covering of forgiveness for sin had to do primarily with God's gracious provision for his people rather than with human actions.

d. The sacrificial system and Day of Atonement took on new meaning as they were reinterpreted in the prophetic writings. For example Isaiah speaks of the sacrifice of the servant for the sins of many (Isaiah 53:4, 5). This passage foreshadows the sacrifice of Christ on the Cross for the sins of the world.

2. New Testament teaching

a. John the Baptist referred to Jesus as 'the Lamb of God, who takes away the sin of the world' (John 1:29), suggesting a sacrifice for sin parallel to the Old Testament concept of Atonement.

b. Through his death on the Cross, Christ became 'our Passover Lamb' (1 Corinthians 5:7; 1 Peter 1:18, 19), 'a sacrifice of atonement, through faith in his blood' (Romans 3:25). His death was for all humanity (2 Corinthians 5:14); he was the servant who became a ransom, the mediator between God and the world (Mark 10:45; 1 Timothy 2:5, 6).

c. Jesus spoke of 'my blood of the covenant, which is poured out for many' (Mark 14:24) and of the necessity for his suffering, death and resurrection (Mark 8:31; 9:31; 10:33, 34).

d. The initiative in the atonement was taken by God in Christ (John 3:16; 10:17, 18; Romans 5:6–8; 2 Corinthians 5:18, 19).

e. The death of Christ on the Cross was prefigured, that is represented beforehand, in the Old Testament sacrificial system but, in contrast to the recurring need for sacrifices of atonement, it was a 'once for all' sacrifice (Hebrews 9:25-28).

◆ *The New Testament writers used familiar Old Testament concepts to explain their understanding of the work of Jesus. What challenges do we face in communicating these truths in today's culture and society?*

◆ *Why did Jesus have to die?*

3. Church teaching and theories of the Atonement
The meaning of the Atonement has been reinterpreted through successive periods of Church history. As followers of Christ have reflected on their experience, they have discovered its relevance within their own cultural and historical contexts and have used various metaphors to explain its significance. The terms used to describe them are highlighted below:

a. Origen emphasised the sacrificial character of Christ's death as a **ransom** paid to the powers of evil. But although it seemed that evil had won, Jesus in his death became victorious over Satan and the powers of evil. Far from being a day symbolising defeat,

Good Friday became a day of victory (1 Corinthians 15:57 described by the Latin term ***Christus Victor***).

b. Athanasius argued that Jesus' **sacrifice** was superior to Old Testament sacrifices because it was complete and permanent, needing no repetition. He also stressed the self-offering of Jesus, for the sake of humanity.

c. Augustine, stressing the need for liberation from the human situation, emphasised the significance of the humble life of Jesus as the mediator of the Atonement. His death therefore provided an example for that same humility in humankind, **a moral influence** from which people might learn. For Augustine, Jesus was both the sacrifice and the priest 'both the offerer and the offering' who mediated between humanity and God.[2]

d. Anselm rejected the possibility that the sacrifice of Christ could be a ransom paid to the devil. Using the language and concepts of his time, he interpreted the Atonement in terms of the honour and satisfaction required by the feudal system. Using metaphors which evoked the image of a balance of accounts, some way had to be found to settle the difference between the standards of God and human inability to satisfy them unaided. Sin was dishonouring to God and God's nature demanded **satisfaction**, which human beings did not have the capacity to provide. Without this satisfaction the fellowship between God and humanity could not be restored. Jesus shared the human and divine natures, and therefore had both the human obligation and the divine ability to make the necessary satisfaction. Thus the death of Jesus restored honour, and renewed fellowship, between humanity and God. Forgiveness and restoration are therefore rooted in the divine righteousness of God, who both demands and makes provision for satisfaction.

e. Peter Abelard (1079-1142 AD) restated the **moral influence** theory so that the incarnation and death of Christ are viewed as the highest expression of **God's love to humankind**, the effect of which is to awaken love in us, and motivate us to live in free obedience to God. 'We are thus joined through his grace to him and our neighbour by an unbreakable bond of love.'[3]

f. Thomas Aquinas (c1225-1274 AD) developed and combined views presented by Anselm and Abelard, arguing that the work of Atonement involves 'a superabundant satisfaction for the sins of the human race'[4] and moves humanity to respond in love. God could have forgiven sins and granted grace without the sacrifice of Christ, but the work of Christ on the Cross is the wisest and most efficient method that God, as the Governor of the universe, could choose to effect Atonement.

g. Erasmus of Rotterdam (c1466-1536 AD) maintained that God, humanity, grace and free will are each necessary to the work of salvation. The grace of God is the primary factor in our salvation, and the exercise of free will the secondary but necessary response.

h. In response Luther taught that salvation involves a new relationship to God, based not on any work of merit on our part but on trust and faith in Christ. Christ has borne our sins and by grace through faith we in turn are made right in the sight of God. Our righteousness, then, is God's gift. For Luther, free will without the grace of God is not free but is the slave of evil.[5]

i. Calvin, like Luther, thought that all people are in a state of ruin meriting only damnation. Some are undeservedly rescued through the work of Christ, who paid the penalty due for the sins of those on whose behalf he died. But this work of **substitution** must also become the personal possession of humanity who are unable to either resist or initiate it. So, for Calvin, salvation is a matter of divine choice; some are saved, but others are lost, also by divine choice.

'By predestination we mean the eternal decree of God, by which he determined with himself whatever he wished to happen with regard to every man. All are not created on equal terms, but some are preordained to eternal life, others to eternal damnation; and, accordingly, as each has been created for one or other of these ends, we say that he has been predestinated to life or to death.'[6]

Note: the substitution theory of the atonement need not inevitably lead to a doctrine of election and predestination.

j. That Calvinistic teaching of election and predestination, and consequently of a limited atonement, produced a strong adverse reaction especially amongst Anabaptists, the most radical group of the 16th century reformers. The fullest expression of that Anabaptist reaction was found in the work of Jacobus Arminius (1560-1609). He believed that Christ died for all of humankind and not only for the elect. 'It cannot be said, "Faith is bestowed on the elect, or on those who are to be saved," but that "believers are elected and saved."'[7] These views, which were developed by theologians of the Dutch Reformed Church, became known as Arminianism and were later largely adopted by the Wesleyan teaching in which Salvation Army doctrine has its roots. For Arminians, all who believe in Jesus Christ are predestined to salvation.

k. John Wesley accepted and developed Arminian views, focusing consistently on Christ as the crucified redeemer who is also *Christus Victor*. A distinctive feature of Wesleyan theology is the affirmation that Christ died for everyone. Therefore the saving benefits of the Atonement are not limited to the elect; all people are able to make a response to God's grace.

'God decrees, from everlasting to everlasting, that all who believe in the Son of his love, shall be conformed to his image; shall be saved from all inward and outward sin, into all inward and outward holiness. Accordingly it is a plain undeniable fact that all who truly believe in the name of the Son of God do now "receive the end of their faith, the salvation of their souls".[8]

This resonates clearly with Doctrine 6, which states that the work of Christ was for the whole world and that salvation is a possibility for all who choose it.

l. Since the 18th century, there has been a shift in the meaning of the term 'sacrifice', so that the commonly understood meaning is no longer associated with a specifically religious ritual slaughter, but with a heroic or costly action by an individual, especially the giving up of life, but not necessarily in a religious context.

m Western thinking at the close of the 20th century and in the early years of the 21st century has developed a culture of suspicion that questions the motives of those in authority, seeking to discover the dominating power that underlies them. This has led to some loss of confidence in the institutions of society, including the Church, and to some loss of hope. Theologian Anthony Thiselton suggests an interpretation of the work of Christ that answers these accusations and restores hope. Describing the grace of God demonstrated by the Cross as 'love without strings', he argues that a love which gives itself for another, in the interests of the other, cannot be an attempt to manipulate or gain power over them.[9] The self-giving of Jesus therefore offers new hope as the individual is loved, accepted and reconciled with God without manipulation or conditions. It gives new meaning to a life in which the image of God is being restored.

◆ *Which theory of the Atonement is most helpful to your understanding of the work of Christ? How does it help to shape your personal faith?*

- *Do contemporary Christians really understand the meaning of the sacrifice of Christ?*

- *Look again at the various theories of the Atonement. What do you see to be their strengths and weaknesses in helping believers understand the doctrine of the work of Christ?*

- *Create a resource that will help a small group understand and reflect upon the meaning of the Atonement in the 21st century.*

C. Issues for Salvationists

The centrality of the work of Christ

In answer to an inquiry as to what was The Salvation Army's principal doctrine, William Booth is purported to have replied, 'the bleeding Lamb'. Christianity makes no sense without the doctrine of the work of Christ on the Cross. This must be seen as fundamental to personal faith and mission.

A gospel for all people

The benefits brought about by the death of Jesus are not limited to a chosen elect, since through grace it is possible for anyone to respond to the offer of salvation through the death of Christ on the Cross (Chapter 8). The possibility of salvation for 'the whosoever' is foundational to The Salvation Army's belief, history and ongoing mission. It must be seen to be a core motivating factor in Army policies, programmes and pastoral concern.

3. Freedom to choose

However, each individual has the freedom to respond either positively or negatively to the invitation given. The Salvation Army's responsibility is to communicate the message and meaning of the atoning work of Jesus clearly, with conviction and in a way that is culturally relevant.

4. Our place in God's mission

'The Salvation Army is called to embody God's immense salvation in a wounded world.'[10] The challenge to each generation of Salvationists is to interpret the message of the Atonement in terms that can be understood, and to live authentically and attractively, embodying the message that they are called to share.

Agnus dei (c1635): Francisco de Zurbaran

◆ *Read Isaiah 53:1-12 and reflect upon the image above in the light of John 1:29. Make a note of your thoughts and feelings.*

◆ *Who are the 'whosoever' in your community? What are their characteristics, their hopes and their needs? What difference, if any, does this make to the way in which you present the doctrine of the Atonement to them?*

◆ *'In mission we express in word and deed and through the totality of our lives the compassion of God for the lost'[11] What strategies are relevant to your culture and context?*

143

◆ *How would you respond to a friend who deliberately chose not to see the relevance of salvation for themselves?*

◆ *In communicating and understanding the experience of salvation, what would you consider to be a proper relationship between an emphasis on the grace of God and our free response to him?*

---

[1] *The Song Book of The Salvation Army* 1986 135:1
[2] Augustine, *Doctrinal Treatises* Chapter 14
http://www.ccel.org/ccel/schaff/npnf103.iv.i.vi.xv.html
[3] Peter Abelard, quoted in Alister E. McGrath, ed., *The Christian Theology Reader 3rd Edition.* Oxford Blackwell: 358
[4] Thomas Aquinas, quoted in Alister E. McGrath, ed., *The Christian Theology Reader 3rd Edition.* Oxford Blackwell: 363
[5] Martin Luther, 2005 (first published 1525) *The Bondage of the Will.* Fort Worth Texas RDMc Publishing: 59 http://www.ccel.org/ccel/luther/bondage.html
[6] John Calvin, *The Institutes of the Christian Religion.* Book 3 Chapter 21
http://www.ccel.org/ccel/calvin/institutes.v.xxii.html
[7] *The Apology or Defense of James Arminius: Nine Questions.*
http://wesley.nnu.edu/arminianism/arminius/Arminius.htm
[8] John Wesley, Sermon 58 *On Predestination*
http://www.godrules.net/library/wsermons/wsermons58.htm
[9] Anthony Thiselton, 1995 *Interpreting God and the Postmodern Self.* Edinburgh: T. & T. Clark
[10] Ray Harris, *The Salvation Army: Its Name and Mission* in *The Officer* May-June 2003: 11
[11] Robert Street, 2008 *Called To Be God's People.* London: Salvation Books :7

Chapter 7

The process of salvation

Repentance, faith and regeneration

We believe that repentance towards God, faith in our Lord Jesus Christ, and regeneration by the Holy Spirit, are necessary to salvation.

A. Repentance

1. In the life and ministry of Jesus

When John the Baptist began his ministry by the River Jordan, he called people to a baptism of repentance for the forgiveness of sins in anticipation of the coming of the Kingdom of God (Matthew 3:1; Luke 3:3). His message was one of preparation for the ministry of the one who would not baptise with water, but with the Holy Spirit (Matthew 3:11; Mark 1:8; Luke 3:16; John 1:26, 27).

When Jesus was baptised by John, it became evident that his baptism was not a sign of repentance, but a moment of recognition and affirmation by the Spirit of God (Matthew 3:16, 17; Mark 1:9-11; Luke 3:21, 22; John 1:33, 34). Jesus was the one for whom John's ministry was preparing people, he was 'the Lamb of God, who takes away the sins of the world' (John 1:29).

As Jesus began his ministry, he too preached repentance and declared the coming of the Kingdom of God (Matthew 4:17; Mark 1:15; Luke 5:32). In his life and work, the Kingdom was becoming a reality (Matthew 11:4-6; Isaiah 35:5-7). In his death, provision was made for the forgiveness of sins, so that anyone who believes may become a citizen of the Kingdom; a Kingdom which will finally be revealed in its fullness when Jesus comes again as judge and King (Matthew 24-25; Revelation 21, 22).

2. As a response to the work of Christ

If we are to experience personally the forgiveness offered by the Atonement, we must respond to the grace of God as revealed in Christ's sacrificial act (Luke 24:47; Acts 2:38; 3:19). That response is repentance and faith, which are twin elements of one action. They may be distinct or woven into one experience, but each is indispensable and neither is possible without the accompanying grace of God.

Our repentance is a gift of grace through the Holy Spirit. Although often accompanied by sorrow, it is essentially joyful, not morbid, because it is our response to the good news of salvation (2 Corinthians 7:10). The Spirit stimulates within us a desire for a change of direction. We become more aware of our sinfulness and this moves us, not down into despair, but upward towards God. We long to turn away from our selfishness and sin and towards the self-giving love of God. We are drawn to confess our sins, renounce selfish lifestyles and to make restitution for the sins of the past.

B. Faith

True repentance, however, must always be accompanied by faith in Christ (Acts 20:21). We can be sorry for acts of transgression and want to leave them behind. We can bear deep guilt over past sins and want to have our conscience cleansed (Psalm 51:1-12; Jeremiah 31:18, 19). We can even make a major change and turn in a new direction. All this may be called repentance, but it is not the repentance that leads to life in Christ. Salvation results only when repentance is combined with faith in Christ as Saviour.

Faith is focused on Jesus the Christ, the full expression of God's grace and mercy (Romans 3:23-26; Galatians 2:20). Faith sees the crucified Jesus and is assured of forgiving grace. Faith sees the

146

resurrected Jesus and is assured of life-changing grace. Sorrow for sins is profoundly deepened when we see Jesus through the eyes of faith. Our change of purpose and direction is given substance when in faith we see the obedient and self-giving Christ and decide to call him Lord (Acts 16:31; Romans 4:16; 10:9-13). Faith transforms the longing for change into genuine repentance that sees the Christ, experiences his forgiveness and follows him unconditionally.

The outcome is justification. We are justified by grace through faith alone. Such faith is not just an assent to the truth of Scripture, but involves a trusting acceptance of God's grace in Christ and confidence in a pardoning God. By faith we know that God in Christ loves us and has given himself for us, and that we are reconciled to God by the blood of Christ (Romans 3:24; Titus 3:5-7). This is the joyful experience of those who are saved (Chapter 8).

C. Regeneration = a total change

The essence of justification by faith is that we are accepted by God. Although we are sinners, our faith in Christ's Atonement leads to forgiveness and hope. We know that God is for us in Jesus. This tremendous change in our relationship with God brings to life new desires for inward purity and love for others. These desires are signs of the experience of new life, the spiritual transformation that we call regeneration.

The blessing of regeneration is described in the New Testament in a number of ways. In the Gospel of John, Jesus speaks of the need for those who would see the Kingdom of God to be born again (John 3:3-8). He is describing the rebirth in the Spirit that comes about through faith. Paul uses the idea of new creation to illustrate the death of the old life and the beginning of the new (2 Corinthians 5:17). The language indicates an inward revolution as well as an outward change in our status before God. The gift of the Holy Spirit is new life.

Regeneration is distinct from justification (Chapter 8) but closely related to it, and the two are inseparable in our own experience.

Justification is God's work for us, the forgiveness of our sins and our change of status before God. It does not depend on our moral renewal. Regeneration is God's work in us, the gift of the indwelling Spirit and the beginning of a life of holiness. It is our call to the Christlike life and involves our moral renewal.

Regeneration means that we die to our old life and come alive to Christ (Romans 6:2-4; Colossians 3:3). We are alive to the presence of Christ with us, we hear his call to follow him and we experience his peace and joy in our hearts. We are sensitive to sin and eager to seek forgiveness. The fruit of the Spirit becomes evident in us as a visible sign of regeneration (Galatians 5:16-26). The Spirit guides us as we reach out to share the love of God with others. We look to the future rather than the past and are filled with hope. We learn to grow in the knowledge and love of Jesus Christ. This regeneration is the first step in a life of holiness in Christ.

D. The work of the Holy Spirit

1. The promise of the Spirit
In Old Testament times, the Holy Spirit spoke through special messengers who were gifted for particular tasks or for prophecy (Judges 6:34; 1 Samuel 10:10, 11; 2 Peter 1:20, 21). The later prophets, especially Joel (Joel 2:28-32), foretold the outpouring of God's Spirit on all people, a prophecy that was fulfilled on the Day of Pentecost (Acts 2:14-36). The prophet Isaiah foretold the coming of one in whom the Spirit of the Lord would dwell perfectly (Isaiah 11:1-5).

2. The Spirit in Jesus
The Holy Spirit was active in the Incarnation: by his power God's Son was born of a woman (Luke 1:35). The Spirit was at work in the life and ministry of Jesus (Luke 3:21, 22; 4:16-21) and in the mighty act of God that commenced the new creation by raising Jesus Christ from the dead.

3. The work of the Spirit in the life of the believer

The Holy Spirit convicts us of our sinfulness and need of salvation (John 16:7-11), and leads us to repentance and faith. Through regeneration, he imparts new life in Christ and enables us to live in the reality of the Resurrection (Romans 8:1-11). He sanctifies us as God's people, enabling us to bear the fruit of the Spirit (1 Corinthians 6:11; Galatians 5:22-25). He calls us to continual repentance. He re-awakens us to the memory of Jesus and continues to remind us that we are sinners saved by grace to live victoriously (Galatians 5:16-18).

The Spirit enlightens and empowers us in spiritual warfare (Ephesians 6:10-18). We are engaged in conflict with the principalities and powers of evil, which seek to overthrow the Kingdom of God, corrupt the Church and thwart its mission (1 John 4:1-6).

We need not be oppressed by, nor preoccupied with, the demonic or the powers of darkness (1 John 4:4; Ephesians 6:11). We can rejoice in our hope of the eventual victorious completion of the struggle against the powers of darkness (1 John 5:4, 5).

The Holy Spirit intercedes for us and gives voice to our prayers, interpreting our unspoken needs at the throne of grace where Jesus Christ represents us before the Father (Romans 8:26, 27).

As the Counsellor promised by Jesus, the Holy Spirit comes alongside to help, witnessing to Christ and bringing to the minds of his followers his example, teaching and love (John 14:26). He gives understanding of our task, equipment for service and empowerment for mission.

The Holy Spirit indwells the believer. He imparts strength, peace, joy and courage to witness, enabling us to live holy lives (John 16; Ephesians 3:14-19; Chapters 9 and 10) and is the guarantor of the life that is to come (2 Corinthians 5:5; Ephesians 1:13, 14).

4. The Spirit in the Church

At Pentecost the Holy Spirit became the creator of the Church through which God initiated the reign of Christ and the mission of his people (John 17:20; Acts 1:8; 2:1-41). In the ongoing life of the Church the Spirit initiates and seeks to guide and sustain genuine religious revival and spiritual renewal (see A Salvationist understanding of the Church).

- He releases and directs new life in the Church (Acts 8:26-40; 10:44; 13:2).

- He creates fellowship (2 Corinthians 13:14).

- He inspires sacrificial love (1 Corinthians 13:1-14).

- He imparts humility (Philippians 2:1-3).

- He provides believers with spiritual gifts (1 Corinthians 12-14; Ephesians 4:7-13).

The freely chosen human actions of repentance and faith, made possible by the grace of God, and the renewing, restoring and re-creating power of the Holy Spirit are each necessary if God's saving action is to be a reality in the life of the believer.

For further exploration 7

A. Essentials of the doctrine

1. The work of Jesus on the Cross calls humanity to repentance and faith

Repentance and faith describe the proper human response to the work of Jesus on the Cross; together they constitute the necessary human action for salvation (Acts 20:21). They are not totally human in origin, but flow from an experience of God's grace which enables the individual to appreciate, and respond to, God's gift in Christ. Nevertheless, it is possible for humanity to ignore, resist or deliberately turn away from this gift. Repentance and faith are always freely chosen.

2. Repentance and faith lead to regeneration

The doctrine points to the regenerating work of the Holy Spirit which brings people to salvation and transforms and renews their life. It describes the spiritual rebirth that is experienced by those who have repented and believed. It is described in various ways, each of which signifies a movement from decay to wholeness. These include a change from death to life (John 5:24; 1 John 3:14), becoming a new creation (2 Corinthians 5:17; Galatians 6:15), being born again (John 3:5-6; 1 Peter 1:23), receiving eternal life (John 17:2; Romans 6:23) and moving from darkness to light (John 8:12; Ephesians 5:8). God's purpose is our re-creation in the image of his

151

Son, Jesus, and our freedom from the power of sin. Through faith in Jesus, we can be led into a free, open and growing relationship with God. We are freed by the Spirit to become our true selves. This process is never completed in this life, but it grows and develops as the Holy Spirit reveals to us more of our own need of the power of Christ. The Holy Spirit as Lord and giver of life makes the risen Christ real to us.

3. The outcome is salvation

Salvation means we are accepted by God unconditionally and promised a new way of life through him; our salvation depends both on the grace of God and upon our response of faith. The doctrine of salvation is vital for our understanding of the nature of God. It shows that we worship a saving God, one who understands our human situation and comes to rescue us.

4. Salvation in community

To be saved is far more than to receive a personal new life: we are part of God's new society, his people called to convey the good news to the world. The Church is the family of those who have been born again by the grace of God and the power of the Holy Spirit and who, together, are the people of God in the world (A Salvationist understanding of the Church).

Furthermore, salvation in the biblical sense does not only concern individuals and communities but affects the entire world order. We are promised 'a new Heaven and a new earth'. All history is moving towards the fulfilment of God's purposes for the entire universe, 'to bring all things in heaven and on earth together under one head, even Christ' (Ephesians 1:10).

◆ *Do you agree that salvation means freedom and new life? How would you explain this to someone of another faith?*

◆ *How would you describe repentance, faith and regeneration to a group of young adults who have little knowledge of the Bible?*

◆ *Look again at the images of regeneration listed in Section 2 above. Would these be easily understood in your culture and context? What other images might be used to describe this experience?*

B. Historical summary

1. The Old Testament

a. Throughout the Old Testament we see God constantly at work to bring his people into a new relationship with himself and with each other. His saving character is revealed through the events of Hebrew history. The Exodus, when the Hebrew slaves were released from oppression in Egypt and guided to the promised land, provides the dominant image of God's intervention to rescue his people (Exodus 3:7, 8).

b. The Exodus experience had convinced the Hebrew slaves that God was on their side. He freed his people from oppression and restored their lost identity. He restored them to fellowship with himself, offering the Covenant, the Law and the sacrificial system to help them in their continuing walk with him. God is the one who vindicates his people, acting on behalf of those who are oppressed, whether by captivity, poverty, injustice or sin.

c. The constant recollection and re-enactment of the Exodus celebrated and revealed the saving nature of God and acknowledged the people's responsibility to be faithful to their Saviour God (Deuteronomy 29, 30). As the history of Israel again led to loss of home and exile, the Jews developed a hope that the one who had saved in the past would continue to exercise his saving grace in the present (Nehemiah 1:1-11).

d. The later Old Testament prophets believed that the ongoing political disasters of the kingdoms of Israel and Judah were caused by the continuing disobedience of God's people (Isaiah 1:2-9). Called into a special relationship with God that they could not maintain, with leaders who constantly failed them (Ezekiel

153

34), the people lurched towards spiritual and political disintegration (Hosea 4). Nevertheless, the message of the prophets was one of hope and love (Hosea 11:1-11); God's people would finally be vindicated and a new world order brought into being (Joel 2:12-32; Isaiah 65:17–66:24). Jeremiah spoke of the hope of inward renewal. God would forgive Israel and make a new covenant in which each individual would know him for themselves (Jeremiah 31:31-34).

e. God could create the means for his people to continue to walk with him in trustful obedience. The sacrificial system and the promise of inward regeneration in the later Old Testament writings were gifts which would enable his people to approach him and to maintain their covenant relationship with him.

2. The New Testament

a. In the New Testament, God is again revealed as the one who saves. His saving grace is revealed in the life, death and Resurrection of Jesus Christ. Jesus' self-offering and death is God's new intervention in history, the new Exodus (Luke 9:31, speaks of Jesus' passion as his 'departure' or 'exodus'). Jesus' death and his Resurrection provide the means whereby all people, not only the Jewish nation, can receive salvation. Their rebellion against God can be forgiven and their relationship with him restored through the gift of the Holy Spirit (Acts 2:38).

b. The New Testament writers show that through Jesus' life and teaching God's grace has been released into the world in a new way. Luke records the ministry of Jesus as a fulfilment of Isaiah's promise of freedom and renewal (Luke 4:16-21 cf Isaiah 61:1, 2). By his actions, Jesus revealed the nature of God's salvation. He fed the hungry, healed the sick, forgave sins and announced the Kingdom of God. His teaching showed that God stood alongside and vindicated those who acknowledged their need of him (Matthew 5:3; 18:21-35; Luke 18:13).

c. Jesus' rejection by the religious authorities and their collusion with the Romans formed the circumstances which led to God's saving act through the Cross. For the New Testament writers, Jesus' self-giving love on the Cross and vindication through the Resurrection offer salvation for all humanity (John 12:31-33; Acts 2:22-39; Romans 3:21-26; 5:18-21; 6:3, 4). This was a new revelation of God's saving character, offering the possibility of a new relationship with him, a new kind of life for those who trust him, a new security in his presence, a new family, a new humanity and a new creation.

d. For Paul, the sacrifice of Christ has brought the twin blessings of liberation and entry into God's new life (Romans 8:2; 2 Corinthians 5:17). Together, this is salvation. Faith in Christ brings deliverance from sin, from the principalities and powers, from the restrictive guardianship of the Jewish Law, from the weakness of our human nature.

e. Salvation is not only concerned with personal freedom from sin, but is also marked by right relationships within the Christian community (Romans 12:4; 1 Corinthians 12:13). The relationships between the members of the Trinity provide both inspiration and a model for human relationships for those who belong to the Body of Christ (2 Corinthians 13:14).

f. The ultimate will of God is to bring 'unity to all things in heaven and on earth under Christ' (Ephesians 1:10). Salvation will eventually affect the whole of creation.

g. The new life begins with Christ and will go on into the new world that God is preparing for his people when Christ will come again (1 Thessalonians 4:13-17).

◆ *Read Deuteronomy 26:6-9. What does this passage tell us about the nature of God and of salvation?*

◆ *How does the Old Testament understanding of salvation help us to understand the death and Resurrection of Jesus? What implications does this have for our teaching and preaching?*

3. Church teaching
Throughout the history of the Church, the doctrine of salvation has been explored and developed in different ways.

● Origen explored the biblical truth of freedom in Christ against the background of a culture ruled by fear of enemies in this world and in the world of the spirits. Salvation was to be freed from such fears by Jesus Christ.

● In medieval times, the fear of hell was widespread and personal freedoms were circumscribed by rigid social structures. The Roman Catholic Church preached salvation by grace, but some of its practices increased fears rather than relieved them (for example, the pressure to buy and sell papal indulgences for the remission of sin).

● The Reformation spoke of the possibility of salvation by faith. Luther's search for a gracious God resonated with the needs of those who believed that sinners could not be accepted by a righteous God. He concluded that God not only requires righteousness, but also provides it.

> 'Faith is God's work in us, that changes us and gives new birth from God (John 1:13) ... It changes our hearts, our spirits, our thoughts and all our powers. It brings the Holy Spirit with it. Yes, it is a living, creative, active and powerful thing, this faith ... Faith is a living, bold trust in God's grace.'[2]

Freedom from condemnation is therefore a gift from God which enables humanity to enter the presence of God (Chapter 8). Faith, according to Luther, is being in right relationship with God. Faith is not merely belief in the historical reliability of the gospels, but involves personal trust in the work of salvation brought by Christ and willingness to act upon this belief. However, the test of faith is not the intensity of belief, but the reliability of the one in whom faith is placed. It must be a constant and enduring feature of life. Faith leads to a mutual commitment between Christ and the believer; as an individual responds completely to God, so this leads to the indwelling of the Holy Spirit in his or her life.

- Pietism, which was particularly associated with 17th century European Christianity, was a challenge to sterile, orthodox religion and correct, but lifeless doctrine. The resulting call to faith which is rooted in personal experience resonated clearly with the doctrine of regeneration. John Wesley who was influenced by the pietist tradition, centred his teaching on the privilege of a changed life for those who are born of God. Faith in Christ brings salvation, that is, freedom from sin and also from its power, 'He who is thus justified, or saved by faith, is indeed born again. He is born again of the Spirit unto a new life ...'.[3]

- Methodist theologian Richard Watson (1781-1833) described regeneration as 'that renewal of our nature which gives us dominion over sin, and enables us to serve God, from love and not merely from fear'.[4]

- 18th and 19th century revivalism was built on these doctrines – salvation from sin through the grace of God, the reality of justification and new life in Christ and the possibility of sanctification. They are the foundation of Salvationist belief, life and mission.

◆ *What images from contemporary society might be used to interpret the biblical image of freedom in Christ to the current generation?*

C. Later theological developments

a. The rise of Existentialism in the 19th century led to a distinction between 'authentic' and 'inauthentic' human existence (Heidegger 1888-1976 AD). Bultmann interpreted these as characterised by faith in God (authentic existence), or being bound by the transient material world (inauthentic existence), arguing that through the gospel proclamation, the *kerygma* (a Greek word meaning proclamation), authentic existence is made possible. A similar approach was developed by Paul Tillich (1886-1965 AD) for whom salvation seems to be related solely to living an authentic personal life. Whilst offering some insight into the authenticity and integrity of the redeemed life this interpretation does not give full attention to the work of God in salvation, and ignores the corporate, social and political aspects of the Christian gospel.

b. A contrasting perspective is that of liberation theology. Many people in contemporary society are not so concerned with individual and spiritual salvation as with the more concrete reality of freedom from physical and material oppression. In the 20th century, women sought to become free from physical, psychological and economic domination by men, ethnic minorities from historical and economic domination, and the poor from the domination by the rich. The phrase 'liberation theology' is usually understood to refer to the Roman Catholic movement in Latin America, dating from the 1960s, where many in the Church declared that God was on the side of the poor and involved in the fight for freedom and justice. Liberation theologians believe that theology must be rooted in critical reflection on practice in the light of the word of God and must seek to transform, rather than explain, the world. Therefore, God's people must follow Christ in service to the poor and involvement in their plight, even if they suffer for it. Some theologians equated salvation with this political liberation, though others maintained that it has consequences for both the spiritual and the material worlds. Gustavo Gutiérrez

(1928-), writing of salvation as new creation, says that the Pauline writings (Romans 8; 2 Corinthians 5:17) present the work of Christ 'simultaneously as a liberation from sin and from all its consequences: despoliation, injustice, hatred'.[5]

c. Feminist theological concerns, which explore theological issues in the light of women's experience, are also relevant in relation to our understanding of sin and therefore the need for repentance. Many feminists have suggested that the categories that are generally used to describe human sin are male orientated, for example inappropriate pride, ambition and self-esteem, and argue that these are the opposite of the experience of women for whom sin is often *lack of* the same qualities. A presentation of salvation in which sin is defined as that which separates from God and which damages, distorts or limits the development of our true human potential, can alleviate this concern.[6]

Salvation has a wide scope, matching the breadth and depth of human need. For Paul, salvation meant liberation from sin as well as from the confines of the Jewish law. For Augustine, it meant freedom from the corruption of the human will; for Luther, from the agonies of a troubled conscience; and for Wesley, from the darkness of the old life. The search for 'authentic' existence resonates with the deep needs of individuals and the critique of social structures that is emphasised by the liberation theologians has relevance to reality. These aspects of the human condition are relevant at any period of history. Salvation is an individual reality but also has a social context. It relates to wholeness of life and well-being. It has to do with material freedoms as well as spiritual ones. It relates to the healing of communities as well as of individuals. Jesus came to set us free from all that binds us.

◆ *Liberation theology argues that theology should not be separated from social involvement or political action. What are the advantages and the disadvantages of this approach?*

D. Issues for Salvationists

1. A freely chosen experience
Salvation requires the personal involvement of the individual in the process of repentance and faith. It involves a free and deliberate choice to re-orientate our life towards God. It may be comprehended differently according to the age, experience and ability of the believer, but perfect understanding is not necessary to repentance, nor to faith.

2. Regeneration is the work of the Spirit
Ultimately, it is the work of the Holy Spirit that brings about the experience of salvation. The Salvation Army has a responsibility to model, preach and teach salvation in ways that make it credible and understandable, but cannot make it happen. That is the work of the Spirit in human life, and is dependent upon the response of the individual who chooses to repent and believe.

3. The Salvation Army
The doctrine of salvation is central to Salvationist teaching and practice. We are a *Salvation* Army proclaiming the good news of salvation through faith in Christ. This salvation is made possible through God's grace and is available to all people regardless of their age, gender, status and cultural background.

4. Salvation is a holistic experience
All our activities, practical, social and spiritual, arise out of our basic conviction of the reality of the love of God and our desire to see all people brought into relationship with him. None of our practices or programmes can be divorced from the reality that salvation is both a promise and a possibility for all people. Our doctrine reminds us that salvation is holistic: the work of the Holy Spirit touches all areas of our life and personality, our physical, emotional and spiritual well-being, our relationships with our families and with the world around us. When we exercise practical care or seek to bring about

healing in families and in communities we are sharing the gospel of Jesus Christ.

◆ *'He ran thus till he came at a place somewhat ascending; and upon that place stood a cross, and a little below in the bottom, a sepulchre. So I saw in my dream, that just as Christian came up with the cross, his burden loosed from off his shoulders, and fell from off his back, and began to tumble, and so continued to do till it came to the mouth of the sepulchre, where it fell in, and I saw it no more.'[7] Does your experience of salvation resonate with Bunyan's image? Reflect upon similarities and differences.*

◆ *'The transformation of an individual leads to a transformation of relationships, of families, of communities, of nations. We long for and anticipate with joy the new creation of all things in Christ. Our mission is God's mission.'[8] How can we ensure that our mission is holistic and inclusive?*

◆ *Is the challenging of unjust or corrupt institutions or political regimes an integral part of the work of bringing salvation to the world?*

◆ *What is the role of the Salvation Army mercy seat in the process of bringing people to salvation? To what extent is a public act either helpful or necessary?*

◆ *Write a song, poem or a letter to a friend which celebrates the experience of salvation (see Luke 1:47-55).*

---

[1] Catherine Booth, undated. *The Highway of our God: Selections from the Army Mother's Writings.* London SP&S: 13
[2] Martin Luther, *Introduction to St Paul's Letter to the Romans* http://www.iclnet.org/pub/resources/text/wittenberg/luther/luther-faith.txt
[3] John Wesley, 1851 *Sermons on Several Occasions.* http://www.ccel.org/ccel/wesley/sermons.v.i.html

[4] Richard Watson, quoted in Alister E. McGrath, ed., *The Christian Theology Reader 3rd Edition*. Oxford Blackwell: 465

[5] Gustavo Gutiérrez, 1974 *A Theology of Liberation*. London: SCM Press :90

[6] For example see Judith Plaskow, 1908 *Sex, Sin and Grace*. University Press of America; Daphne Hampson, quoted in Alister E. McGrath, ed., *The Christian Theology Reader 3rd Edition*. Oxford Blackwell: 479-482

[7] John Bunyan, 1965 *Pilgrims Progress*. London: Penguin: 69-70

[8] Robert Street, 2008 *Called to Be God's People*. London: Salvation Books: 7

Chapter 8

The nature of salvation

Justification, grace and faith

We believe that we are justified by grace through faith in our Lord Jesus Christ and that he that believeth hath the witness in himself.

If the transforming grace brought about by the Atonement is to save us, we must experience the power of the universal work of Christ on the Cross for ourselves. This comes about, not by understanding the doctrine, but by trusting in the God who saves.

Those who come to God in true repentance and faith discover the overwhelming reality of his freely offered forgiveness. The result is a transformation of life, a revolution that can only be described as a new creation (2 Corinthians 5:17).

A. Justification

The word justification describes the act of God which changes the relationship between ourselves and him. Although we are sinners, God declares us righteous because of our faith in Jesus Christ (Romans 3:22). We are accepted by God as we are. We do not deserve such acceptance, neither can we earn it, or repay it. We can only experience the joy of forgiveness and reconciliation with God. Like the returning prodigal in Jesus' parable, we are treated as one who has the right to the Father's fellowship and esteem (Luke 15:17-24). We know ourselves to be children of God, and are affirmed in our relationship with him and with one another. We are fully adopted into the family of God, having the hope of eternal life (Galatians 4:3-7; Titus 3:4-7).

Our justification depends upon the character of God, the saving work of Jesus Christ and our faith in him. God, who is righteous, merciful and true, has reached out in the person of Jesus Christ to save the guilty and helpless. We are acquitted of our sin, accepted by God and our sins are forgiven because God is gracious and merciful. This is the gift of God.

Jesus taught the gracious fatherhood of God and the need for humble faith in his mercy. Paul's teaching used the image of justification to describe God's way of restoring all people to a right relationship with himself through faith in Christ (Romans 1:17; Galatians 2:16; 3:24). Justification is central to the good news of the gospel.

It is helpful to recognise that there is a paradox in our relationship with God that the twin blessings of justification and regeneration address. Justification speaks of a decisive change in our relationship with God through faith in Christ, from alienation to acceptance. Regeneration speaks of the life of the Spirit imparted to us; the ongoing work of grace in our lives in which we must co-operate. We know both the joy and the pain of the growth to which true righteousness invites us. Both regeneration and justification are true; though God calls us on to holiness of life, he always accepts us as his children and through the Spirit reassures us of our place with him.

B. Justified by grace

God seeks us before we even desire to seek him. His grace is totally unmerited (Hosea 11:3-4, 8-9), this is a characteristic of God's dealings with us at all times, seen supremely in Jesus Christ (1 Corinthians 1:4). It awakens us, convicts us of sin, convinces us of hope, enables us to respond and leads to new life.

However, we cannot presume upon God's forgiveness. He does not provide an automatic pardon for unrepentant sinners. It is by his grace that we are awakened to our need of salvation, and the necessary response is our repentance.

The term 'prevenient grace' describes this preparatory work of the Holy Spirit. It is the grace that comes before conversion. Our moral sense, or conscience, although imperfect because of ignorance and sin, can act as a stimulus to spiritual awakening. God gives a measure of moral enlightenment to all human beings, and the teaching of Jesus assures us that those who hunger and thirst for righteousness will be satisfied (Matthew 5:6). All this is a work of the Spirit who can transform natural remorse or human moral philosophy into a true awareness of God.

It is through the grace of God that the Holy Spirit convicts of sin. He reveals our real and appropriate guilt as opposed to feelings aroused by cultural or religious factors or excessive introspection. Grace that leads to this conviction has positive results – repentance, forgiveness and new life.

Our justification is by the grace of God. It is the grace of God that saves us when we first exercise justifying faith (Romans 3:24; Ephesians 2:4-10). Life in Christ demands continual reliance on the grace of God and not on our own goodness to earn God's favour. We are always in God's debt, always undeserving, always accepted by grace alone. God's saving grace will be complete only when our life reaches its final conclusion with Christ (Ephesians 1:13, 14).

C. Justification through faith

1. The nature of faith
Faith is our personal response to the grace of God. It is a trusting acceptance of the good news of the gospel, that God accepts us because of Jesus Christ. It involves commitment to him, an obedient response to his goodness and a desire to follow him in the way of discipleship (Romans 5:1, 2).

Therefore, faith is more than intellectual belief. Though faith in Christ requires the use of our minds, it is possible to assent to a creed without trusting the Saviour. Justifying faith involves heart, mind and will, and is made possible by God himself who bestows faith on those who desire it.

2. Faith and works

Faith is not a human achievement that wins or earns reward. It is the God-given channel through which grace flows. It is an attitude rather than an action.

Those who attempt to win acceptance with God by their own performance are doomed to continual frustration and unease because the greatest human effort can never fulfil all the requirements of true righteousness. Even if our outward lives appear to be flawless in conduct, we know that our thoughts and motives fall short of pleasing God. Greater striving may make us more self-centred and less God-directed, more judgmental and self-absorbed. A host of good works cannot build up a credit balance in God's accounting nor outweigh our sin (John 6:28, 29). Nevertheless, the outcome of genuine Christian faith will be good works as the believer lives obediently and faithfully (James 2:14-26).

When we abandon human efforts and cast ourselves in repentance on the merciful grace of God, his grace is freely given (Psalm 37:3-6). We are freed from guilt and accepted as righteous in and through Jesus Christ. Then, confidently resting on God's mercy, we discover the new way of righteousness, based not on human striving but on the life-giving grace of God (Romans 3:21-26).

D. Assurance

We believe that God, who has accepted and saved us and given us eternal life, has given us also the assurance of our right relationship with him. The Holy Spirit is the seal and guarantee of our salvation and assures us of the truth of the gospel message and its effectiveness for us. Our new life, our determination to obey God, our break with the past and our new spiritual direction give evidence of our adoption into God's family (Romans 8:14-17). We can be assured because the Holy Spirit speaks to us and our lives have been changed (1 John 5:1-12).

Our confidence is based not on changing moods or feelings but on the word of God. When we accept the biblical promises of God concerning our justification and regeneration, and our acceptance into God's family, we base our trust on the faithfulness of God who has given his promise and who can be trusted (Psalm 138:7, 8; Hebrews 10:19-23).

Assurance does not mean that we may never be troubled by doubt following our conversion or that we shall always be consciously aware of the work of the Spirit within us. However, at times when we do not feel consciously assured of our salvation we remember that an ongoing union with Christ depends on his work and not on our feelings (1 John 3:19-24).

Some people receive their assurance in a moment of intense experience; with others the assurance is quietly and slowly given. Such assurance must be affirmed daily by obedience and never made an excuse for carelessness or complacency. The changed, and changing, life is evidence for the work of grace within (2 Corinthians 13:5-7; Philippians 1: 4-6).

It is God's will that his children should know they belong to his family and so continue on their way with confidence (Romans 8:35-39). The gospel call to salvation is to faith, not fear.

E. A salvation to be claimed

We are justified by grace through faith in our Lord Jesus Christ, and are born again by the Holy Spirit, who testifies to salvation in our hearts as we continue in an obedient faith-relationship with Christ. The mission of the Church is to invite the world to share in this salvation. The Church that has received the good news of grace has the privilege of preaching it to a world which does not know or understand its truth. The Church that has learned to trust in Jesus has the joy of inviting to faith those who no longer trust. The Church that has the assurance of sins forgiven has the confidence to bring the message of God's reliable provision.

For further exploration 8

A. Essentials of the doctrine

1. Counted righteous before God

The Greek word which is translated as 'righteousness' (*dikaiosune*) has the same root meaning as the word which is normally translated 'to justify' (*dikaio*), that is 'to declare righteous'. Thus, when the Bible states that we are justified it means that God is treating us as though we are righteous.

2. God's action and human response

Justification is an act of God; it is his gift to us in that he treats us as if we are righteous (that is justified), even though we cannot deserve it, or earn it by following the law, or by living a particular lifestyle. The proper human response to God's justifying action is faith, which enables us to receive this gift (Philippians 3:7-11).

3. Jesus enables justification

The work of Jesus on the Cross met the conditions for human justification (Romans 4:24, 25; 5:18; Chapter 6).

4. The doctrine of assurance (1 John 5:10)

This provides peace of conscience, both in the objective truth that Jesus Christ provided atonement for sin and therefore justification

169

is a possibility, but also in the subjective sense of knowing the experience of justification as an individual believer.

5. For all people
The doctrines of justification by faith and assurance can be effective in the lives of all human beings who choose to believe in the atoning work of Jesus Christ.

◆ *Spend some time reading and reflecting on Ephesians 2:4-10. What does the passage say that God has done for us? What does it say about why he did it? How do these verses help you to understand the phrase 'the grace of God'?*

◆ *Find songs that describe the joy of the Christian's spiritual homecoming and acceptance by God. Make a list that you can use as a resource for meeting preparation and for personal devotions.*

B. Historical summary

1. The Old Testament
Old Testament teaching is consistent with the doctrine of justification

a. It shows that sin is universal (Psalm 14:3) but forgiveness is provided by God (Psalm 130:3, 4).

b. Abraham's belief in God's promise to give him an heir was 'credited to him as righteousness' (Genesis 15:6).

c. The image of a court of law as the means by which God provides for human salvation is evident in the Old Testament (Psalm 43:1).

2. The New Testament
a. The means of human salvation is through justification by grace through faith in Christ (Romans 3:21-26). This concept is

developed in Romans and Galatians, where Paul's concern is to explore the demands that should be placed on Gentile Christians with regard to the Jewish law. Should they have to obey the law in order to be counted as righteous? Paul argued that this is not a condition of Christian faith or living. We are justified, that is restored to a right relationship with God, solely by faith in Jesus, the crucified and risen Messiah (Romans 3-5; Galatians 3:23–4:7).

b. In a Jewish context righteousness was concerned with the law. The righteous person is one who is acquitted, who has secured a 'not guilty' verdict before God. This is only achievable through the Atonement (for further exploration 6B3). Righteousness is not concerned with what people do or with their intrinsic worth, but with their status before God.

c. The believer is therefore 'justified'. This is both a position, which is described by a changed status, as the relationship between God and humanity is restored, and a process, as the relationship continues. Our justification is brought about by faith as we accept that the work of Jesus on the Cross has made possible this change of status.

d. This takes place in the context of grace, God's gift to undeserving humanity (1 Corinthians 15:10; Ephesians 2:8).

e. There is nothing that needs to be added to faith in Christ, and people of all races and social situations may come to him and be made new through his grace (Galatians 3:28). God's freedom is for all.

f. Some commentators contrast the writings of James with those of Paul, suggesting that James 2:24 claims the possibility of justification by works. A careful reading of James 2:14-26 shows that works are the evidence of justifying faith. We act according to what we really believe, thus faith that is not worked out in our lifestyle is lifeless and worthless.

g. The believer can be assured of salvation (1 John 3:24; Romans 8:16). This is the work of the Spirit in the life of the believer. Similarly, Paul describes the Holy Spirit as a 'seal' (2 Corinthians 1:22; Ephesians 1:13; 4:30). This can imply ownership, but also suggests security and promise for the future.

3. Church teaching

a. Paul's teaching on justification was taken up in early Christianity by Augustine whose teaching centred around the primacy of God's grace. Augustine believed human beings to be by nature morally frail and susceptible to evil (for further exploration 5 B3), therefore our salvation comes to us only by the grace of God. 'But this grace of Christ, without which neither infants not grown persons can be saved, is not bestowed as a reward for merits, but is given freely [gratis] which is why it is called grace [gratia]'.[2]

b. However, Augustine followed this to its logical conclusion, suggesting that we cannot choose whether to be justified, nor can we reject the salvation that is offered. God's grace leads us to faith in Christ. It is then that we are free to love and choose the good and are restored to a right attitude towards God. We are made right and justified by grace. Thereafter, we live in this new relationship wholly by the grace of God.

c. In contrast to Augustinian theology, Salvation Army doctrine, while affirming the necessity of God's grace in human justification, is consistent with the Arminian viewpoint that salvation is also conditional on human response (For further exploration 6B3j and k; For further exploration 9B3b). We must choose to accept the gift that is offered.

d. In the 16th century the rise of humanism led to new emphasis on the importance of the individual and to new questions about how the individual Christian could have a personal relationship with

God. Luther came to an understanding of justification through personal experience and new insight into the biblical text. Despite his efforts to live a blameless life as a monk, Luther's conscience was troubled and he still believed himself to be a sinner before God. Eventually, while reading Romans 1, he realised that the phrase 'the righteousness of God' (1:17) referred not to God's desire to punish, but to save. 'I began to understand that in this verse the justice of God is that by which the just person lives by a gift of God, that is by faith.'[3] God graciously gives the righteousness which human beings cannot attain. The sole requirement is trusting faith. This discovery brought personal liberation to Luther. His subsequent teaching of salvation by faith alone brought him into conflict with the Roman Catholic Church and led to the Protestant Reformation.

e. Augustine had spoken of justification as being made right with God, this is sometimes described as 'imparted righteousness' because God's gift of righteousness actually becomes part of who we are – we *are* righteous. For Luther, justification does not make us righteous, so much as count us righteous. This is 'imputed righteousness'. Our salvation involves taking upon ourselves the righteousness of Christ which is never our own, but his. Therefore God treats us *as if* we are righteous.

f. Luther spoke of our 'alien' righteousness. Through faith we are 'clothed' in righteousness (see Ezekiel 16:8). Both Luther and Calvin used the image of putting on new robes: our sin is like a set of filthy clothes which we exchange for the robes of Christ. The 'clothes' belong to Christ, so the sinful nature remains beneath the 'covering' of Christ. 'A man will be justified by faith when ... by faith [he] lays hold of the righteousness of Christ, and clothed in it appears in the sight of God not as a sinner, but as righteous.'[4] We can be sinners in our own eyes, but righteous before God. In this way, we realise that we are always dependent upon the grace of God.

g. The nature of faith is significant. It is always personal and is not just an historical understanding of the gospel narrative. Faith requires active belief in Jesus Christ crucified and risen for us. It must also be understood as trust: the Christian does not only give mental assent to the truth, but is willing to rely upon and act upon their belief. Finally, faith unites the believer to Christ. It is the complete response of the complete person to God. This is not to say that faith leads to justification, but that through faith justification is received. The initiative and the provision are God's, for even faith is a gift of God.

h. The doctrine of justification by faith has had a profound effect upon Protestantism, for it leads directly to the question of how the justified Christian is set free to become in reality what he already is in Christ. Some believers appear to have suggested that behaviour and lifestyle are not relevant, and possibly even that continuing to sin would allow for an increase of grace (Romans 6:1). This was one of the fears of those who challenged Luther's doctrine of justification in the following centuries: the fear of moral laxity – antinomianism. This issue is addressed in the doctrines of regeneration and sanctification.

i. John Wesley made a significant distinction between justification, which he sees in terms of imputed righteousness, and being actually made just and righteous, which he equates with sanctification (Chapter 10). Suggesting that sanctification is the fruit of justification, Wesley argues that God in justifying us does something for us through the Son; when we are sanctified the Spirit does the work in us.[5]

j. Another significant blessing of salvation is the Holy Spirit's gift of assurance (1 John 5:10). Because of God's great mercy, we can have confidence that our salvation is secure. This is particularly Protestant evangelical teaching. In Roman Catholic teaching, human conviction is viewed as fallible: it is seen to be rather presumptuous to be sure of God's favour. In contrast, Protestants stress the trustworthiness of God. The giver of the promise can be trusted (Hebrews 10:22, 23).

The Return of the Prodigal Son by Rembrandt c1669

◆ Read the story of the prodigal son in Luke 15:11-32 and try to imagine it from the point of view of the father and then of each of his sons. Think about the scope of the father's love and the response of the brothers. A group could role play the story to similar effect. How is this story related to Doctrine 8?

◆ John Wesley sought and found assurance in his 'Aldersgate experience' of 24 May 1738: 'About a quarter before nine, while he (the one who was reading Luther's preface to the Epistle to the Romans) was describing the change which God works in the heart through faith in Christ, I felt my heart strangely warmed. I felt I did trust in Christ, Christ alone, for my salvation, and an assurance was given me that he had taken away my sins, even mine, and saved me from the law of sin and death.[6] How would you describe your experience of justification and assurance?

◆   No condemnation now I dread;
                  Jesus, and all in him, is mine.
                  Alive in him, my living head,
            And clothed in righteousness divine,
          Bold I approach the eternal throne
      And claim the crown, through Christ, my own.[7]

Plan a Bible study or discussion group which explores the doctrinal implications of this verse.

C. Issues for Salvationists

1. By grace

It is God's gift to bring us into a right relationship with him, to justify us. We cannot earn our salvation. The Salvation Army's social action and advocacy for social justice can only be properly understood when beginning from this premise. Our actions are a consequence of our salvation, not the way in which we prove ourselves worthy of it.

2. Through faith

Doctrine 8 clearly states that personal faith is the means through which we know ourselves to be in a right relationship with God. This deep trust in, and willingness to base our lives upon, the action of God in Jesus Christ is the foundation for an ongoing and individual relationship with God. Faith is an action which goes beyond mental or intellectual understanding. It is available to all who believe, and a necessity for all who would claim to be Salvationists.

3. We can know that we are saved

For those who choose to accept the grace of God and place their trust in him there is the possibility of knowing that we are saved. Our life can be based upon this confidence and our living must reflect this truth. Our salvation does not depend upon how we feel but upon the promise and action of God. In the climate of religious, political and cultural uncertainty which forms the environment of many Salvationists, the assurance of salvation is a vital facet of our doctrine and can offer the possibility of security and stability in the face of ambiguity.

◆ *Read Romans 3-5; Galatians 3:23–4:7 in conjunction with the notes above. What are the challenges of communicating the meaning of justification by faith in the 21st century?*

◆ *Review your faith journey so far. To what extent has the assurance of your salvation enabled you to 'live above feeling'?[8]*

◆ *Discuss the activist heritage of The Salvation Army. How is it possible to guard against an attitude that seems to imply that salvation can be achieved or maintained by our good works?*

---

[1] *The Song Book of The Salvation Army* 1986 371:2
[2] Augustine quoted in Alister E. McGrath, ed., *The Christian Theology Reader 3rd Edition.* Oxford Blackwell: 416

[3] Martin Luther, *Preface to the Complete Edition of Luther's Latin Works* (1545)
http://www.iclnet.org/pub/resources/text/wittenberg/luther/tower.txt

[4] John Calvin, *Institutes of the Christian religion Book 1*
http://www.ccel.org/ccel/calvin/institutes.v.xii.html

[5] John Wesley, *Sermons on Several Occasions*
http://www.ccel.org/ccel/wesley/sermons.v.v.html

[6] John Wesley, *The Journal of John Wesley*
http://www.ccel.org/ccel/wesley/journal.vi.ii.xvi.html

[7] Charles Wesley, *The Song Book of The Salvation Army* 1986 283:4

[8] Lucy Milward Booth-Hellberg, *The Song Book of The Salvation Army* 1986 773:4

Chapter 9

Maintaining salvation

Continued obedient faith

We believe that continuance in a state of salvation depends upon continued obedient faith in Christ.

A. The blessings of salvation

The word generally used to describe becoming a Christian is conversion. It indicates a change of direction, an about-turn, a change of heart. It means entering into a new relationship with God in which unbelief is replaced by belief and trust, resulting in new life.

This new relationship brings great joy and many blessings. There is open communication between the individual and God: the pain of separation is past. We are aware of new desires for good and new power to realise them. We enjoy a sense of confidence in God's presence and feel that we are part of a new family. We long for more of God and his reality in our present and our future. Such blessings as these have been expressed in the language of Christian doctrine, for example: justification, regeneration, assurance, adoption and sanctification. The terms are important in identifying the nature of our personal experience and grounding it in the universal experience of Christian believers.

God's purpose in saving us is to create in us the likeness of his Son, Jesus Christ, who is the true image of God, so that we may 'participate in the divine nature' (2 Peter 1:4). It is to make it possible for us to glorify God as Christ's true disciples. It is to make us holy (Ephesians 4:22-24).

B. Backsliding

Assurance (Chapter 8) does not mean that our salvation is guaranteed to us against our free will. It is possible to cease to obey Christ and so forfeit our hope of eternal life. This is consistent with our understanding of the grace of God, who always leaves us open to respond freely to him. Freedom to live by grace includes freedom to turn away.

This doctrine reminds us that the Christian life requires a combined commitment of faith and obedience (Jude 20, 21) and a willingness to be led by the Spirit of God (Romans 8:14). The Gospel of John uses the image of the vine and the branches to signify the deep and sustained connection that is necessary between Jesus and his disciples.

'Remain in me, and I will remain in you. No branch can bear fruit by itself; it must remain in the vine. Neither can you bear fruit unless you remain in me' (John 15:4).

When this relationship is broken, backsliding is possible even for true Christians. It can be described as an expression of human unresponsiveness or opposition to the will of God, and can occur through the deliberate rejection of Christ, or, more insidiously, when we drift from the way of discipleship or neglect our spiritual life (Hebrews 2:1-3). It may happen when we fail to do what we know to be right, or when we deliberately and continuously choose what we know to be wrong (Hebrews 10:19-39). This does not mean that every time we sin we slide away from the grace of God. A wrong action is not backsliding. What is important is the attitude which follows the act. Our many failures will not deprive us of the Holy Spirit's presence if we turn to him for forgiveness and restoration. Yet this does not mean that we can be careless or complacent in our attitude to sin (Romans 6:1-4).

Ultimately, consistent backsliding results in loss of connection with Christ; this brings lasting consequences (Matthew 5:13; John 15:6; Hebrews 10:26-31; Revelation 2:4, 5; 3:1-6, 14-22).

To develop and nurture a life secured by a total trust in God's grace, we should not be daunted by the possibility of being tempted beyond our powers (1 Corinthians 10:6-13). Our obedient faith, which enabled us to know Christ as Saviour, will not be sustained by over-anxiety about staying saved, or by limiting our involvement with life for fear of backsliding. Our faith will be assured as in obedience to Christ's call to serve we keep close to him: to risk our lives wherever there is human need, challenge sin and dare to live the Christian life in all its fullness.

C. Continued obedient faith

When we live a life of continued obedient faith in Christ we will not fall from grace and be eternally lost. This life involves the spiritual disciplines of prayer, Bible study and self-denial, as well as openness to the ministry of the Body of Christ through worship, teaching, caring and service. However, obedient faith, although dependent upon human commitment and action, also requires the continued inward working of the Holy Spirit in the life of the believer (Philippians 2:13; Hebrews 13:20, 21).

Our salvation is assured as long as we continue to exercise faith in Jesus Christ. Such faith is expressed in obedience to his leadings, will and commands. Obedience as a free will choice is a consequence of faith, and without it faith dies.

Our conversion inaugurates a journey during which we are being transformed into Christ's likeness. Thus salvation is neither a state to be preserved nor an insurance policy which requires no further investment. It is the beginning of a pilgrimage with Christ. This pilgrimage requires from us the obedience of separation from sin and consecration to the purposes of God (Colossians 2:6, 7; 1 Thessalonians 5:12-22). This is why 'obedient faith' is crucial: it makes pilgrimage possible as we cooperate with God, allowing him to do his work within us. It is completed by God's deepening action within us to make us holy (Chapter 10).

Our Christian pilgrimage is a faith-journey inviting us to a life of discipleship which will be evident in our daily life (Romans 12). Through prayer and the study of God's word, we grow in our relationship with him. By following Christ we learn to put into practice what we hear through the Spirit. We grow in obedience and faithfulness to God (2 Peter 3:18; I John 5:1-5). We begin to discover that obedient faith is given by God's grace, rather than achieved by our superlative efforts.

We become aware of the sanctifying work of the Holy Spirit.

For further exploration 9

'If faith is the trusting of one's sinful life to God for salvation,
it is also the trustful dedication of one's redeemed life in
obedient service to him.'

Frederick Coutts[1]

A. Essentials of the doctrine

1. Continuous faith

This doctrine underlines the fact that Christian discipleship requires
constant cooperation with God. Faith is not a single action at the
point of salvation but an ongoing commitment and way of life.
Doctrine 9 is complemented by Doctrine 10 which speaks of the
work of sanctification that God will do in the life of the obedient
believer.

2. Obedient faith

Faith requires obedience. Our commitment to God requires that we
choose to do his will (Matthew 6:9, 10). However, God provides the
resources to live in obedience to the Spirit (Romans 8:3, 4).

3. The marks of obedient faith

Obedient faith is marked by a desire to know the will of God,
prayerful dependence upon him (2 Corinthians 12:9, 10) and
dedication to living a life that is consistent with his known will
(Romans 12:1, 2).

4. The possibility of failure

Throughout our lives we retain the ability to make our own choices.
God's gift of free will is never removed. If we disobey the revealed
will of God we fail (Luke 6:46-49). Continual and unrepentant

disobedience can result in loss of faith, and loss of our status in Christ. This is known as backsliding.

◆ *Reflect upon your own experience of 'continued obedient faith'. What have been the greatest joys and the most difficult challenges?*

B. Historical summary

1. The Old Testament

a. From the earliest times the covenant relationship between God and the people of Israel required continued obedience to the Law and to the will of God (Exodus 20:1-17; Deuteronomy 6:1-25).

b. The determined efforts of the people of God to turn from God and therefore fail to keep their part of the covenant relationship are described as backsliding. 'And my people are bent to backsliding from me: though they called them to the most High, none at all would exalt him' (Hosea 11:7 *KJV*).

c. God's love and faithfulness remained constant, despite continual failure by the people (Jeremiah 31:3; Hosea 11:1-11, Ezekiel 37:23).

2. The New Testament

a. Christian discipleship is described in various terms which indicate that it is a continuous relationship. They include remaining in Christ (John 15:4), living in Christ Jesus (Colossians 2:6), walking in the Spirit (Galatians 5:25), and growing in grace and knowledge of Christ (2 Peter 3:18).

b. Continuous and obedient faith is dependent upon the empowerment of God (Philippians 2:13; Hebrews 13:20, 21).

c. If there is need for 'continued obedient faith' it must be possible for a genuine Christian believer to choose to turn away from their faith, to backslide (Matthew 5:13; Luke 8:13; 9:62; John 15:6). Hebrews 6:4-6 describes the eventual consequences of this choice.

d. Possible reasons for backsliding include the influence of other people (1 Kings 11:4), preference for secular life (2 Timothy 4:10), and neglecting the word of God and the spiritual life (Luke 8:13).

e. Ultimate salvation is promised to those who continue in the faith (Matthew 10:22; 24:13; Colossians 1:22, 23; Hebrews 3:14; Revelation 2:10).

◆ *'Demas, because he loved this world, has deserted me' (2 Timothy 4:10). Discuss the influences in your 'world' that may induce a believer to abandon their faith. What strategies can help to guard against this?*

◆ *Write a parable which expresses the truth of Doctrine 9.*

3. The Calvinist-Arminian debate

In chapters 5-8 reference has been made to different and sometimes divergent views relating to the human condition and the doctrine of salvation. The Calvinist-Arminian debate, which is named after the two theologians whose work and legacy largely characterise the opposing views, John Calvin and Jacobus Arminius, is particularly relevant to Salvation Army theology.

The debate can be summarised in five points, which, in English, are often known by the acrostic TULIP, relating to the Calvinist perspective.

	Calvinist views	**Arminian views**
a.	Total depravity	Total depravity
b.	Unconditional election	Conditional election
c.	Limited atonement	Unlimited atonement
d.	Irresistible grace	Prevenient grace
e.	Perseverance of the saints	Conditional preservation

185

A summary of the similarities and differences and their relationship to The Salvation Army Articles of Faith appears below:

a. Total depravity – as a consequence of the fall (Genesis 3) all human beings have a disposition to sin, and no area of human nature is unaffected. People are inclined to follow and serve their own interests rather than God (For further exploration 5B3). Human freedom to respond to God is impaired. Although not all theologians subscribe to the doctrine of total depravity it is the major point of agreement between Calvinists and Arminians and is specifically stated in Salvation Army Doctrine 5.

b. Unconditional election – This Calvinist doctrine asserts that God chooses those whom he will bring to himself. This is not based on any virtue, merit or good works, but only on his mercy and grace. Predestination is therefore related to the individual believer who is chosen by God (for further exploration 6B3i). As with each of the five Calvinist beliefs, the seeds of this approach can be found in the teaching of Augustine. His emphasis on the supremacy of God's grace led him to understand salvation as being given wholly at God's discretion (for further exploration 8B3b). God's grace is a gift, which some may receive and some not. So, although sin is universal, grace is particular. Augustine called this 'election'. This leads inevitably to the conclusion that some will be saved – by God's grace – and some not. Some are 'elected' to be saved. John Calvin in his *Institutes of the Christian Religion* took this notion to the logical conclusion that some must therefore be elected to be damned: 'All are not created on equal terms, but some are preordained to eternal life, others to eternal damnation'.[2] In contrast, for Arminians, election is conditional upon faith in Christ. God therefore saves all those who freely choose to fulfil the predestined condition of salvation. Predestination therefore becomes a corporate rather than an individual issue, 'It cannot be said, "Faith is bestowed on the elect, or on those who are to be saved," but that "believers are elected and saved."'[3] All people who have chosen faith in Christ are predestined to salvation. Salvation Army Doctrine 7 implies the Arminian belief in conditional election – those who choose salvation are the elect of God.

c. Limited atonement – A logical consequence of unconditional election is the belief that only certain individuals will be saved. Augustine uses the image of the potter, arguing: 'The potter has authority over the clay, of the same lump to make one vessel for honour, and the other for contempt.'[4] This, coupled with an understanding that all those who are the elect will necessarily be saved, summarises the Calvinist doctrine of limited atonement. Arminian theology maintains the universal character and scope of the Atonement. The Salvation Army's Arminian roots are shown clearly in Doctrine 6, which states that 'whosoever will may be saved'.

d. Irresistible grace – The doctrine of irresistible grace argues that the saving grace of God will always be effective for those he has elected to save, so that in God's timing any resistance will be overcome and they will be brought to faith. The Holy Spirit is able to overcome any resistance to salvation. While affirming the doctrine of prevenient grace, that grace which 'goes before' and prepares the human being for salvation, and acknowledging the role of the grace of God in all aspects of the experience of salvation, Arminian theology denies the notion of irresistible grace and affirms the possibility of human choice and decision. For The Salvation Army, the phrases 'whosoever *will* may be saved' and 'repentance toward God, faith in our Lord Jesus Christ … are necessary to salvation' (Doctrines 6 and 7), clearly indicate the importance of human decision making and agency in the process of salvation.

e. Perseverance of the saints – This doctrine implies that our salvation is so 'secure' that it cannot be negated in any way

187

through our personal behaviour or response to God. It is supported by biblical interpretation of texts such as John 10:28 (see also 6:37, 40), Philippians 1:6 and 1 John 2:19. Calvin believed that, in view of God's election, it is impossible for those who have been truly saved to backslide, for that would be to deny the grace of God. Those who apparently fall away will either return, or were never truly saved. In opposition to this, Arminians maintain that backsliding is possible. 'Continuance in a state of salvation depends upon continued obedient faith in Christ' (Doctrine 9). God graciously gives free will, so that we may respond to his grace and also, if we desire, turn away from it.

In summary, it is evident that the Salvationist articles of faith echo Arminian theology. This is largely due to the roots of The Salvation Army in Methodism and the strong influence of Wesleyan theology upon William and Catherine Booth and other early Salvationist thinkers.

Nevertheless it is important to remember that both Calvinism and Arminianism are systems of theology which were developed by godly, scholarly, biblically-focused Christians. Both trace their roots to the Bible and contain elements of the truth. The Calvinist emphasis on the absolute sovereignty of God can be traced in Scripture, as can the Arminian insistence on the free will of humanity. Although theological systems are important for the development of both understanding and the spiritual life, they may never be fully reconciled on an intellectual level, because God, his dealings with human beings, and the mystery of the Atonement, cannot ultimately be apprehended by reason, but must be experienced by faith.

◆ *Review the sections of this book that address the Calvinist-Arminian debate. Ensure that you would be able to explain the main arguments to a new Christian who has expressed a wish to understand these issues.*

C. Issues for Salvationists

1. Guarding our relationship with God

The commitment of faith made at the point of salvation must be followed by a continual development of our trusting and obedient relationship with God. The moment of salvation must lead to a lifestyle which reflects our understanding of God's will for our lives. Salvation Army teaching must facilitate the development of this obedience, by guiding and nurturing all who make a commitment to follow, holding them accountable for their personal faith journey.

2. Personal spiritual disciplines

It is the responsibility of all Salvationists to ensure that their spiritual life is nourished appropriately, in corporate worship and fellowship and by participation in individual spiritual disciplines. This may include personal prayer and Bible reading, attendance at conferences and retreats, mentoring, spiritual direction and other helpful aids to the development of the spiritual life.

3 The possibility of turning away from God.

Salvation must never lead to complacency. There are no Christians for whom the possibility of turning away from God is irrelevant. Anyone could, gradually or suddenly, choose to reject the salvation they have claimed and abandon their relationship with God. All members of Salvationist communities have a responsibility to be alert to signs of disobedience, disinterest or disillusionment in their own lives or those of other people and to challenge any attitude or behaviour that is contrary to this doctrine.

◆ *'I believe that if I deliberately turn my back on God and keep walking away from him there will come a point where the relationship is severed and I am no longer "in Christ"'.[5] How do we recognise the signs of backsliding in ourselves or other people?*

189

◆ *How would you design a Bible study series for young people aged 15-18 years on the lifestyle implications of 'continued obedient faith'?*

◆ *Think of people you know who were once Christians but no longer either worship or profess belief. Commit yourself to pray for them, and, if appropriate, to work actively for their return to faith and fellowship.*

---

[1] Frederick Coutts, 1969 *Essentials of Christian Experience*. London: The Salvation Army: 44-45

[2] John Calvin, *Institutes of the Christian Religion*
http://www.ccel.org/ccel/calvin/institutes.v.xxii.html

[3] Jacobus Arminius, http://wesley.nnu.edu/arminianism/arminius/Arminius.htm

[4] Augustine quoted in Alister E. McGrath, ed., *The Christian Theology Reader 3rd Edition*. Oxford Blackwell: 414

[5] Grant Sandercock-Brown, *Blessed Assurance* in *The Officer* May/June 2009: 48

Chapter 10

Full salvation

The doctrine of holiness

We believe that it is the privilege of all believers to be wholly sanctified, and that their whole spirit and soul and body may be preserved blameless unto the coming of our Lord Jesus Christ.

A. The sanctifying Spirit at work

1. Sanctification

During the experience of salvation the regenerating power of the Holy Spirit becomes a reality in the life of the believer, enabling us to move from the point of conversion and new life towards mature experience as a Christian. The experience of justification is not a destination, but is the beginning of a journey which should be characterised by growth and development.

This is not an automatic process, but one which requires that we are open to the need for change, so that we begin to live according to God's will and purposes rather than our own, and are willing to allow the Holy Spirit to work within us to achieve this end. In response to the command of God to 'Be holy, because I am holy' (1 Peter 1:16) we are called to holy living as a corollary to our salvation.

Sanctification by grace through faith enables holy living. The terms 'sanctification', 'sanctify' and 'sanctified' are translations of the Hebrew and Greek words of Scripture used to describe the holiness of God and the action by which God's children are made holy and set apart for God's purposes. The 10th Salvation Army statement of faith particularly relates to this action of God: 'We believe that it is the privilege of all believers to be wholly sanctified, and that their whole spirit and soul and body may be preserved blameless unto the coming of our Lord Jesus Christ' (quoting 1 Thessalonians 5:23 *KJV*).

Discovering and appropriating for ourselves the sanctifying power of the Holy Spirit is not a new experience unrelated to saving faith and the experience of regeneration. The same grace at work in our lives both saves and sanctifies. The experience of holiness enables us to address the challenges faced when we discover the powerlessness, disillusionment and guilt that may come when we realise that our experience of salvation does not protect us from temptation but does make us more aware of the power of sin, and the reality of human weakness. Nevertheless, by the power of the Spirit we can overcome these challenges and can advance towards the fulfilment of that which our conversion promises – victory over sin, the life of holiness and mature Christian living.

2. God's gracious provision

By God's gracious provision the Holy Spirit works within us and calls us to that holiness which is the privilege of all believers.

We are called to reflect the holiness of God. God is holy, awesome in his majesty and in the beauty of his character. His children are called to reflect his holiness and be dedicated to his service, becoming like him in character (1 Thessalonians 4:1-8).

This is not a call directed to an elect few, nor to an élite who have particular spiritual qualifications, nor does the phrase, 'the privilege of all believers' mean it is optional. It is God's intention for all his people. God calls all Christians: 'Be holy because I am holy' (1 Peter 1:16).

The life of holiness is not mysterious or overwhelming or too difficult to understand. It is becoming like Christ who is the true image of God. He is the truly holy one, who revealed the holiness of God in the wholeness and fullness of his human life and in the manner of his self-offering to God (John 17:15-17). To see him is to understand the nature of holiness, and to follow him is to be marked by it. Holiness is Christlikeness.

Holiness is the realisation of the Christ-life within us. It is the present purpose and positive benefit of our salvation. It is the renewal of our humanity according to the pattern or image of God our Creator. The power of the sin that was cancelled on the Cross is now broken. The Christian is enabled by the power of the Holy Spirit to live a life of discipleship (Romans 8:1-17).

This work of God makes it possible to live according to the purpose for which we were created: to enjoy the gifts of God, to serve and worship him through our living, and to share human fellowship in love and service. God sanctifies us so that we may share fellowship with him to his pleasure, live fulfilled human lives and carry out his mission in the world.

3. By grace through faith

The sanctifying Spirit makes this experience possible. In regeneration, we receive the Holy Spirit who creates new life in Christ and fills us with joy and the assurance of salvation. The Spirit then remains with us. His sanctifying work becomes a reality for us through the life of faith which involves both trust in and continued obedience towards God. We become increasingly transformed into the people God intends us to be (2 Corinthians 3:17, 18).

Even though the Holy Spirit is at work in our lives, he never imposes himself on us or undermines our freedom of choice. The desire for holiness must be in us, and the sincerity of this intention must be affirmed by dedicating our lives to Christ (Romans 8:1-11). As we act in faith, we experience sanctification. The possibility of holiness becomes a reality only through faith, by trusting the grace of the sanctifying God and obeying his word.

4. A radical life-change

The Cross is at the heart of the holiness experience. It points the way to new life. Scripture describes our decisive dying to the old self and to sin in dramatic terms, as we identify with Christ in his death for us and recognise that in a profound sense we died in him (Romans 6:1-14).

God's sanctifying work is a life-changing experience whereby we are empowered to make radical changes of direction in our lives (2 Corinthians 5:14, 15) so that the Spirit of Christ comes and lives his life in us (Galatians 2:20; Ephesians 3:14-19). Sometimes a compelling glimpse of the holiness of God opens our eyes to our need of purity. We may be stimulated to seek to live a holy life because we long for a more satisfying relationship with God. The call to service may lead to a deeper desire for sanctifying grace. We may experience the pain and agony of encountering evil and sin lurking within us. We may become aware of our inclination to give in to temptation or relax our guard. The Holy Spirit's leading and our own desire for more of God may in such circumstances lead to a spiritual crisis.

At such times the Holy Spirit is overwhelmingly present with power for holy living. We experience a moment of grace that leads to spiritual breakthrough. We move to a new level of relationship with the holy God, with others and with ourselves (Philippians 1:9-11).

Such life-changing moments are widespread, but dramatic experiences are not always a feature of our growth in holiness. The Holy Spirit deals with us as individuals and leads us into holiness in the way he sees fit.

We should judge the growth of our spiritual life by the quality of our obedience, and by a deepening and transforming commitment to love for God, other people and ourselves (Romans 12:1, 2; Colossians 3:5-14), rather than by the depth and intensity of our spiritual experiences.

5. A lifelong process

There is a crisis/process dynamic in the life of holiness. Often experienced as a crisis, that is a decisive turning point and decision, sanctification becomes a lifelong process. We are in the process of becoming what we already are in Christ through justification. The holy life, however, will always be marked by an 'already but not yet' reality. We are already sanctified but not yet sinlessly perfect.

Sanctification by the Holy Spirit can extend to the whole or entire personality with no area of life unaffected, just as the pervasive effects of sin have penetrated every area of human life. However, the doctrine of entire sanctification does not mean that in this life we ever arrive at a point where further spiritual progress is unnecessary for those who have been sanctified, even as total depravity does not mean that the unredeemed are as bad as they can be.

The truly holy life is marked by the signature and seal of Christ himself. 'He anointed us, set his seal of ownership on us, and put his Spirit in our hearts as a deposit, guaranteeing what is to come' (2 Corinthians 1:21, 22). In response, first and foremost we seek a close spiritual relationship with God, marked by openness, obedience and connection to him (John 15:1-7). As a result of this relationship we become more like Christ (Romans 8:29; Ephesians 4:13-15; 2 Peter 3:18; 1 John 3:1-3) and his holiness becomes evident in our living. This deepening bond is evidence of our commitment and longing for holiness. Paul describes it as 'Christ living in me' (Galatians 2:20). We experience the presence of the crucified and risen Christ in our own lives.

Christ's presence changes us as we live in and through him. Our self-image undergoes a change. We rest in the knowledge of the love, grace and acceptance of God and this sets us at peace and brings us self-acceptance. Our relationships are marked by those qualities of life which are described by Paul as 'the fruit of the Spirit' (Galatians 5:22-26).

As we follow Jesus, who came to seek and save the lost, we sense the call to serve others in Christ's name. We build relationships with the lost, the abused, the forgotten and the powerless. In them we see Christ. We are drawn to search for truth and justice and the righting of wrongs in the name of Christ.

The holy life is a sacramental life. Reflecting Jesus, it is an open and visible sign of the grace of God. It is a fulfilled human life, a life of close communion with God and self-forgetful service to others. It is a life that anticipates our final sanctification when we are glorified, as eternity breaks through and God becomes all in all (1 Corinthians 15:28).

B. The life of holiness

1. The restoration of the covenant

As the Fall resulted in the fragmentation of all relationships, so the restored image of God in us expresses itself in the renewal of our relationships. This restoration is crucial to holy living. Since God is a covenant-making and a covenant-keeping God, our relationships should be characterised by the requirements of covenant responsibility. This means that our relationships, both with God and with others, must be built on love and faithfulness.

In the Bible, the concept of covenant underlies all relationships. A covenant of obedience to God results in righteous living marked by loving relationships, care for others and faithfulness to moral values. Seeking to glorify God and value people, it pursues love within the God-given intention of the relationship.

We are first and foremost in covenant with God who faithfully keeps his covenant of love with us. As we respond to that love, our relationship with him deepens and we are drawn closer to him. As this love grows, it expresses itself in the life of discipleship. The sanctified believer is empowered by love and guided by obedience to keep covenant.

As our relationship with God unfolds, love for God draws us to other people, and obedient discipleship motivates us to put love into action. Our participation in caring fellowship overcomes our selfishness, challenges our self-righteousness and leads us on to love, humility, wholeness and a desire to see others brought into covenant with God.

Our relationship with God's world is also transformed. We see the beauty and reflection of God in it and acknowledge that it is his world, the fruit of his creation. Hostility towards the created world disappears, and we come to understand our role as stewards.

Holiness, then, expresses itself socially in covenants. It both places us in the social arena and transforms our relationships.

2. Holiness and ethics

Ethics deals primarily with important relational issues. Holiness is true love, nurtured and expressed in relationships. For this reason, Christian ethics is an extremely important dimension and discipline of holy living. It provides the principles and guidelines for the fullness of love in all our relationships.

Jesus Christ is the fulfilment of all that the Old Testament law had promised and anticipated. He taught that the Law was, in fact, fulfilled in love (Mark 12:28-31). This was the ethic of love. To realise Jesus' radical ethic of love is to treat all our relationships as holy covenants (Matthew 5:43-48; Luke 10:25-37; 1 John 4:7-21). God is able to love through us. This transformation is what makes social holiness possible and what enables us to live by the radical ethic of love.

3. Wholeness, health and healing

The God who sanctifies is the healing God who makes us whole (Psalm 30:2; 103:3). The term 'wholeness' points to the comprehensiveness of God's saving work in Christ and of the Spirit's sanctification.

The Gospels reveal that Jesus cared about every dimension of human life and how sin has distorted it, and that his ministry demonstrated a healing response to human suffering and disease in all its forms (Matthew 20:34; Mark 1:32-34, 40-45; Luke 7:11-17). Again and again, the New Testament as a whole records the healing work of the Holy Spirit. The restoration of the covenant required the restoration of health in every relationship of human life: spiritual, emotional, social, physical (Mark 2:1-12; Luke 4:18; 7:22; Ephesians 2:11-22).

This means that there is no holiness without wholeness. Holiness can only be seen as redemptively touching all of life. This does not mean, however, that all those who are physically healthy, or emotionally stable, or socially adjusted, or economically prosperous are holy. Nor does it mean that those who suffer from physical infirmity, emotional turmoil, social maladjustment or economic deprivation are thus sinful. What it does mean is that in claiming holiness we claim the promise of wholeness in all of life. The holy life is then the Spirit-led journey toward wholeness in Christ.

As Jesus refused to attribute illness to specific sin (John 9:3), so we see every form of disease or infirmity only as a manifestation of the overall human condition. And as he did not heal all diseases and restore every broken relationship, so we recognise that the sanctified do not manifest the signs of complete healing in every area of life. The healing we rightfully claim is profound, the effects may await eternity.

As God's holy people we are concerned not only about our own wholeness and health but also that of others. Thereby we who know healing for ourselves become a healing community engaged in a healing mission in anticipation of the final healing to be experienced in the New Jerusalem (James 5:13-16; Revelation 22:1, 2).

4. A holiness to be lived out in mission

The holy life is expressed through a healing, life-giving and loving ministry. It is the life of Christ which we live out in mission. God sanctifies his people not only in order that they will be marked by his character, but also in order that the world will be marked by that character. God changes the structures of society through a variety of means, but he changes them as well through the mission of his sanctified people, empowered and gifted by his Holy Spirit.

The mission of God's holy people encompasses evangelism, service and social action. It is the holy love of God, expressed in the heart and life of his people, pointing the world to Christ, inviting the world to saving grace, serving the world with Christ's compassion and attacking social evils. Holiness leads to mission.

Sanctification by grace through faith is the privilege and calling of all who profess Jesus Christ as their Lord and Saviour and who accept the power of the Holy Spirit to lead a life of holiness.

For further exploration 10

A. Essentials of the doctrine

1. For all believers

Salvation begins with repentance, faith and regeneration (Chapter 7)
and must be sustained by obedient faith (Chapter 9). The
development of life 'in Christ' (2 Corinthians 5:17) is explored in
Doctrine 10. Holiness is not an optional extra for some believers,
but is available to all who accept Jesus as Lord. While described as
a privilege, this does not imply that it is a requirement for only some
Christians.

2. The will and work of God

It is God's intention that human beings will be holy (1 Peter 1:16);
it is also his work in the life of the believer that enables them to be
holy (1 Thessalonians 5:23, 24). Sanctification, being made holy, is
a logical and natural continuation of the process of salvation.

3. Human choice

Although holiness is achieved by the work of God in the life of the believer, it is also a product of human choice. God will not make people holy against their will. Holiness, like salvation, must be freely chosen. This is sometimes described as consecration, although there is not always a clear distinction between the terms used for God's action to make the believer holy and the human pursuit of holiness.

4. Restoring the image of God

Holiness is concerned with a restoration of wholeness and full humanity. Growth towards holiness sets us in the direction of recovering the true image of God in us as we allow him to live his life in and through us. Jesus Christ made true humanity visible by his living. As we move towards wholeness, it affects every aspect of our being, including our relationships with God and other people, our self-image, our attitude to the created order and our being in society.

5. Separation for the purposes of God

The root meaning of the biblical words used to describe holiness suggests separation. This was applied to both people and things, which were set apart from the ordinary, secular world and dedicated to God for worship or service. They became holy by their association with the purposes of God. Holiness is therefore characterised by dedication to God in order to fulfil his wishes.

6. Ethical and social consequences

However, for humanity, holiness is not only concerned with separation, but also has a moral dimension as the believer begins to reflect the character of God. Holiness stresses the ethical and social consequences of salvation. It focuses on the grace of God as a costly grace which calls for changed attitudes, motivation and lifestyle as we begin to reflect the character of God in our daily living.

7. Holiness is not sinlessness

Sanctification does not mean the elimination of all possibility for sinning. Although it is possible through the Holy Spirit not to sin, even when we experience the fullness of God's sanctifying power sin remains a possibility. There are still remnants of behaviour patterns which can recur. There is still the human tendency to give in to temptation.

In the same way, we must not claim sinless perfection in this life. Temptation is part of the human condition, but, by the power of the Holy Spirit, we can successfully resist temptation and not sin. However, we cannot say that those who are sanctified cannot, or will never, sin.

Neither can we say that those who experience a fullness of God's sanctifying power inevitably sin. Those who insist on the sinful imperfection of all believers fail to acknowledge the full benefit and work of the Atonement. When we are born again of the Spirit, sin is not inevitable: salvation brings freedom from the power of sin in the life of the believer.

To insist that believers are necessarily sinful, or that they continue to be prone to personal sin, is to limit the power of the Atonement to bring about a thorough change of character and a comprehensive victory over sin. We may sin, but when we do, we recognise that sin is contradictory and foreign to who we are in Christ. When we confess it to God and to anyone we have wronged, we are renewed in grace.

◆ *As we grow in holiness the image of God is being restored in our lives (Chapter 5). How will this be practically demonstrated in our actions and attitudes?*

◆ *What does being set apart for God's purposes mean for you?*

◆ *Why do some Christians think that only 'special' people can ever be holy? How can we re-educate them so they understand that sanctification is a natural consequence of salvation?*

◆ *Identify an ethical issue that is significant in your context. How can the doctrine of holiness help to shape a Christian response?*

B. Interpretations of the holiness experience

The experience of holiness has been expressed in a number of different ways, none of which reveals the whole truth. Some claim too little and some too much. Care should be taken to avoid gloomy defeatism on the one hand, and pretentious perfectionism on the other. Among the most well known are the following:

1. Entire sanctification

The term 'entire sanctification' is derived from 1 Thessalonians 5:23 (*KJV*). It expresses the belief that sanctification affects the whole personality and reaches the depths of the soul. The term should not be used, however, to suggest a state of sinless perfection. Rather, it means that we are whole or complete, and are conscious that sinning is foreign to our new being in Christ. If we do commit sin, we acknowledge it honestly, confess it before God, make restitution and move on. Entire sanctification means that, while we abide in Christ, we are free from the power of sin to undermine, destroy or divide us. We are free to be what we are called to be (2 Thessalonians 2:13-17).

2. Full salvation

'Full salvation' refers to the completion of Christ's saving work in our hearts. At our conversion, we may not grasp the fullness, nor claim the full benefit of, the Atonement. Our attempts to live the Christian life may sometimes meet with failure. This failure may cause us to discover that saving grace is also sanctifying grace: that we can be cleansed from all sin, and that we can have victory and fulfilment as disciples of Jesus. We claim – and by the power of the Holy Spirit we experience – full salvation.

The concept of full salvation, however, should not be understood as a state of spiritual saturation beyond which we cannot, or will not, receive further grace. It simply refers to our faith in, and openness toward, the full gift of God's grace. A life founded on this full gift, and changed by its powerful content, is a holy life.

Neither should full salvation be confused with final salvation which will be realised only beyond our earthly life.

3. Infilling of the Holy Spirit

The infilling, or fullness, of the Holy Spirit is a phrase used to describe the fullness by which we are empowered to live the Christian life and to be witnesses to our faith. As a result, the joy of the Lord expels and replaces defeatist attitudes. Holiness is fullness in the Spirit. In using the term 'infilling', care should be taken not to depersonalise God by likening him to fluid that can be poured into us as empty vessels. Furthermore, this, and other interpretations of the work of the Holy Spirit, should not be taken to mean that other persons of the Trinity are excluded. Rather, the term, 'infilling of the Holy Spirit' means that God himself comes into the life of the believer by the agency of the person of the Holy Spirit.

4. Baptism of the Holy Spirit

The holiness experience is sometimes described as the 'baptism of the Holy Spirit'. Baptism is a symbol of dying to ourselves and emerging as new persons in Christ which was used by the Early Church to describe the reception of the Holy Spirit at regeneration. 'We were all baptised by one Spirit into one body' (1 Corinthians 12:13). The 'baptism of the Holy Spirit' may therefore be considered as distinct from being 'filled with the Holy Spirit'. Baptism happens once at the beginning of Christian experience, while infilling happens repeatedly throughout the Christian life.

However, sometimes baptism and infilling are equated, with the phrase 'the baptism of the Holy Spirit', suggesting a movement beyond forgiveness of sins to a Spirit-filled newness of life. We must be careful not to place Christian experiences into separate compartments. God's sanctifying power is a benefit and work of the same saving grace, whether it is experienced at conversion or subsequently.

The term 'baptisms in the Spirit' has also been used to describe repeated experiences of infilling or endowments of spiritual power. The use of the term either in the singular or the plural sense can be confusing, leading to lack of clarity.

5. Second blessing

The term 'second work of grace' or 'second blessing' has been used in holiness movements, including The Salvation Army, to distinguish the experience of sanctification from the experience of justification and regeneration, following the teaching of John Wesley. We should be cautious about requiring for every Christian a 'second work of grace' that must be chronologically subsequent to the 'first work of grace'. The sanctifying grace of God is not limited to human timetables or explanations of its effects. For some people, full salvation may be experienced at conversion while for others it happens subsequently. A 'second blessing' does not imply that there are only two blessings, or that a second blessing is the final completion of Christian maturity and development. The Wesleyan doctrine of the second blessing relates to experiences of significant spiritual challenge, decision and growth, subsequent to conversion. As a vision of the potential for all believers in Christ, it is a powerful means of encouraging all Christians to partake in the fullness of the grace of God.

6. Blessing of a clean heart

'Heart cleansing' or the 'blessing of a clean heart' is a term used to emphasise the removal of unworthy, self-centred attitudes of the mind and heart. 'Heart cleansing' implies that our motivation has been purified and all our actions are now driven by love. The concept of purity of motives, however, must be used with great care. Using purification of motives as the basis, we may refuse to admit and confess any specific personal acts of sin: only 'mistakes' are admitted. Purity is a love-gift to which we open ourselves, and which we allow to claim us, but never use to our own advantage.

7. Perfect love

'Perfect love' is perhaps the most comprehensive description of holiness, although a description which can be simply expressed. Through his sanctifying power, the Holy Spirit fills us with God's perfect love, so that we begin to love, not with our own, seriously flawed love, but with the unselfish love of Christ. We are thereby equipped for the path of fulfilling Christ's commandment: 'Love the Lord your God with all your heart and with all your soul and with all your strength and with all your mind' and 'love your neighbour as yourself' (Luke 10:27).

◆ *Express your personal experience of holiness in writing, music, art or dance. Which, if any, of the descriptions listed above resonates most closely with your life?*

◆ *How would you describe what it means to be holy to a new convert who has no Christian background? Would you use these descriptions, or is an explanation using more contemporary and culturally relevant language necessary?*

◆ *Search your Salvation Army Song Book to find songs which use these expressions. How might you explain them in worship?*

C. Historical summary

1. The Old Testament

a. In the Old Testament holiness is an attribute of God, but not of humanity. Sanctification is the act or process by which people or things are cleansed and dedicated to God ritually and morally. In ritual understanding sanctification, or consecration, is a cleansing as preparation for an encounter with God (Exodus 13:2; Joshua 3:5).

b. The Hebrew root of the word *qodesh*, denoting holiness, appears as a verb, noun or adjective more than 850 times in the Old

Testament; this suggests its importance. It means to be cut off, or separated. Something or someone is holy if they are set apart for, and dedicated to, the service of God. This can be seen in the covenant relationship with Israel. God's setting apart of the people makes them 'a kingdom of priests and a holy nation' (Exodus 19:4, 5; Deuteronomy 7:6).

c. The holiness of Israel is to include a moral dimension. The people are to consecrate themselves to God, and in so doing become holy, as God is holy (Leviticus 20:7).

d. The outworking of the covenant relationship is seen in the Holiness Code (Leviticus 19-20) in which holiness is seen to be conditional on keeping the law given by God.

e. Embedded in the concept of holiness in the law and the prophets is the idea of personal righteousness, which is expressed in covenants made and kept with God, and within human relationships. Righteousness is understood as faithfulness in covenant relationships. This faithfulness characterises the person who is holy. To be dedicated to God is to live as God desires (Jeremiah 31:31-34).

2. The New Testament

a. New Testament Greek includes two words which are translated as 'holy'. *Hagiasmos,* sometimes translated as 'sanctification,' denotes the notion of being set apart for God. The second word is *hosiotes (hosios)*. This is to do with qualities of life. It signifies being righteous and pure before God, both inwardly and in our actions. Both together make up a New Testament picture of holiness, which includes moral and spiritual purity as well as consecration to God and separation for his use.

b. Jesus is the model. Named as the 'holy one of God' by demons (Mark 1:24), Jesus' holiness is revealed in relationships and holy living and most perfectly in love. He accepts and acknowledges the authority of God the Father (John 17:11); is devoted to fulfilling the Father's will (John 8:29); his life and death are free of self-interest (Mark 10:45, John 17:17-19); and he shows total integrity in his lifestyle and his dealings with people. Paul describes Jesus as the model of our holiness and the source of our life in God (1 Corinthians 1:30).

c. In the New Testament, holiness is an attribute of God that the people of God are urged to reflect in their lives. It is a restoration of the image of God in the believer through union with Christ (Colossians 3:9, 10). Holiness means to be at God's disposal for his mission in the world and to be Christlike in character and attitudes.

d. The New Testament understanding of holiness redefines the Old Testament emphases of cleansing (Hebrews 9:13-14); dedication (Romans 6:19; 15:16); and covenant faithfulness (Hebrews 8:6-13).

e. For Paul, sanctification is the moral equivalent to the sacrificial offerings of the Old Testament, where people or things are set aside or set apart for God (Romans 12:1, 2). It is important to note that believers have been chosen for, and dedicated to, holiness. It is God's will for them, and without holiness no one will see the Lord (Hebrews 12:14).

f. Sanctification is seen as the work of God the Father, of Christ and especially of the Holy Spirit. Christians are sanctified by being 'in Christ' through regeneration and therefore Paul calls all Christians saints, that is 'holy ones'. This does not refer to those who are special, and therefore nearly or fully morally perfect, but simply to the believers in a particular place (Romans 1:7; 1 Corinthians 1:2; Ephesians 1:1; Philippians 1:1, 4:21; Colossians 1:1). It is a word used almost exclusively in the plural.

The saints are the people who belong to God. This is an inclusive term which indicates the relational aspect of holiness. It is not to do with being perfect, but with being perfected, being brought to maturity in Christ. To be a saint is not to be a finished product, but to be a work in progress. The saints of the New Testament are imperfect people (Romans 1:7, cf 2:1; 1 Corinthians 1:2, cf 10), but they will finally be completed (Philippians 1:6; 1 John 3:2, 3).

g. The letters of Paul assume that right belief will naturally result in right moral actions. His letters often follow a pattern which has been described as the 'indicative-imperative' structure. Doctrinal teaching is followed by the practical implications required to live a Christian life. The two sections are often linked by the word 'therefore' or 'then' (Romans 12:1; Ephesians 4:1; Colossians 3:12). Salvation leads to holiness, and holiness is evidenced in right living and particularly in community relationships (1 Corinthians 5–8; Ephesians 4–6:9; Colossians 3:12–4:1).

h. The Church is called to model what a true community of God must be like because the world knows of God only through the reality of the sanctification of the people of God (John 17:17, 18).

i. The believers have been made holy and continue to live in holiness; therefore believers are both passive and active in their sanctification.

3. The Early Church
a. In the Early Church we meet radical discipleship and a call to a holy life. There were two reasons for this. First, the gospel was understood as calling believers to live in a way that was fundamentally different from the lives of non-believers. Second, there was urgency in mission, as the early Christians expected the imminent return of Christ and the establishment of the Kingdom of God.

b. The doctrine of holiness is very evident in the early Christian writings. Christians lived in a pagan environment and they were called to holiness in the midst of the world. Here they had to witness to God and glorify him by their daily behaviour. For the writer of the *Didache*, ordinary holiness, living the 'Way of Life', is required in the context of extraordinarily difficult times.[3] Similarly, the *Letter of Clement to the Corinthians* calls Christians to do 'those things that pertain to holiness'[4] so that their good actions are a witness to others.

c. However, as the Church became established and supported by the ruling powers of society, the urgency of the call to holiness was nearly forgotten in mainstream Christianity. As a consequence of this development holiness came to be seen as the prerogative of the elect few. The call to holiness did not significantly touch the laity. Holy living was expected only from those chosen to be saints on behalf of the people. Around 270 AD St Anthony moved into the desert and began a life of solitude and fasting. Soon there were a number of hermits, who were venerated as holy men. Some developed strange beliefs and practices.

d. By the 3rd and 4th centuries groups of ascetics began to live in communities, and this eventually developed into the monastic lifestyle. These religious communities were groups of people who were looking for communion with God through spiritual journey and struggle. They also advocated the way of the Cross, with denial of self or possessions and life in community, but this was a minority, and holiness was no longer the concern of the total community of believers. By the 6th century, monasticism had become organised, as in the Rule of St Benedict which was built around work and prayer.

e. Early Celtic Christianity – which was nurtured in Ireland and was the most significant movement in replanting Christianity in England, Scotland, and Western Europe following the fall of the

Roman Empire in the 5th century – taught a radical holiness. This was a way of life which encouraged purity alongside compassion for others and involvement in every dimension of human life.

4. The Middle Ages

a. During the Middle Ages holiness again came to be seen as the normal and natural outcome of the Christian life. Both Bernard of Clairvaux (1090-1153 AD), and Thomas Aquinas (1225-1274 AD), focused on the Pauline meaning of holiness as a moral and ethical value. Francis of Assisi (1181-1226 AD) rediscovered holiness as a simple, but radical, lifestyle of compassion, joy and powerlessness.

b. The Waldensians were founded by Peter Waldo (c1140-c1218 AD), a rich merchant of Lyons, who in 1173 obeyed the command of Jesus to sell all he had and give to the poor (Matthew 19:21) and began an itinerant life, preaching and calling people to discipleship. A revival movement of lay people developed. It was marked by extreme poverty and an emphasis on preaching, by both men and women. After the Reformation the Waldensians became aligned with the reformed church.

c. The writings of Joachim of Fiore (1132-1202 AD) have provided inspiration for individuals and groups, including the holiness movement of the 18th and 19th centuries. Joachim's concept of the eternal gospel, *evangelisms aeternum,* as the indestructible fruit of faith, which is left after having been through the cleansing fire of the Holy Spirit, has caught the imagination of many. This broad concept has been filled with different meanings according to the viewpoints and beliefs of the persons or groups concerned. Linked to this concept is his division of history into three stages: the time of the Father (Old Testament times), the time of the Son (New Testament times), and the time of the Holy Spirit, which will be marked by the eternal gospel and by an overwhelming outpouring of the Spirit. This, together with his prophecies and interpretations of the book of Revelation made an impact on people in the following centuries. At times his influence seemed to disappear only suddenly to surface again.

5. *The Reformation*

a. A significant outcome of the Reformation was the development of the concept of the priesthood of all believers. Luther wrote 'It says in 1 Peter 2, "You are a chosen race, a royal priesthood, a priestly kingdom." In this way we are all priests, as many of us as are Christians'.[5] Therefore, there is no necessity for a priest to act as an intermediary between individual Christians and God; the only mediator between God and humanity is Jesus Christ (1 Timothy 2:5). The Church collectively is a 'royal priesthood' and therefore each believer has a vocation and a ministry to fulfil. Nevertheless this does not mean that all can fulfil the 'priestly' functions, rather that each Christian must fulfil his or her own function within the Church. Holiness is therefore relevant to all Christians, who must be willing to contribute to the work and service of the body of Christ.

b. As with the doctrine of justification, the Reformers believed that holiness is not our own achievement, it is solely the work of God. Calvin wrote that we receive a double grace, reconciliation to God and sanctification, which cannot be separated.

> 'It is certain that no man will ever know him aright without at the same time receiving the sanctification of the Spirit; or, to express the matter more plainly, faith consists in the knowledge of Christ; Christ cannot be known without the sanctification of his Spirit: therefore faith cannot possibly be disjoined from pious affection.'[6]

6. *Pietism and Puritanism*

a. The Puritan and Pietist traditions in the 17th and 18th centuries focused on holiness of life and were the foundation on which the Wesleyan Movement of the 18th century and the Holiness Movement of the 19th century were grounded.

b. The publication of Philip Jacob Spener's book *Pia Desideria* (*Pious Wishes*, 1675) inaugurated the Pietist movement. Spener's proposals for the revitalisation of the Church, most significantly through personal Bible study, proved influential. Pietism reacted against the supremacy of doctrinal orthodoxy, balancing this with a faith which relates to and addresses the realities of life. John Bunyan's (1678-1684 AD) book *The Pilgrim's Progress* also had a widespread influence upon authors, writers, preachers, churches and individual Christians through its images and examples. The extended analogy of the Christian life as a journey which involves personal commitment and struggle captures the pietist ethos and emphasis.

c. The Puritans of 16th and 17th century England advocated personal piety and purity of worship and doctrine. Their criticism of both the Church of England and the monarchy meant they were subject to arrest and imprisonment and therefore many chose to emigrate to the American colonies, where they became a major shaping force of American Christianity. The most significant American Puritan theologian was Jonathan Edwards (1703-1758 AD), who was a central figure of great revivals in the 1730s and 1740s. His books were widely read, paving the way for understanding holiness as a separate experience.[7] In 1740 George Whitefield (1714-1770 AD) was invited to join the revival which was later called The First Great Awakening.

d. At the same time pietists in Halle in Germany, especially Nikolaus Ludwig Graf von Zinzendorf (1700-1760 AD), the founder of the Moravians, had a strong influence on the development of the holiness movement in Europe. John Wesley's holiness teaching was influenced by Zinzendorf, who stressed that sanctification as well as justification is 'by faith'.

7. *Methodism*
a. John Wesley was greatly influenced by the community in Halle. In particular Peter Böhler (1712-1775 AD) played a great part in

Wesley's spiritual development leading up to his Aldersgate experience (For further exploration 8 B3) in which his doubt and fear were replaced with peace, trust and victory, as he read the preface to Martin Luther's Commentary on Romans.

b. Wesley's understanding of holiness grew out of experience; it is not a systematic theology. He argued that there is no medium way. 'We cannot be holy in parts of our lives, every part must be dedicated to God. 'Every part of my life (not some only) must either be a sacrifice to God, or myself, that is, in effect, to the devil.'[8]

c. Wesley saw holiness as being a part of the complete way of salvation, the *via salutis* which begins with regeneration, the new birth which accompanies justification. From that instantaneous work it increases gradually until there is another work in which cleansing from sin results in a heart of 'perfect love', by which Wesley meant purity of motivation or intent, a sincerity of love. The sanctifying process then continues until its completion at the believer's death or glorification.

d. Wesley took the notion of perfection from his reading of William Law's books *Christian Perfection* and *Serious Call*. His definition of perfection was not that a person could be so good that they had no room for growth or improvement, but it had the biblical sense of achieving the desired end, fulfilment of the task for which we are created, a sense of completion, of maturity (thus reflecting the Greek word *teleios* which is translated into English as 'perfect' but literally means end, goal or target). So Wesley defined perfection as 'that love of God and our neighbour which implies deliverance from all sin'.[9]

e. Wesley noted: 'Exactly as we are justified by faith, so we are sanctified by faith. Faith is the condition, and the only condition of sanctification exactly as it is of justification.' The believer knows that they are sanctified 'by the Spirit that he hath given us.'[10]

f. For Wesley, sanctification expressed itself in practical ways. There was a clear ethical impulse in his holiness teaching in that the 'perfect love' which characterised his understanding of holiness included bearing the burdens of others. 'Christianity,' he said, 'is a social religion; and ... to turn it into a solitary one is to destroy it.'[11] Although this refers specifically to the Christian's contact with society as a whole, he also acknowledged the need for a Christian community to sustain the spiritual life. To that end he set up three support groups for his converts – the Society, the Band and the Class Meeting. Wesley wrote: [if] 'you unite together, to encourage and help each other in thus working out your salvation, and for that end watch over one another in love, you are they whom I mean by Methodists'.[12]

g. The years leading up to the birth of The Salvation Army were marked by a great holiness revival. It began in 1858 in the United States of America as a prayer meeting revival, spreading to Canada and then to the United Kingdom (1859). Charles Finney and James Caughey were influential preachers. The revival affected most churches, including the evangelicals within the Anglican/Episcopal Church, Methodists, the Congregationalists and the Presbyterians.

h. Walter C. Palmer and his wife Phoebe Palmer were Americans who held campaigns in the United Kingdom from 1859-1863. The teaching and revival meetings of both, and the books on holiness by Phoebe Palmer, were a source of inspiration for William and Catherine Booth.

i. This great revival influenced mission initiatives to different parts of the world. The Evangelical Alliance, which had just been founded (1846), became closely linked to the holiness revival.

8. The Salvation Army

a. Belief in the possibility of living a holy life and of encountering the sanctifying Spirit of God is integral to Salvation Army teaching and faith. It is strongly influenced by the teaching of John Wesley. Preachers of the Great Awakening as well as the Holiness Movement leading up to the time of the birth of the Army were also significant. Early Salvationist leaders, including William and Catherine Booth, Bramwell Booth and George Scott Railton made holiness teaching a priority. Writing in 1902, William Booth underlined its importance: 'I regard the enjoyment and publication of the Blessing of a Clean Heart as being essential to my own peace, power and usefulness, and as necessary to the progress and prosperity of the Army as it ever was.'[13]

b. As early as 1881 Railton had suggested that the blessing of sanctification is essential to the Salvation Army officer:

> 'It is impossible to be an efficient officer without the enjoyment of this blessing. Almost every officer has, at one time or another, possessed it, too; so that those who do not possess it must be in a fallen condition, and more or less wretched and untrue.'[14]

c. Samuel Logan Brengle wrote extensively on holiness. Describing holiness as 'perfect love', 'pure love' and 'Christ in you' (1896), Brengle took an eradicationist position, believing that cleansing from all sin, so that there is no evil desire or tendency in the heart, is a possibility. Holiness is a state in which God is trusted with a perfect heart, and Christian perfection is being and doing what God requires. This is achieved by 'a second work of grace, preceded by a whole-hearted consecration and a definite act of faith as that which preceded his conversion'.[15]

d. In the 1960s Frederick Coutts gave renewed impetus to our holiness teaching through his thinking, teaching and writings. In

The Call to Holiness he emphasises 'Christlikeness' as his definition of holiness:[16] 'Where Christ is enthroned, there is true holiness.' He believed that any decisive moment or crisis must be followed by a process of increasing reception of the fruit of the Spirit in the life of the believer.

> 'The crisis must be followed by a process. In the initial act of surrender I receive the fullness of the Spirit according to my capacity to receive. But that capacity grows with receiving ... A full surrender is the beginning of the life of holy living; the end of that experience I do not – I cannot – see.'[17]

e. Contributions to Salvationist holiness teaching through the 1970s and 1980s include Edward Read, 1975 *Studies in Sanctification;* Clarence Wiseman, 1978 *Living the Holy Life;* Arthur Pitcher, 1987 *Holiness in the Traffic;* John Larsson 1983 *Spiritual Breakthrough;* Chick Yuill 1988 *We Need Saints.*

f. John Larsson summarised late 20th century understanding as follows:

> 'It would be fair to say that the dominating thought today is not of a process leading to a culminating crisis, but rather the reverse, the crisis is seen as "triggering off" the process of sanctification. Somewhere in the foothills, the pilgrim experiences a spiritual crisis which sets him a climbing the hill of holiness. The crisis has become the gateway not the goal. And the crisis is not therefore for the few athletes of the spirit who have nearly made it to the top. It is the way in to spiritual progress, and is therefore meant for everybody.'[18]

g. Spiritual progress is a natural consequence of following through our salvation and learning to live a more Christlike life. But for most people this takes time and patience. Shaw Clifton likens this experience to that of the 'saints' (C2f) of the New Testament who were 'set apart' – called out from the world for the purposes of God – but were still flawed human beings. They were holy by status, but not always holy in the reality of their living.

> 'It was one thing to be holy in name or by status, but another for their lives to be holy by results. This is just as true for modern Christians. As soon as you were saved you belonged to Christ. You became holy by status in the same sense that Paul says the far-from-perfect recipients of his letters were holy. For most Christians the gap between holy status and holy living is at first a very wide one. Growing in grace and in spiritual maturity is about closing that gap, steadily but surely.'[19]

God requires that we allow the status conferred by our salvation to produce in us holy results. For many people this will require a subsequent moment of decision (or more than one) when they move towards a deeper commitment and understanding of what God wants them to be, but for all it is a learning process as we become 'saints' in reality as well as by status.

h. The International Spiritual Life Commission (1996-1998) confirmed and reinforced the commitment of The Salvation Army to holiness:

> 'We call Salvationists worldwide to restate and live out the doctrine of holiness in all its dimensions – personal, relational, social and political – in the context of our cultures and in the idioms of our day while allowing for, and indeed prizing, such diversity of experience and expression as is in accord with the Scriptures.'[20]

The affirmation which followed noted: 'We resolve to make every effort to embrace holiness of life, knowing that this is only possible by means of the power of the Holy Spirit producing his fruit in us.'

i. In the early years of the 21st century, The Salvation Army continues to explore what this means for individuals and for the Salvationist community. Contemporary scholarship which focuses upon the Trinity as a community in relationship (Chapter 3) and therefore a model for human Christian relationship, coupled with a renewed focus upon Christian community as a response to contemporary society has led to discussion of issues of social and relational holiness. Philip Needham writes:

> 'If holiness is, as we Salvationists have claimed, perfect love, then it is meaningless outside a community in which the love of God can be experienced, expressed and learned.' If we love one another, God lives in us, and his love is perfected in us' (I John 4:12). We must be that kind of community or our holiness is empty ... holiness must be seen as a personal journey only as part of a journey in fellowship with other believers. We are "citizens with the saints ... and members of the household of God" (Ephesians 2:19). The New Testament allows me a holiness which is both singular and plural.'[21]

The need for holiness remains at the centre of The Salvation Army's life and thought. Drawing on our early heritage and that of the wider Church, Salvationist preachers, teachers and writers continue to seek to make its meaning accessible, relevant and attractive to the lives of all Salvationists. Holy living, in which the Spirit lives his life in and through believers, so that their influence works to bring about the transforming influence of the Kingdom of God in other people and the world, remains a priority for The Salvation Army.

◆ *Holiness is an action of God and not our own accomplishment. Is this true? Why?*

- Find a piece of art which for you reflects the sanctifying Spirit at work.

- To what extent has the idea that holiness is not the concern of the 'normal' Christian persisted into the 21st century? (C3cd)

- What counsel would you give to a young person who is struggling to live out holiness in one particular aspect of their life? (C7b)

D. Issues for Salvationists

1. The privilege of all believers

In the same way that salvation must be seen as a possibility for any human being who chooses to believe in the atoning work of Jesus, holiness must be viewed as a possibility for all believers. In addition, it cannot be seen as an optional spiritual experience for those who are more spiritual or more enthusiastic, but must be embraced as the natural corollary of salvation. It is God's will for all his people. Salvationist teaching and corps life must reflect this truth.

2. The holiness experience

There are no certain routes to holiness. The development of the inner spiritual life is vital in order that it will sustain our life in the world, but we cannot systematise the experience, which is known by its fruits rather than by the way in which it is received or the name we give to it. Salvationists will be known as a holy people only when they live holy lives and not because they have had certain religious or spiritual experiences.

3. Holy living

In holiness teaching one finds the very essentials of Salvationism, which are the intimate relationship between spirituality and service, the holy life and mission. A Salvationist understanding of holiness expresses itself as practical and social holiness as well as personal spiritual experience and development. The holiness of Salvationists must be evident in their interactions with other people, in their moral standards and in their contribution to society.

4. A holy community

Holiness teaching stresses the need to develop an inner personal spiritual life to feed on for living a holy life, a life in community with others and a life of restored relationships. The Salvationists in any community must learn to model what this means. The 'saints' in the New Testament are always plural; one cannot be holy as an individual without being holy in interaction with others. This does not mean that Salvation Army corps or centres will be without fault, but it does mean that our relationships should be determined by our holiness.

5. Holiness and society

The implications of this understanding of holiness are far-reaching. They lead to an involvement in society on many levels: direct involvement with people in their needs, both spiritual and practical; engagement in advocacy for social justice and human rights; awareness of the importance of an ecological balance in our surroundings, a global sharing of resources and a willingness to work towards this end; and responsibility for the weak and poor, the vulnerable and the marginalised, thus demonstrating a Christian world view in all of life.

6. Holiness and works

The experience of holiness results from the indwelling and work of the Holy Spirit in the life of Christians as they are open to him. It leads to growing discipleship and changed patterns of living as the life of Christ infuses and transforms their human life. As believers grow in holiness, both individually and in community with other Christians, their lifestyle will reflect this growth. Commitment to worship and personal devotion will be accompanied by commitment to God's mission in the world by evangelism, social service and social action. However, works of piety or compassion cannot achieve or earn holiness, but are its effects.

◆ Holiness is not a special state for the few 'saints' but the life to which God calls human beings. 'It is a quality of character to which God calls his people, and if he calls us to it, it must be possible.'[22] Why have so many Salvationists believed that holiness is unattainable? How can we counteract this misunderstanding?

◆ 'Holiness demands that we get our hands dirty while asking God to keep our hearts clean.'[23] What does this mean in your life? Do you need to make any changes?

◆ What impact does your understanding and/or experience of holiness have on your everyday decisions and actions?

◆ How should the doctrine of holiness impact upon The Salvation Army's response to contemporary ethical issues?

◆ How would you explain the Army's emphasis on holiness to a Christian friend of another tradition that does not emphasise the call to holiness or does not see a life of holiness as a real possibility for the Christian in this life?

◆ Is there any danger that Salvationists may act as if they can earn holiness by their 'good works'? How can we guard against this possibility?

◆ Does the language of the doctrine of holiness resonate with contemporary society? How might you restate it in order to make it more understandable for people who do not know the traditional religious vocabulary?

---

[1] Samuel Logan Brengle, 1902 2nd edn. *The Way of Holiness.* Salvation Army Book Department:2

[2] Colin Fairclough, *The Song Book of The Salvation Army* 1986: 479:3

[3] http://www.earlychristianwritings.com/text/didache-roberts.html

[4] *Letter of Clement to the Corinthians* http://www.ccel.org/ccel/schaff/anf09.xii.iv.xxx.html

[5] Martin Luther, 1520 *Babylonian Captivity of the Church-* Ordination http://www.ccel.org/ccel/luther/first_prin.v.iii.vii.html

[6] John Calvin, http://www.ccel.org/ccel/calvin/institutes.v.iii.html

[7] Jonathan Edwards, *The Life and Diary of David Brainerd* 1745 and *Charity and its Fruits* 1746

[8] John Wesley, *A Plain Account of Christian Perfection:* www.ccel.org/w/wesley/perfection/perfection.html:1

[9] John Wesley, *A Plain Account of Christian Perfection:* www.ccel.org/w/wesley/perfection/perfection.html: 17

[10] John Wesley, *The Works of John Wesley, 14 vols.* reprinted., Grand Rapids, Michigan.: Baker Book House, 1978, 11:420.

[11] John Wesley, http://www.godrules.net/library/wsermons/wsermons24.htm

[12] John Wesley, *Advice to the People Called Methodists* http://www.godrules.net/library/wesley/274wesley_h14.htm

[13] William Booth, 1902 *Purity of Heart.* London SP & S :15

[14] quoted in John Larsson, 1983 *Spiritual Breakthrough.* London: The Salvation Army: 53

[15] Samuel Logan Brengle, 1896 *Helps to Holiness* Salvationist Publishing and Supplies Ltd:8

[16] Frederick Coutts, 1957 *The Call to Holiness* London: Salvationist Publishing & Supplies Ltd :25

[17] Frederick Coutts, 1957 *The Call to Holiness* London: Salvationist Publishing & Supplies Ltd :36-37

[18] John Larsson, 1983 *Spiritual Breakthrough.* London: The Salvation Army: 46

[19] Shaw Clifton 1997 *Never The Same Again* Alexandria: Crest Books:114

[20] *The Report of the International Spiritual Life Commission* Appendix 4.

[21] Philip Needham, 2000 *Integrating Holiness and Community: The Task of an Evolving Salvation Army. Word and Deed* Fall 2000: 11,14

[22] Eva Burrows, in Shaw Clifton, 2004 *New Love:* Wellington, New Zealand: The Salvation Army 125.

[23] Robert Street, 2008 *Called To Be God's People* London: Salvation Books: 84

Chapter 11

Kingdom of the risen Lord

The doctrine of last things

We believe in the immortality of the soul; in the resurrection of the body; in the general judgment at the end of the world; in the eternal happiness of the righteous; and in the endless punishment of the wicked.

A. The Christian hope

The Christian hope in life after death depends upon belief in the Resurrection of Jesus Christ. Belief in the Resurrection asserts that death does not have the last word over human destiny; God does. Jesus conquered death, and so death does not finally separate us from God. He was raised from death to a new order of life, an eternal life given by God. The Christian hope is that as God raised Jesus Christ from death, so God will raise us from death to eternal life with him.

For the Christian, belief in the Resurrection is radical trust in the one eternal God. The God of the beginning is also the God of the end. At the beginning there was God, who called the world into being out of nothing and created us in his own image. At the end there is God, not nothing; a God who calls us into new Resurrection life with him. God, our Creator and Perfecter, completely fulfils his purpose for us.

As Jesus did not die into nothing, neither do we. We die into the life of God.

1. The triumph of the Kingdom of God

The completion of God's purposes for the whole universe can be illustrated in the biblical language of the Kingdom of God. This language is a way of describing the rule of God in human affairs, and is demonstrated when lives and human communities are transformed by Christ. The Bible looks forward to that transformation being made complete and visible in a new world order under God. This hope is clothed in vivid pictures which attempt to describe the ultimately indescribable, the entire cosmos in mutual harmony and at peace with its Creator (Isaiah 11:6-9; Isaiah 65:17-25). There are descriptions of a new creation where all live in love, share an abundance of good things and know great joy. Images of banquets and wedding feasts, of water that never runs dry, of life-giving trees and an ever-welcoming eternal city, express hope in concrete terms (Revelation 21:1-7; 22:1-5). They remind us that God plans for us a whole, fully personal, eternal life together.

Jesus came preaching the coming of God's Kingdom and in his ministry of teaching, preaching and healing revealed a foretaste of the coming joy (Luke 4:18, 19; 7:22; 11:14-20). In Christ's Resurrection from the dead and the outpouring of the Spirit, the life of the Kingdom of God was released into the world (Acts 2:32-36). Therefore the good news of the Kingdom became the central theme of the message of the Early Church (Acts 8:12; 19:8; 28:23-31). All who accept Christ through faith can live in its reality and look forward to its completion at the end of time, when Christ returns (1 Peter 1:3-5).

2. Eternal life

The life beyond death which beckons the Christian is eternal life. This is a quality of life in the presence of God, not simply unending time. It begins now as we follow Christ (Mark 10:17-22; John 3:16; 10:27-30; 11:25; 17:1-3). It is the life everlasting of which the Bible speaks, life with no end and love with no end. It is abundant life beyond our imagination (1 Corinthians 2:9). All we can say is that God will be all in all (1 Corinthians 15:28).

Eternal life focuses on unending adoration and enjoyment of God. We find our destiny and experience that for which we were created: to see God, to be like him, to love him and to enjoy him for ever (1 John 3:2).

B. Death and Resurrection

To have a hope for Heaven is not to disguise the reality of death. Death is part of our human condition as biological beings. Death is God-given, a limitation on fallen human existence. But the reality of death should not deprive us of hope in the reality of death's defeat. Death does not separate us from God (Psalm116:15; Romans 8:38, 39). Jesus has conquered death (1 Corinthians 15: 20-26).

We will still die physically, yet because of Jesus Christ we need not be dead to God. When Paul writes about death being the 'wages of sin', he is not referring to physical death but to the spiritual death that threatens those who reject God (Romans 6:23).

1. The immortality of the soul

Christians have often expressed belief in life after death in the phrase, 'the immortality of the soul'. This phrase needs to be clearly understood. It is usually employed by Christians to mean that death is not the end, and this usual understanding is certainly essential to the gospel. It is important to recognise, however, that apart from God's action there is no part of us that naturally survives beyond death.

Our eternal existence is totally dependent on God. That is true for the righteous and the unrighteous. The Christian doctrine of immortality affirms that we are whole persons, originally brought to life by God (Genesis 2:7), and because of God's action there will be no loss of integrated, embodied personality in the life beyond present existence. God brings us all into eternity to participate in the general resurrection and submit to the final judgment of Christ (Matthew 25: 31-46; Romans 2:5-11; 1 Corinthians 15:50-54; 1 Timothy 6:13-16).

2. The resurrection of the body

The phrase, 'the resurrection of the body' is the biblical way to express Christian belief in life after death. In the Bible the word 'body' means the whole person. The phrase safeguards the integrity of the human person (Job 19:25-27). We do not look forward to becoming mere disembodied spirits, but whole persons, fully alive with Christ in God.

We all die, but death is not the end for either the believer or the non-believer (Psalm 73:24; Daniel 12:2). For all will be raised to judgment (John 5:25-29; Revelation 20:11-15). Our life beyond the grave is entirely dependent upon the mercy and judgment of God, who has planned for those who trust in Jesus a re-creation into a new humanity, perfectly fulfilling his will (John 14:1-14; 1 Corinthians 15:49).

Our resurrection depends upon the Resurrection of Christ and follows a similar pattern. Jesus died a real death on the Cross. His Resurrection was a re-creation, not a resuscitation. He was not raised like Lazarus, only to die again (John 11:17-44). He had a Resurrection body that was different from his human body, yet recognisable. Our resurrection, too, through Christ, will be a total re-creation. Belief in a personal resurrection affirms our faith in God, Creator and re-creator, who has made us, and will re-make us, out of love and for love (1 Corinthians 15).

C. Ultimate accountability

As Christians we believe that world history is not purposeless but is moving towards an ultimate crisis, which biblical writers sometimes describe as 'the Day of the Lord' (Isaiah 2:12-21; Joel 2:30-32). In the Old Testament the prophets used the term to look forward to the time when God's righteousness would be ultimately realised on earth, the day of triumph and transformation. The God of Israel would be revealed to all nations, for blessing and for judgment (Amos 5:18-27). The revelation of Jesus Christ changed the shape of this hope, though not its content, so that we now look forward to the time when Christ will be exalted and universally acknowledged as Lord (Philippians 2:9-11).

1. Judgment

It is in this context that we can speak of judgment. Judgment is the fulfilment of God's promises. It is the fullest affirmation of God's righteousness, of the liberating message of the New Testament, of the trusting faith of those who believe in a loving God. Judgment manifests the triumph of good over evil, the righting of wrongs, the validation of the truth, the victory of love over fear, the new Heaven and the new earth.

Judgment is also the fullest affirmation of universal accountability. All are accountable to God, during life and beyond death. This is the clear message of the New Testament. We have personal responsibility for our lives, for the choices we make, for our attitude and actions towards our fellows, for the stewardship of what we have received, for our ultimate destiny (Matthew 25:31-46). This accountability is essential to our dignity as bearers of the divine image: God takes us seriously.

God alone is the judge. Because our judge is also our Saviour, we can face judgment with confidence. His judgment will validate our faith-response (1 John 4:17). We can rest with assurance in the mercy and grace of God, as well as in his absolute justice (Psalm 9:8; 1 Corinthians 3:13-15). We cannot dictate to God who will be saved and who not. But we can trust to the judgment of God the lives of all those whose life and experience, personal creed and spiritual opportunities are different from our own because he is the loving Creator of all (Romans 2:12-16; Chapter 5).

2. Hell and Heaven

To believe in judgment is to accept the reality of Hell and Heaven. Biblical pictures of Hell are terrifying and vivid and remind us that to choose to reject the grace of God must issue in a separation from him that reaches into eternity (Matthew 13:24-30). Ultimately, our God-given freedom includes the freedom to make choices with eternal consequences (Matthew 25:1-13; 31-46). As Hell refers to the anguish of those who face eternity without God, so Heaven describes the bliss of those who enjoy the full experience of his presence. Biblical references to Heaven and Hell are only faint glimpses of the greater realities, of the final abode of the saved and the lost (Mark 9: 42-48; 2 Thessalonians 1:6-10; 2 Peter 3:8-13).

A hope to be shared

Christian life is marked by a hope that reaches beyond this life to life with God in his eternity. It is a life of joy in the presence of Christ, anticipating the life to come. It is a life of trust, full of confidence in the ultimate purposes of God in Christ.

For us, the future hope is already part of the present, as the Holy Spirit brings to us the living Christ who makes his Kingdom a present reality. As we live out this future today we invite others to share in our hope.

Doctrine 11 summarises the final consequences of the choices we make in relation to God and the atonement offered by Jesus Christ. The beliefs we hold concerning last things are based on God's power, on his justice and on his love, as these have been revealed through Jesus Christ and through the biblical message. This includes Christ's return in glory, the completion of God's Kingdom, the resurrection of the body, the final accountability of all persons to God, the endless despair of those who reject salvation and the eternal happiness of those who are righteous through faith.

For further exploration 11

'Finish then thy new creation,
Pure and spotless let us be;
Let us see thy great salvation,
Perfectly restored in thee.
Changed from glory into glory,
Till in Heaven we take our place,
Till we cast our crowns before thee,
Lost in wonder, love and praise.'

Charles Wesley[1]

A. Essentials of the doctrine

1. Last things

Doctrine 11 deals with eschatology, that is the study of last things. This does not only refer to death, Heaven, Hell and judgment, but also to the final fulfilment of the Kingdom of God, bringing to completion his plans for creation and for human history. This highlights a characteristic Christian belief that time is linear, not cyclical. History had a beginning, and will ultimately also have an end.

Eschatology can be distinguished from apocalyptic, which is used to refer to a type of writing that generally focuses on the expectation that God will intervene in history to vindicate his people, destroy their enemies and replace the present world order with a restored creation. Emphasis is placed on visions and dreams in which the writer learns the secret plans of God. Although some eschatological writing is apocalyptic in style, the doctrine of last things may also be expressed in different ways.

2. Hope

The doctrine is grounded in hope, a hope that transcends the border between life and death and predominates even when faced with death. The gospel is a gospel of hope for redemption now and in eternity. The reality and pain of death is not denied but is infused with hope because, in the Resurrection of Jesus we see the first fruits, that is the anticipation, of the defeat and final destruction of death (1 Corinthians 15:20, 25, 26, 55; Revelation 21:4).

3. The Kingdom of God

The coming of the Kingdom of God is the dominant theme in the teaching of Jesus. By implication the doctrine looks forward to the complete fulfilment of God's reign and suggests that the final transformation of the believer will be a part of this process (1 Corinthians 15:22, 50-57). The victory of God and the establishment of his new creation are certain.

4. The consequences of human free will and the reality of judgment

Our choices in life have eternal consequences; therefore everything shall be decided upon in the light of the Kingdom of God. Belief in the Resurrection, in eternal life, in ultimate accountability, gives value, dignity and meaning to life and to us as individual persons. It gives us a vision extending beyond the limits of time. However, we cannot, and must not, pre-empt that judgment. Only God can judge and he will do so in the light of his justice and his grace.

◆ How can a belief in last things be reflected in our choices in life?

◆ Have you ever encountered death at close hand involving one of your loved ones or friends or colleagues? If so, how did Doctrine 11 help you to respond?

◆ Why is it important to witness to a faith that transcends this life?

Historical summary

1. The Old Testament

a. In Old Testament thought there is little discussion of any kind of life after death. Humanity was created as a wholeness of body and soul and also died in this wholeness. Hope was vested in the land and the people, and after death individuals were believed to be 'gathered to their fathers' (Genesis 25:8) with no thought of resurrection. However, although the primary focus of Old Testament teaching about the Kingdom, or reign, of God is this world, different interpretations of the possibility of a future life developed (Ecclesiastes 3:21; Daniel 12).

b. The root of belief in the **resurrection** in the Old Testament is the faith that as God masters life he also masters death. As God has created, so he can recreate (1 Samuel 2:6; Deuteronomy 32:39; Isaiah 25:8).

c. The earliest texts which envision a real resurrection of the righteous and a belief that God will overcome death for ever are found in Isaiah (Isaiah 24-27, see also Daniel 12:1-3), where Jerusalem is seen to be the focus and location of the reign of God (Isaiah 24:23; 27:13), and it appears that a bodily resurrection is envisaged (Isaiah 26:19).

d. The place for the dead was described as Sheol, which in its essence is 'non-life' or the opposite of life (Psalm 16:10). In the Septuagint (a Greek translation of the Old Testament from around 200 BC) Sheol was translated as Hades (the final abode of the dead in Greek mythology) and this appears in the Greek New Testament as a provisional place for the ungodly (Revelation 20:13, 14).

e. The expression **'the Kingdom of God'** does not occur in the Old Testament, but the notion of God as King is pervasive, and his Kingly control encompasses past, present and future (Psalm

145:13). In the midst of national disaster and exile, the prophets announce a time when God will manifest himself as King. This great future, realised through the work of the Messiah, will mean salvation and blessing for all nations (Isaiah 2:1-4; 11:9; 40:10; 52:7, 8; Micah 4:1-5).

2. Between the Testaments

a. In the period between the Old and New Testaments, as the nation suffered political martyrdom, belief in a life hereafter developed. The Jews came to believe that God's suffering people would be vindicated in a future place of justice. In the books of the Apocrypha we can see how physical **resurrection** became part of the hope of the nation. God as Creator, will re-create, redeem and vindicate (2 Maccabees 7).

b. However, some writings from the same period have no reference to life after death, focusing completely upon God's action in the present time. These include 1 and 3 Maccabees and Ben Sirach. Others speak of immortality in a disembodied sense, that is the continuation of the soul, rather than an embodied resurrection (4 Maccabees, Jubilees 23).

c. By the time of Jesus, the aristocratic, priestly Jewish religious leaders, the Sadducees, denied any kind of future life (Matthew 22:23). The Pharisees, who were experts in both oral and written law, and many ordinary Jewish people, believed in an eventual resurrection and new world order (Acts 23:8; John 11:24).

d. For those who did believe in a future life, this included a place of **judgment** which was called Gehenna. In the Old Testament, the Valley of Ben Hinnom (Gehenna) marked the border between the tribes of Judah and Benjamin and after the captivity it marked the northern border of Judah. This valley was the scene of worship of the Canaanite gods Molech and Baal. Jeremiah especially paints in vivid pictures what was happening there. The worship involved sacrifices of children who passed through fire into the hands of the gods (Jeremiah 7:31; 19:4, 5; 32:35).

3. New Testament background

a. By the time of Jesus, Gehenna (the Valley of Ben Hinnom) had become an ever-burning rubbish dump. This developed into a metaphorical understanding of Gehenna, translated as Hell (Matthew 5:22, 29-30; 10:28; 18:9; 23:15, 33; Mark 9:43, 45, 47; Luke 12:5). It was considered to be the place of the wicked after the final judgment; an everlasting fiery punishment, also awaiting the devil and his angels. The fire would never be quenched.

b. In the New Testament 'the Kingdom of God' or 'the Kingdom of Heaven' forms the central theme in the proclamation of Jesus (Mark 1:15). The Greek word *basileia* is translated as 'kingdom'; this is sometimes thought to imply something static, whereas it more properly refers to the act of reigning, to kingship. In announcing the Kingdom, Jesus declares the realisation of Israel's hope. The new and final order of history has arrived.

c. The Kingdom is present reality, but also has a future aspect. This relates to the immediate future, arriving through the death and Resurrection of Christ (Matthew 17:9; Mark 9:9), and to distant future at the time of the final judgment (Matthew 8:11, 12; 13:37-50; 25:31-46). Thus the one, eschatological, Kingdom arrives in successive stages. It is important to be aware of, and understand, the aspect of the 'already, but not yet' in the announcement of the Kingdom (Mark 4:30-32).

d. The eschatology in the letters of Paul also shows a tension between 'now' and 'not yet'. He emphasises the coming of a new age with the Resurrection of Jesus, so the 'new creation' that has begun (2 Corinthians 5:17) will finally be completed (Philippians 1:6), both in individuals and in the world (Romans 8:19-23).

233

e. The central focus of the New Testament is the **resurrection** of Jesus Christ and its consequences for humanity. The Resurrection of Jesus showed the Kingship of God as a power which could become present in the lives of Christians, radically changing their lives and their outlook. The weak and fearful disciples became strong witnesses because they lived in the reality of this power (Acts 4:13-20). They longed for and expected the return of Christ when that power would be unfolded in its fullness (Ephesians 1:18-23; Philippians 3:20, 21).

f. The **coming of Christ in judgment** would confirm the new life of the believers and their victory over sin and death. The Church appears to have used an Aramaic term *maranatha* (meaning 'Our Lord, come!') to express their hope (1 Corinthians 16:22). The future coming of Christ is described by the Greek word *parousia* (1 Thessalonians 4:15; 1 Corinthians 15:23) which literally means 'presence' and was used to describe the mysterious presence of a god, or the visit of a powerful, royal ruler. Both have significance for the coming again of Jesus.

g. The disciples awaited the return of Christ in their own lifetime (1 Thessalonians 4:13–5:11). It was a cause of bewilderment when this did not happen. Paul encouraged the Christians in Thessalonica not to believe in rumours and speculations (2 Thessalonians 2:1-3).

h. The early Christians had the sure conviction that they would soon be with Christ either by his coming again or by themselves dying into Christ. As a result of this conviction they faced persecution and martyrdom. They knew they did not die into nothing: they died into Christ. They believed that as Jesus had been raised from the dead so they would be raised (1 Corinthians 15:20-22). In its fullest sense resurrection is God's raising of persons from the realm of the dead to a new and unending life in his presence. It is an event leading to a state of clarity, fullness of life and total communion with God (1 Corinthians 13:12).

i. **Resurrection to eternal life** is a privilege reserved for the righteous, not a right for all or a general property of the human soul (Romans 2:6-7, 10; 1 Corinthians 15:23, 42, 51-54). John's Gospel suggests a final resurrection of all, but distinguishes between those who will rise to life and those who will be condemned (John 5:25-29).

j. The Jewish understanding of the totality of human life was the foundation for belief in the resurrection of the body. The resurrected body is of divine origin; it is a spiritual body. This does not mean that it is composed of spirit but that it is animated and guided by the Spirit (1 Corinthians 15:44, 46). It is imperishable, glorious, powerful and free from sickness and decay (1 Corinthians 15:42, 43).

k. The Holy Spirit is closely associated with the believer's resurrection, as he is 'the Spirit of life' (Romans 8:2) and the one who imparts life (2 Corinthians 3:6). For Paul, the Spirit is the pledge and means of a future resurrection, and the one who will sustain resurrection life (Romans 8:10, 11; 2 Corinthians 5:5; Ephesians 1:13, 14).

l. The believer is raised to a state of eternal life, which is sometimes described as **immortality**. We were created for immortality, not with immortality. We receive immortality as a divine gift (Romans 2:7) and will be immortal through grace. It is a future inheritance, not a present possession. God can clothe our mortality with immortality (1 Corinthians 15:53).

m. There will be a **judgment day**, but judgment does not only happen in the future. It is already present (John 3:18; 5:24; 12:31; 16:11; 1 Corinthians 11:29, 32). On the day of judgment all people will be raised to a judgment that leads either to life in abundance, to perfect communion with God, or to eternal death, isolation from God (John 3:36; 5:28-30).

n. One concern might be the extent to which judgment should apply to those who have not heard the gospel. Whereas the Bible indicates that God has not left himself without testimony in creation and through moral law (Acts 14:17; Romans 1:18-32; Romans 2: 14-16), it also suggests that people will be judged according to their opportunity to know God through Jesus (Matthew 11:20-24; Romans 2:1-24; 2 Peter 2:21). The justice and grace of God will form the context in which judgment is made.

4. Church teaching and other influences

a. **The immortality of the soul:** The spread of Christianity in the Hellenistic world (ie the world influenced by Greek culture, language and thought forms), brought it into contact with new influences. In anthropology which is influenced by the ideas of Plato (Platonic anthropology), a human being is perceived as a dualistic being with a soul and a body which are two opposing entities, rather than as a holistic human being, as in Jewish thought. The dualistic view not only separates humanity into two substances, but sees the human body as of lesser value than the soul. Only the soul, which is spirit, is immortal.

b. This had consequences for the way Christians explained the belief in everlasting life. A negative view of the body as inherently evil and belief in immortality as a quality belonging to the individual soul secured a foothold in the Church. Through the influence of Platonic thinking, immortality became part of the teaching of the Church, even though it was never reflected in the classical creeds. It was included in the 17th century Westminster Confession of Faith and from here the expression, but not the Platonic meaning, has become part of Salvation Army doctrine.

c. God alone is immortal (1 Timothy 6:15, 16). Humanity is mortal, and it is the clear teaching of Paul that immortality is a divine gift which will be given only through a future resurrection

(1 Corinthians 15:53-55). In The Salvation Army, as in other Protestant churches, immortality is seen in this context and not as an inherent quality of humanity.

d. In some Christian traditions, the immortality of the soul has been used to explain what happens between death and resurrection, sometimes called 'the intermediate state'. It is an attempt to explain what is outside time in terms of time. This has led to such traditions as praying to and for the dead, and a belief in 'purgatory' as a place for the soul to be purified and for a second chance to repent and embrace the gospel. There is no substantial biblical foundation for such beliefs, which do not form part of Salvation Army doctrine. The Bible is clear that divine judgment is solely based on one's life on earth (Matthew 25:31-46). The New Testament stresses that we die to be with Christ. We do not engage ourselves in speculative details; the reality is as far beyond our understanding as it is outside the limits of time. We can trust that we will be safe in the hands of God.

e. Augustine of Hippo, in his influential work *City of God*, when referring to the intermediate period between the incarnation of Christ and his coming again, described the Church as in exile in the 'city of the world'. Here it is called to maintain a distinctive ethos while surrounded by disbelief, and to live according to a future hope in which the Church will be delivered from the world in order to become part of the 'city of God'. In the meantime the Church shares the fallen nature of the world and is composed of both saints and sinners. Salvation is inaugurated in this life, but will be brought to completion only at the end of history.

f. John Wesley particularly emphasised the present reality of the **Kingdom of God**, an emphasis that was subsequently followed by William Booth in The Salvation Army. Wesley was concerned for the establishment of the Kingdom of God on earth as he preached the gospel of salvation by faith. He taught that as individual lives are transformed by the grace of God, they will experience the life of the Kingdom in the present and that this would be completed in glory. The Kingdom is 'a state to be enjoyed on earth: the proper disposition for the glory of Heaven, rather than the possession of it'.[2]

g. But in Wesley's view the establishment of the Kingdom of God on earth goes beyond the internal religion of those who have accepted his Kingship and rule in their hearts. That acceptance entails an outward expression of love which will have an impact on the world at large as followers of Christ fulfil his ideal for them to be the 'salt of the earth' (Matthew 5:13). Wesley commented that we are to season whatever is round about us with the 'divine savour' which is in us.

h. The Christian must have an impact on society at large and thus contribute to the establishment of God's Kingdom on earth. Wesley included the social dimension of grace and the teaching of holiness in his preaching and practice. Social action and social reform are essential to evangelism, for in his view, solitary religion is not to be found in the gospel of Christ, nor is there a solitary holiness that excludes the social dimension: 'The gospel of Christ knows of no religion, but social; no holiness but social holiness.'[3]

i. The rationalist mood of the Enlightenment led to scepticism about the doctrine of last things and particularly about the validity of a future hope which could not be proven, and which could lead to a lack of responsibility for improving conditions in this life. Nineteenth century liberalism abandoned the idea of the intervention of God to end history and bring about a new creation in favour of an evolutionary doctrine of hope which looked for the gradual development of moral and social perfection in this world. The notion of the Kingdom of God became linked to the development of moral values and a just society.

j. During the 20th century there was a general loss of confidence in human society as a source of hope and progress. The injustices and horrors of two world wars raised doubts about the liberal agenda and a new interest in eschatology emerged. Three general positions summarise the scholarship; futurist eschatology sees the Kingdom of God as being brought about by a dramatic intervention in human history at some point in the future; inaugurated eschatology suggests that the Kingdom is already present but will be fully realised in the future; and realised eschatology claims that the Kingdom of God is already fully present in the coming of Jesus. The second of the three, inaugurated eschatology, is most consistent with the biblical message and has the greatest support.

k. Also during the 20th century, discomfort with the notion of a final judgment with eternal consequences led to a growing emphasis on universalism, the belief that ultimately all people will be saved by the mercy and grace of God. Whereas ultimately God is a God of grace, he is also a God of justice and this view is not consistent with New Testament teaching which indicates that the choices humans make on earth will have eternal consequences. However, this is not to assume that the symbolic pictures of the end times in the Book of Revelation and elsewhere in Scripture are to be interpreted as literal descriptions of actual events and places.

l. Scholars continue to wrestle with the theology of the end times. Bultmann argues that the biblical text has existential meaning, so that judgment does not refer to the end times, but to our own judgment of ourselves based on our knowledge of what God has done in Christ.

m. Jürgen Moltmann in *Theology of Hope* (1964) argued for a rediscovery of a conception of Christian hope which is not primarily about the private transformation of the individual but a corporate hope in which God will transform and renew the whole of creation.

n. Beginning from a theology grounded in the biblical text and knowledge of the context in which it was written, Tom Wright summarises the Christian hope as a hope for 'God's new creation' already come to life in Jesus and providing a sound basis and motivation for mission in the world. In the time between the Resurrection of Jesus and his final coming the Church must build for the Kingdom as it speaks hope through redemption and healing and announces the Lordship of Christ.

> 'Our task in the present … is to live as resurrection people in between Easter and the final day, with our Christian life, corporate and individual, in both worship and mission, as a sign of the first and a foretaste of the second.'[4]

This view resonates with Salvationist belief, ethos and activist approach to faith and mission.

◆ *In what way can you say that you live in the reality of the Kingdom of God? Does it make sense to speak of that in your everyday life, in your business, studies, work and home? How does it affect your decisions and your life goals?*

◆ *How would you explain the resurrection of the body to your friends? What biblical passages would you use to support your explanation?*

◆ *Compare Isaiah 2:12-17 and Philippians 2:9-11. Discuss the similarities and differences between them. What do they say about human response?*

◆ *In today's world many people relate their faith in life after death to reincarnation, which originates with Hinduism. Why do you think that is the case? In what ways is the doctrine of reincarnation incompatible with a biblical Christian faith?*

◆ *Why is universalism an attractive theory for some people in the 21ˢᵗ century?*

C. Interpretations of the return of Christ

1. The Parousia

The return of Christ is often referred to by the Greek term, *parousia*. This is usually translated as 'coming' but literally has a sense of 'presence' as opposed to 'absence'. Throughout the centuries some parts of the Church have emphasised Christ's return in glory, making it a priority in theology and worship. The Salvation Army has avoided speculation about details of the return of Christ. Salvationists prefer to emphasise the Christian responsibility to live in a state of expectation and hope. We should be constantly open to the presence and judgment of God in Christ, and fully involved in the mission of God for the salvation of the world.

2. The millennium

The millennium refers to the thousand-year reign of Christ on earth which is mentioned in Revelation 20:2-7. Although explored at various times in Church history, it does not have universal acceptance among Christians, nor is there a common interpretation.

3. A-millenialism

Some Christians interpret the millennium symbolically to mean not a period of time as such, but Christ's reign on earth through his people. It is a symbol of perfection and completeness but has no implications of time. This is usually known as a-millennialism.

4. Post-millenialism

Post-millennialists teach that there will be a period of the Kingdom of God on earth, or a thousand years of 'power for the gospel' followed by the return of Christ. The implication is that this will be a period in which universal acknowledgement of Christ is pursued and established. Supporters suggest that this is implied by Matthew 28:19, 20 and by the notion of the triumph of the Church (Matthew 16:18). However, it is difficult to reconcile with verses which suggest times of persecution and unbelief before the end (Matthew 24:6-14; Luke 18:8; 2 Thessalonians 2:3-12; Revelation 13) and with Jesus' warning that his return will be unexpected (Mark 13:32-37).

5. Pre-millenialism
In contrast, pre-millennialists teach that Christ will return to earth to reign for a thousand years before Satan's final overthrow. Although evil will still be present, it will be restrained and both humanity and creation will enjoy a time of blessing. However, this will be followed by a final battle in which Satan is defeated before the universal judgment and the inauguration of the new creation. The major source of this belief is Revelation 20 (but see also Isaiah 2:2-5; Zechariah 14: 9, 16-21) but interpretation is not straightforward and other meanings are possible.

6. Dispensationalism
Dispensationalists take the pre-millennial view further. They see the millennium as a further dispensation, or period in God's dealings with humanity. In their understanding, the coming of Christ will be preceded by the 'rapture' of the Church. This concerns the expectation that the believer will be taken up 'in the clouds' to meet Christ at the time of his return (1 Thessalonians 4:15-17). The millennium itself will be the time of the literal fulfilment of the Old Testament promises to Israel.

The differing interpretations suggest that the Bible leaves us with the mystery of God and his purposes for us, which are finally beyond speculation. Our best response is to be silent before the mystery, confident in the good purposes of a loving God and in the redemption offered in Jesus Christ.

◆ *Ensure that you understand each of the above concepts so that you could explain the similarities and differences to a new Christian.*

D. Issues for Salvationists

1. The whole person

In Salvationist faith and practice the wholeness of the person is crucial. It is reflected in the combination of our evangelistic and social work. The doctrine underlines this wholeness as we believe in a resurrection of our total being. There are many different beliefs concerning life after death and there is always the danger that beliefs reflecting the 'spirit of the time' can slip unnoticed into Christian thinking. Any dualistic thinking which separates soul and body, often suggesting that the body is either less important or evil, must be resisted as it can lead to unhealthy or immoral practice. Salvationist teaching must clearly present the wholeness of the individual as a basis for personal spiritual life and mission in the world.

2. Life and death

We live in a time when, within some Western cultures, there is a rejection of the reality and pain of death. There is an expectation that there will be a cure for every illness and frailty, and that life can be extended endlessly. Death has been institutionalised, or hospitalised, and therefore, to a certain extent, hidden. It is no longer a natural part of life as many people have never been present at the moment of death of their loved ones, seen a dead person or taken care of a dead body. At the same time the media revels in death 'pornography' showing pictures of maimed and tortured bodies, of violence leading to death, or focusing on funerals exposing people's grief as if it was a showpiece. Salvationists are not immune to these influences. This doctrine is vital because it points to death as a reality and then looks beyond death. It encourages us to reflect upon crucial questions which face every human being. What is the meaning of life? Is there anything on the other side of death? How do I cross over from life to death? Is there anything which can carry me through death? Do I face death on my own? Therefore it is vital to keep the focus on resurrection and accountability. Resurrection underlines the wholeness, the reality of death, the one life we have as a gift from God and for which we are accountable now and on the judgment day.

3. Accountability

To know that we are accountable and will be judged on the basis of our choices will shape our attitude towards others as well as our judgment of them. God judges us all by the light we have and on the truth of Christ (Romans 2:1-4). As Salvationists we must be aware that we should use our God-given free will wisely. We must learn to choose Christ continually, aware that our decision will ultimately have significance not only for ourselves but in the Kingdom of God.

4. Mission

This doctrine helps us to get our perspectives right. Because of our deep involvement with social questions and work, our focus can easily be limited to the matters of this world, but this doctrine broadens our horizon and gives an eternal aspect to all we do and are. It urges us to pursue God's mission, offering hope and healing to a world which, through the Resurrection of Jesus Christ, will one day be made new.

5. God's final purposes

Salvationists believe in the perfection of individuals in Glory as part of a redeemed creation. This is nothing less than belief in the Resurrection of Christ, for the redeemed society is no other than the glorified Body of Christ (Revelation 21:1-7). That is why our resurrection, like our present salvation, is more than individual. It is all of that, there is no loss of personal identity or integrity, but it is more than that. The doctrine is, above all, a sign of hope, that one day God will bring about his own purposes and creation will be fully healed and redeemed as the Kingdom of God is finally realised and his will is accomplished on earth.

◆ *Are Salvationists ever guilty of dualistic attitudes which deny the reality and integrity of the whole person? What potential dangers are there with this attitude and how might we combat them?*

◆ *In what ways does the reality of the final triumph of the Kingdom of God affect our lifestyle and attitudes?*

◆ *How does belief in the final judgment give urgency and focus to your witness?*

◆ *If you were asked, in a pastoral context, by the family of someone who is nearing the end of life, to explain the meaning of Doctrine 11, what would you say?*

◆ *Do you think the answers the doctrine gives satisfy the questions of people today on the meaning of life and death? What are your reasons for your answer?*

◆ *Express your belief in last things in the way most relevant for you – for example, a statement of faith, art, music, creative writing, dance or drama. Share what you have prepared with a friend or at your corps.*

1 *The Song Book of The Salvation Army* 1986: 438:3
2 John Wesley, *Notes on Matthew*
   3:2http://www.godrules.net/library/wesley/wesleymat3.htm
3 John Wesley,
   http://www.divinity.duke.edu/wesleyan/docs/jworiginalcollections/04_Hymns_and_Sac
   red_Poems_(1739).pdf
4 Tom Wright, 2007 *Surprised by Hope*. London: SPCK:41

A Salvationist understanding of the Church

Of this Great Church of the Living God we claim, and have ever claimed, that we of The Salvation Army are an integral part and element – a living fruit-bearing branch in the True Vine.'[1]

The Church is the fellowship of all who are justified and sanctified by grace through faith in Christ. Membership in the body of Christ is not optional for believers: it is a reality given to all who know Christ, the Head of the Church. It is a benefit of the Atonement through which we are invited into fellowship with God and with one another.

Salvation Army doctrine implies a doctrine of the Church. Each doctrine begins: 'We believe ... '. 'We' points to a body of believers, a community of faith – a church.

One very important change since the 11 Articles of Faith were formulated and adopted is the evolution of the movement from an agency for evangelism to a church, an evangelistic body of believers who worship, share fellowship, minister and join in mission together.

Salvationists are members of the one body of Christ. We share common ground with the universal Church while manifesting our own characteristics. As one particular expression of the Church, The Salvation Army participates with other Christian denominations and congregations in mission and ministry. We are part of the one, universal Church.

The corps is The Salvation Army's local congregation. It is a visible expression of the Church. It has its own ways of worshipping, training and serving, based on the teaching of the Bible, the guidance of the Holy Spirit and the nature of its mission. Its purpose is consistent with the calling and teaching of the one, universal Church. Its three key strengths are its missional zeal, its commitment to holiness and its strong community outreach.

A. The Body of Christ

When we speak of the Church as the Body of Christ we mean that all believers are incorporated in spiritual union with Christ who is their Head (Colossians 1:18), and with one another as fellow members working in harmony (Romans 12:4, 5; Ephesians 4:4-6, 15, 16). We mean that the Church is Christ's visible presence in the world, given life by the indwelling of the Holy Spirit and called to grow in conformity to Christ.

Scripture teaches that every member of the Body has an essential part to play if the whole is to function to the glory of God, and that without the presence and participation of every member, the Body suffers (1 Corinthians 12:12-30).

B. The people of God

The Old Testament describes how God called out an identifiable company, the Jews, not for favouritism but to be his people, to make known his grace to all and to be examples of faith and obedience (Exodus 19:5, 6; Deuteronomy 27:9, 10).

The New Testament recognises that the Church is called to a comparable faith and obedience (Acts 5:29; Titus 2:11-14; 1 Peter 2:9, 10). As a pilgrim people, the Church proclaims the universal message of the grace of God and invites people everywhere to become fellow-pilgrims with those throughout the ages who have responded to God in faith.

C. The Church as community

1. A community of reconciliation
The Church demonstrates that community has been restored through Christ. As the Fall brought division and deception into

human relationships, so the restoration brings healing, honesty and love into those relationships. The Church is a fellowship in which we learn to risk being vulnerable with one another, because on the Cross Christ conquered sin by making himself vulnerable for our sakes (Galatians 6:2). The Church is called to demonstrate to the world that God has accomplished reconciliation through the Cross (Ephesians 2:11-22; Colossians 1:1-22).

It must be admitted that there are many examples of Christian congregations failing to embody the reality of reconciliation both between believers and towards those outside the Church (1 Corinthians 1:10-17; 11:17, 18). In consequence, some people have withdrawn from active participation in congregational life. However, total withdrawal from fellowship is failure to participate in of one of the most significant benefits of the Atonement, the possibility of authentic human community (Luke 14:15-24).

But the Body of Christ is not in bondage to its failures. Throughout the Church's history, where fellowship has been risked within the security Christ gives, spiritual transformation in human relationships has resulted (Ephesians 4:25-32). This has been made possible through the work of the Holy Spirit who creates, empowers and renews the Church (Chapters 3, 7 and 10).

2. A continuing community

As an integral part of its mission to continue the ministry of Christ, the Church passes on the gospel from one generation to another (Psalm 145:4-7). While subject to the authority of Scripture, the Christian community, led by the Spirit and with the presence of Christ (Matthew 18:20), provides a consensus of interpretation that ensures the preservation of the gospel message.

The Church is one, though diverse in its expressions. Differing over certain matters, Christians are united in proclaiming Christ as the only Lord and Saviour, and the Church preserves a tradition of worship and devotion that originated with the first Christians and their response to the risen Lord.

249

Again and again in the New Testament we are reminded of the unity we already enjoy in Christ while, at the same time, we are warned against division and are exhorted to seek the greater completeness of that unity. All Christians are called constantly to pursue and express the unity God gives to his people.

The unity of the Church depends upon incorporation in Christ, not necessarily in a single unified church body (John 17:20-26). The challenge to unity reminds us that we live in a 'now but not yet' situation.

3. A gathered community

a. The Church is created by the Holy Spirit for fellowship.

Together we are God's household, his family, as we abide in Christ and he in us (John 15:1-17). This intimate community exists by the command of Christ and the work of the Holy Spirit (John 13:34, 35; 1 John 4:7-12). It is he who enables us to gather in fellowship as one, sharing life together, growing up into Christ our Head, discovering in him freedom from prejudice and sin.

Its importance can hardly be overestimated. Within this community we can experience healing, spiritual growth, happiness and a deep fellowship of giving and receiving (Acts 2:42-47; 4:32-35; Ephesians 2:19-22). As holiness is relational, holiness of life is to be realised in community. As Christians we make our spiritual journey as part of a company. The New Testament speaks of 'saints' only in the plural (Romans 1:7; 2 Corinthians 1:1; Ephesians 1:1). John Wesley taught that holiness is social: it is nurtured in the fellowship of Christians and then dispersed throughout society (Chapter 10).

b. The Church is created by the Holy Spirit for healing.

Within Christ's healing community, the Holy Spirit enables us to care for each other, to respond to one another's hurts and to experience healing. Through the congregation the Spirit supports us in times of trial or loss; our personhood is affirmed and our worth enhanced (James 5:13-20). As we are being made holy and are helped and healed, we discover that the Church is a community which is marked by deep joy which no-one can take from us.

c. The Church is created by the Holy Spirit for nurture.

Within the Christian fellowship the Holy Spirit enables us to build each other up in the faith, to instruct, to bear each other's burdens, to encourage, forgive, celebrate, share, comfort and challenge one another (Galatians 6:1-5; Ephesians 4:25-32; Colossians 3:12-17; Philemon verse 7).

Such strong support helps us to grow in Christlikeness and holiness and to cultivate the fruit of the Spirit. Described in Galatians 5:22, 23 as love, joy, peace, patience, kindness, goodness, faithfulness, gentleness and self-control, the fruit of the Spirit is the manifestation of the nature of Christ in each of us through the sanctifying Spirit. It is the fruit that all Christians are called and empowered to bear; the fruit that marks us as true disciples of Jesus Christ.

We are also nurtured by the worship of the congregation. In worship, God edifies his people, enabling them to respond to the Holy Spirit for themselves and to reach out in faith to others. Prayer, preaching, music and artistic expression all combine to glorify God and nurture his people (Colossians 3:15-17).

d. The Church is created by the Holy Spirit to equip for ministry and mission.

In the congregation we discover and deploy our individual gifts for ministry and mission. Each member of the Body of Christ receives gifts for ministry and is called by God to develop and deploy them for the benefit of all (Acts 6:1-6; 13:1-3; 1 Corinthians 7:7; 12:4-11). Gifts are given both to build up the Church and to make possible its mission in the world (Romans 12:3-21; Ephesians 4:11-16). The community of faith recognises our gifts and commissions our service. As we then deploy our gifts in ministry and mission, God is glorified (1 Peter 4:7-11).

4. A scattered community

a. The Church gathers that it may be sent out in mission.

The Church is not a self-absorbed society brought together for security and socialising. It is a fellowship that is called by Jesus to release its members for pilgrimage and mission (Matthew 9:35–10:16; 28:16-20; Mark 16:15; Luke 9:57-62). The Holy Spirit creates the Church not only for our benefit, but also to make our witness and mission possible.

b. The Holy Spirit empowers the whole Church for witness.

Our Christian pilgrimage demands an enduring commitment to a life of discipline and a tentative relationship to distracting world values. The Church is the community where Kingdom values are taught and lived, thereby encouraging us to sustain a radical lifestyle in keeping with our calling.

We are all called to live holy lives in the world and to see ourselves as set apart to be ministers or servants of the gospel. All Christians have direct access to God through the priesthood of Christ (1 Peter 2:4-10). All are called to exercise the challenging ministry of intercession on behalf of one another and for the world. In Christ, all Christians share in the priestly ministry. All vocations are important opportunities for expressing discipleship (Ephesians 4:1-24). In that sense there is no separated ministry.

Within that common calling, some are called by Christ to be full-time office-holders within the Church. Their calling is affirmed by the gift of the Holy Spirit, the recognition of the Christian community and their commissioning – ordination – for service (Acts 13:1-3). Their function is to focus the mission and ministry of the whole Church so that its members are held faithful to their calling.

They serve their fellow ministers as visionaries who point the way to mission, as pastors who minister to the people when they are hurt or overcome, as enablers who equip others for mission, as spiritual leaders.

c. The Holy Spirit empowers the Church for mission.

In affirming and sanctioning our callings, the Church sends us out to share in the mission of God who sent Jesus to reconcile the world to himself.

As members of Christ's Church we carry out God's mission in Christ's name in various ways including:

- By our presence in the world (Matthew 5:13-16)

- By our public proclamation of the gospel (2 Timothy 4:1-5)

- By personal evangelism (Acts 8:26-40)

- By pointing to evidence of the Holy Spirit's power to transform lives (Acts 2:38)

- By identifying with and offering compassionate service to the poor and disadvantaged (Matthew 25:31-46; Luke 10:25-37)

- By working with the oppressed for justice and liberty (Luke 4:16-21)

All these ministries seek life-transformation. When any of them is ignored or neglected the mission of the Church suffers. As members of Christ's Church we are all engaged in mission to the whole person and the whole world through the power of the Holy Spirit.

5. A community renewed for the future

The Church lives by hope. It is caught up in the movement from Pentecost to the Parousia, from the beginning of the Church to the return of Christ and the fulfilment of his promises. The Holy Spirit frees God's resurrection people from the grip of past failures and renews them for God's future in Christ (Romans 8:18-39). The Bible looks to the future. In the Old Testament the restoration of Israel was promised (Jeremiah 31:1-14). The New Testament sees this restoration on a universal scale: all things brought together under Christ (Matthew 8:11; Ephesians 1:9, 10; 1 Peter 1:3-9; Revelation 11:15; 21:1-4).

In the Church, both militant on earth and triumphant in Heaven, God's future is not only hoped for, but also lived out. As such it is a sign of the coming Kingdom. The Church lives with its mind set on those things which are 'above'. It invests its talents and gifts to express that future and actually to live by its reality. The Church lives expectantly in the light of the dawn of Christ's future (1 Corinthians 15:50-58; Colossians 3:1-4; 1 Peter 5:1-11). Its mission is to open that future to the world.

The Church: study notes

A. Essential characteristics

1. The study of the Church

The study of the theology of the Church is called ecclesiology. The term comes from the Greek words *logos* (which means word, mind, or doctrine), and *ekklesia* (church), which in turn is comprised of two other Greek words, *ek* (out of) and *kaleo* (I call). It was used in the pre-Christian period to indicate the summons of an army for battle, and also for the duly-constituted assembly of free citizens for the self-governing of their city. Early Church writers chose the term *ekklesia* in preference to the Jewish term *sunagoge* (from *sunagein*, meaning 'to bring together') to describe the fellowship of believers. Perhaps the choice is significant. It appears that being 'called out' was seen as more representative of the Church than 'bringing together'.

2. Local and universal, visible and invisible

Since New Testament times the word 'church' has been used to describe both the local congregation (Revelation 2-3 'to the angel of the church in ... '), and in the generic sense, denoting the total number of Christian believers (Colossians 1:18). This indicates that there is one universal Church which functions in local and diverse settings. Calvin made a distinction between the visible, earthly Church of present experience, which is flawed and fallible, made up of both the elect and those who are not chosen (Chapter 9), and the invisible, eschatological, true, 'one' Church, consisting only of the elect, which will come into being at the end time. Although the Calvinistic notion of the Church consisting only of those individuals who have been elected by God for salvation is not consistent with Salvation Army faith and belief, this model does highlight future hopes and expectations which centre on the total company of the redeemed, through time and in the age to come.

3. Gathered and scattered

Our understanding of the Church keeps two important activities in perspective – 'gathering' and 'scattering'. The gathering activities of the Church are crucial. God's people need to come together to be nurtured, encouraged and equipped for ministry and mission. This is complemented by the 'scattering' of the Church in order to fulfil God's mission in the world. Worshipping God, learning in community and the development of spiritual gifts are essential to the life of the Church. The Church gathers together to receive the presence of God and to prepare and equip itself to be scattered in the world. In so doing it must be a leavening influence, a courageous witness, an evangelistic mission, a compassionate servant and a prophetic voice.

4. Life in community

The doctrine of the Church seeks to keep us faithful to the scriptural understanding of human life as being properly lived in community. All people need a community where they can be at home and can find roots, place and belonging. It is the Church, and not a highly individualistic Christianity, that responds to these needs. We have no real identity other than as human beings in relationship to others. We are who we are as members of the Body of Christ. The gospel offers the world true community in Christ and guards against destructive, presumptuous, self-centred individualism. A theology of the Church offers the foundation for this understanding. We discover who we are, what our gifts are, and what our mission is within the context of the Christian community.

5. A community of reconciliation

Viewed from the New Testament perspective the Church is the community of those who have found forgiveness, the peace of Christ and new life free of destructive inner forces of hostility. The Church is where the disconnection caused by sin is being healed. The Church gives proof to the reality and power of reconciliation through Christ. It demonstrates the positive alternatives to relationships and societies that are built upon power, unhealthy competition, conformity and repression. It demonstrates the true humanity to which God calls us.

6. The guardian of the faith

The Church is the guardian of the faith. It must teach responsibly, ensuring that there is a place for both the wisdom of the past and proper development in the present. As such, it sustains orthodox – that is agreed and established – faith, discerns heresy and ensures a dynamic approach to Christian theology as new understandings emerge. We must recognise, however, that expressions of the Church have sometimes been, and still can be, corrupt or negligent, not guarding the faith as they should. The community of all believers must accept responsibility to ensure the integrity of the Church, which is accountable to God through the judgment of Scripture.

7. A community in culture

Although the Church is part of the surrounding culture, it must understand itself to be a radically different kind of community. It must comment on and sometimes oppose the allegiances, values and lifestyles of contemporary culture. It cannot compromise its own holiness; it must live in the freedom of Christ and not become absorbed by the present world order. At the same time the Church must relate the gospel message to the hopes, needs and life struggles of those in contemporary culture without losing its prophetic edge or weakening the integrity of its witness. It must seek to be culturally relevant without compromising the gospel and its values.

8. Unity and diversity

The theology of the Church affirms unity in diversity. It is important, therefore, that all Christians acknowledge that we are one in Christ.

This oneness centres on the essentials of a common faith, love for one another, a shared call to holiness and a united commitment to mission. This unity must be affirmed within each congregation, within the denomination and within the universal Church.

Within the unity of the Body of Christ we become willing to express and celebrate our difference in personalities, gifts, methods, cultural expressions and points of view. The variety of denominations is a visible, corporate sign of this diversity within unity.

The tension between belief in 'one' Church and the existence of a multiplicity of congregations and denominations is problematic for some. It has generally been resolved in one of four ways: to claim that one denomination is the true Church and that all others are false or approximations of what they should be; to draw a distinction between the 'ideal' and the 'real'; to suggest that the current disunity will be abolished on the last day; or to take an organic approach, suggesting that the varied Christian expressions are analogous to the branches of the tree, which are united by their connection with a common root system (John 15).

A common theme in the ecumenical movement, which is concerned with the fostering of Christian unity, is to point to Christ as the source of that unity, following a maxim derived from Ignatius of Antioch (c35 or 50 – between 98 and 117AD) 'where Christ is, there is also the Church'.

◆ Read, and carefully consider, Ephesians 2:11-22. What is the connection between reconciliation with God and reconciliation in a community? What are the 'dividing walls of hostility' that we face in the Church today? Is your own worshipping community in need of reconciliation? If so, why is this? How might it be resolved?

◆ Discuss how your experience as a participant in the Body of Christ, the fellowship of believers, has had a significant impact on your life.

◆ How do you understand the relationship of the Church to contemporary society? What can be done to ensure that relevance does not compromise the integrity of faith?

B Historical summary

1. The New Testament

a. Biblical religion is always corporate. The Bible tells the history of a people and their relationship with God. Although the faith and action of individuals is significant, it is properly understood only in the context of the community. Jesus is seen as the Saviour of his people (Matthew 1:21); his own ministry is conducted in the company of a group of 12 followers, who can be seen as the nucleus of the New Israel. He refers to the 'Church' that will be established (Matthew 16:18; 18:17) and his final commission implies a continuing communal context (Matthew 28:19, 20).

b. The Acts of the Apostles records the development of the community. Although the day of Pentecost was experienced by individuals, it is essentially a corporate experience which leads to the formation of an ongoing fellowship of faith and witness (Acts 2:1-4).

c. The Church is seen as the new people of God, the New Israel. As a body this Church comprises 'a chosen people, a royal priesthood, a holy nation' that has been called 'out of darkness into his wonderful light' in order to 'declare the praises of him who called' (1 Peter 2:9). All Christians have a place and a calling within this people. The Church is the miracle by which God in Christ takes those who 'were not a people' and transforms them into 'God's people' (1 Peter 2:10).

d. In addition, other biblical images help to define the character of the Church. These include the Body of Christ (Colossians 1:18; Romans 12:4, 5; Ephesians 4:4-6,15, 16); the building of God (1 Corinthians 3:10, 11, 16; Ephesians 2:20-22); the family of God (Ephesians 2:19; 1 Timothy 3:15); the flock of God (1 Peter 2:25; 5:4; Hebrews 13:20); and the vineyard of God (John 15:1-8).

2. The Early Church

In the first two centuries Christians understood the Church as a holy community with a radical lifestyle. It would not compromise with the values of society and was therefore persecuted for its unwillingness to accommodate. The Church of that day can be seen as an alternative society warring against the principalities and powers that shaped the lives of individuals and social structures – an army committed to uncompromising obedience to Jesus Christ as Lord. In this climate there was little interest in, or energy for, formulating a theology of the Church. Nevertheless, some elements achieved wide consensus. The Church, as a spiritual society, replaces Israel as the people of God in the world and despite differences of gender, race or culture, all Christians are one in Christ. In addition, the Church, in which true Christian teaching is located and proclaimed, gathers the faithful for nurture and growth in holiness.

3. The Nicene Creed

The Nicene Creed (Appendix 1) contains the affirmation, 'We believe in one holy, catholic and apostolic church'. The four adjectives became known as the four 'marks' or 'notes' that are the distinctive features of the Church and they have shaped many approaches to ecclesiology in the intervening centuries. They emphasise the qualities that should be evident in the Church, even if in practice the Church may fail to achieve them. Thus the Church should be 'one' despite the plurality of expression and denominations; holy, that is set apart for the purposes of God, even though both individual members and the institution sometimes fail to be holy in their life and actions; catholic, often now described as universal, but also meaning complete in its proclamation of the gospel, for all people and able to meet every human need; and apostolic, or deriving from the teaching of the apostles.

4. Church and state

When Christianity became legalised under the Emperor Constantine by the Edict of Milan (313 AD) and then the state religion of the

Roman Empire under Theodosius 1 (392 AD), it began rapidly to accommodate itself to the cultural values and practices of society and to identify with many of them. Membership began to be increasingly less focused upon radical commitment. Citizenship and the state became equated with membership in the Church. Rather than being 'the sacramental community', the Church largely became 'the dispenser of sacraments'.

The pattern of Church organisation increasingly followed that of Roman civil government and gradually became part of its structure. This was to prove an advantage because it enabled the Church to survive the chaos of the Roman Empire's dissolution. But it also proved to be a limiting factor because of the concentration of power and participation in the hands of a minority, the clerics, thereby severely limiting the participation of the majority of Christians in creative discipleship and leadership.

5. Sacred and secular

From the fourth century until the end of the Middle Ages, society was understood as being divided into two realms, the sacred and the secular. The Church was seen as the authority, guardian and arbiter of the sacred realm. However, it also wielded considerable political and economic power in the secular realm and often became involved in the political process, sometimes strongly influencing, or even determining, the outcome. At the same time, radical Christian groups, often persecuted by the established Church, sought to preserve and live by the dynamics of discipleship which they discovered in the New Testament. For example, the early Celtic Church developed a spirituality of great depth that affirmed the presence of God in daily life, transforming pagan cultures by the power of life-affirming holiness and compassionate community.

6. Reformation

The Reformation (16th century) sought the recovery of true biblical spirituality. However, in time, many of these Reformation churches themselves became State churches, often compromising with culture and weakening the ministry of the laity.

The Reformers initially thought that the reforming movement would return to the Roman Catholic Church and influence it from within, but when it became evident at the Colloquy of Ratisbon, held at Regensburg in 1541, that there could not be reconciliation or compromise between the Reformers and the Church, it was necessary to develop an ecclesiology for the Protestant movement. Calvin argued that the marks of the true Church are that the word of God is preached and that the sacraments should be rightly administered. 'Wherever we see the word of God sincerely preached and heard, wherever we see the sacraments administered according to the institution of Christ, there we cannot have any doubt that the Church of God has some existence, since his promise cannot fail…'[2] This definition was later to prove problematic for the acceptance of The Salvation Army in some contexts.

The Radical Reformation that followed sought the recovery of the Church as the radical, non-accommodating community of faith. Distinct from the present world order, the Church was to give witness to the transforming power of the gospel by living as God's holy colony on earth.

7. Revival and mission

The 18th century Wesleyan Revival saw the Church as the community of the sanctified that nurtured holiness and gave itself to mission for the world. The Church became holy as its members allowed God the Holy Spirit to sanctify them (Chapter 10). In the latter part of the 19th century, the first Salvationists understood themselves as a radical militant people of God called to holiness and holy warfare (evangelism and social involvement).

The 19th century also saw the significant expansion of world missions. Many denominations and other groups of individuals created missionary societies dedicated to bringing the gospel to non-Christian lands. A considerable degree of educational, medical, and social work was also undertaken. This became the modern missionary movement. It was driven by an expansionist understanding of the Church committed to evangelising and serving the world. As significant and sacrificial as many of these missions were, they often exported Western culture as well as the gospel. They sometimes encouraged dependency and paternalism. The 20th century has seen a gradual reaction away from cultural imperialism as the churches in these countries have taken control of their own destinies.

8. Secularisation and migration

During the 20th century, church attendance in the West has declined and society has become secularised. With diminishing numbers and support, the Western Church may be forced to see itself once again as a small counter-cultural community of witness. Although this may mean that the Church is no longer viewed as one of the major institutions of society, it may also allow it to reclaim its prophetic voice, speaking from the margins to comment upon and challenge the accepted wisdom and practice of the age. Meanwhile, in many parts of the Two-Thirds World, the Church continues to grow and free itself from the Western paternalism of earlier years.

Another significant phenomenon of the latter part of the 20th century has been the immigration of African, Asian, West Indian and South American peoples to Western nations. This has created new opportunities for Christian mission. First, Western Christians have undertaken cross-cultural mission with these groups, often with great success. Second, Christians from within the immigrant groups themselves are increasingly evangelising others in the West. It has also allowed for the establishment of indigenous congregations within the host culture, thus adding to the diversity of the ecumenical fellowship and allowing for mutual understanding and enrichment.

9. Spirituality and the consumer culture

In many cultures the end of the 20th century and first few years of the 21st century have brought a rising interest in spirituality as the secular agenda has failed to bring fulfilment and peace. However, this is most often marked by a turning to alternative spiritualities rather than to Christianity. A consumer approach to religion, in which individuals choose the elements of the spiritual life that most appeal to them, is common. This does not easily resonate with the Christian message, particularly the obedient love and dedicated lifestyle that is a result of a personal response to the Atonement of Jesus. Nevertheless, the Church has opportunity to react creatively to this openness to the spiritual life.

◆ *Identify a number of New Testament descriptions of a church or congregation (see study notes B1d for examples). Which ones best describe your corps or worshipping community, or what it aspires to become? What steps can be taken to bring your corps or community closer to the spiritual reality to which these word pictures point? Which picture is most challenging?*

◆ *A friend says she is a Christian, has an experience of salvation through Christ and believes the Bible, but does not attend a church because the Church is full of hypocrites who do not live what they profess. She has decided to practise her faith privately and is clearly seeking approval for her decision to withdraw from church fellowship. What would you do and say?*

◆ *Discuss ways in which church association with secular powers, particularly the state, can be either an advantage or a disadvantage to the local worshipping community.*

◆ *Read John 17:20-26. Why did Jesus pray 'that they may be one as we are one'? What are the consequences when unity is absent?*

◆ *What strategies are necessary for the Church to be an effective and attractive witness in the 21st century?*

C. The Salvation Army and the Church

1. From mission to spiritual home

It is clear that the early Salvationists did not envisage creating another church or denomination. Nineteenth-century churches were perceived by some to demonstrate lack of concern for a largely unsaved world (especially the poor and working classes), materialism, compromised living, complacency and unwillingness to adapt to the needs of other classes and cultural groups. These tendencies were in direct opposition to the aims of William Booth and his people. The early Army could be described as a para-church (*para*, beside, alongside), that is, a group or agency that serves alongside the churches and carries out a specific mission about which it is very passionate and for which it is especially equipped. In effect this was an agency to evangelise the poor and working classes.

However, the people who came to faith needed a 'church home', a fellowship of believers in which they could be nurtured, discipled, trained and encouraged. Most of the church congregations proved unable to accommodate the culture of poverty and provide the needed support. The converts returned to the mission and made it their spiritual home. Unless Christians have a community of faith which serves as their spiritual support system, their conversions will probably be short-lived. In reality, The Salvation Army became a church with a missional emphasis.

2. 'A living, fruit-bearing branch of the True Vine'

However, many within our movement have been reluctant to call the Army a church. George Scott Railton summarised the reasons: 'We are an Army of Soldiers of Christ, seeking no church status, avoiding as we would the plague every denominational rut, in order perpetually to reach more and more of those who lie outside every church boundary.'[3] With a slightly different perspective, Bramwell Booth wrote: 'Of this Great Church of the Living God, we claim and have ever claimed, that we of The Salvation Army are an integral part and element – a living fruit-bearing branch in the True Vine'[4] but he does not actually use the term 'church'. As a para-church movement we certainly believed ourselves to be 'an arm of the Church', and some churches today who are familiar with our social work, perhaps even our evangelistic work, but are largely ignorant of our congregational life, still see us that way.

3. What kind of church?

Today it would be difficult to deny that The Salvation Army is a fully authentic and adequate fellowship within the spectrum of Christian denominations. Writing in 1987, Phil Needham suggested that: 'Many within the movement feel the need to develop an ecclesiological understanding that will enable Salvationists better to understand the nature and calling of the Church, the particular calling of the Army as a branch of the Church, and the contribution of the Army to the Church.'[5] The international mission statement defines The Salvation Army as follows:

> The Salvation Army, an international movement, is an evangelical part of the universal Christian Church.
>
> Its message is based on the Bible. Its ministry is motivated by love for God. Its mission is to preach the gospel of Jesus Christ and meet human needs in his name without discrimination.[6]

The New Testament Church was called by God to be his people and to carry out his mission in the world. By this definition, The Salvation Army would claim to be a church. As a part of God's people, The Salvation Army is biblically orthodox and non-sectarian, having doctrines and practices that are consistent with universally-accepted creeds, and which fall within the mainstream of Church teaching. The missional emphasis is consistent with the great commission of Jesus and the biblical emphasis (Matthew 28:19, 20; Acts 1:8).

4. A gathered and scattered community

While it is clear from Salvation Army history that the need for a gathered community for its converts led to the emergence of the denomination, nevertheless the Army has almost always thought of itself more in terms of mission rather than fellowship – it is a scattered community. Emerging at a time when the Church seemed overall to be in retreat, especially among the marginalised, the Army saw itself as an invading evangelical force called out of the perceived comfort and introspection of mainline Christianity. The emphasis on mission remains. The Salvation Army can only be properly understood in the light of its mission, although a second key focus of the movement, its emphasis upon the development of holy and distinctive living, underlines the fact that the worship and fellowship of the gathered community is vital if it is to be effective in its scattered mission.

5. An ecclesiology for The Salvation Army

At the beginning of the 21st century The Salvation Army takes its place in the Christian Church, bringing a distinctive contribution and focus. The 2006 Theology and Ethics Symposium in Johannesburg took ecclesiology as its theme and 2008 saw the publication of *The Salvation Army in the Body of Christ: An Ecclesiological Statement* which states:

> 'Through the years Salvationism has moved on in its emerging self-perception, and in the perceptions of others, from being a para-church evangelistic revival movement (at first known as The Christian Mission) to being a Christian church with a permanent mission to the unsaved and the marginalised. Salvationists remain comfortable in being known simply as "the Army", or a "mission", or a "movement", or for certain purposes as a "charity". All of these descriptors can be used alongside "church". With this multi-faceted identity the Army is welcomed to, and takes its place at, the ecumenical table at local, national and international levels.'[7]

♦ *Why is it appropriate to describe The Salvation Army as a church?*

♦ *What can we learn from the historical story told in C1 that can inform our participation in God's mission in the 21st century?*

♦ *Write notes which you could use with a group of young people who want to explore the identity of The Salvation Army in relation to the Universal Church.*

D. Spiritual gifts

1. The Gifts of the Holy Spirit

Spiritual gifts are given by the Holy Spirit to unite the Christian fellowship in its life together and in its mission. As such, they are to be recognised as evidence of God's loving generosity to his people and of his desire that they be fully equipped to share in his mission. Gifts are diverse, yet each person is important and each has a responsibility to deploy their gifts in the fellowship (Romans 12:3-8)

In the New Testament there are a number of passages in which specific spiritual gifts are identified. They speak of the many differing ministries that the Spirit has given to sustain the life of the Church. There are gifts that enable Christians to proclaim the gospel message, such as preaching, teaching and prophecy. Others are given so that Christians may serve people in Christ's name, for example gifts of service, healing, generosity and hospitality. Some are gifts of leadership. Some are gifts which enhance and encourage devotion to God, such as gifts of prayer, faith and speaking in tongues. Whatever our gifts, they are to be used to serve one another and to glorify God (Ephesians 4:7-13; 1 Peter 4:7-11).

2. Misuse and abuse

It follows that the use of spiritual gifts to promote competition or to further individualism is misuse. We must beware, then, of the elevation of certain gifts as proof of spiritual superiority and the consequent undervaluing of other gifts.

Speaking in tongues is the clearest example of a gift that is overvalued in some Christian fellowships and undervalued in others. This gift is overvalued when it is regarded as the definitive evidence of the baptism in the Spirit and so becomes a measure of spiritual accomplishment. It is undervalued when it fails to be acknowledged as a true gift of God's Holy Spirit (1 Corinthians 12-14).

3. The Salvation Army and spiritual gifts

The Salvation Army recognises all spiritual gifts. However, in the light of the susceptibility of some to abuse in public worship, the Army emphasises those gifts that encourage the clear proclamation of the gospel and draw into the circle of worship everyone who is present.

The New Testament shows that spiritual gifts are exercised in different ways in different congregations, often because of different circumstances and needs. It also emphasises the special value of those gifts that enable the Church clearly to present Jesus Christ as Lord and Saviour.

◆ *Study the New Testament teaching on spiritual gifts in order to ensure that you have a balanced and biblical understanding.*

◆ *Identify your spiritual gifts. In what ways are you already using them? How might you enhance or develop your contribution?*

E. The Sacraments

1. A sign of grace

A sacrament has been described as 'an outward and visible sign of inward and spiritual grace'.[8] It is a sign of grace that can be seen, smelled, heard, touched, tasted. It draws on the most common human experiences to express divine gifts.

A sacrament is an event in which the truths of faith move into something that is quite beyond theological formulation and human attempts at comprehension. It enables the believer, through experience, to set aside intellectual caution and rationalisation and to allow God's incomprehensible grace to enter and transform their ordinary life. Sacraments deal with the extraordinary, that is the 'inward and spiritual grace', experienced through the ordinary, or the 'outward and visible sign' – extraordinary things like God's saving sacrifice, his inclusive fellowship, his call to discipleship, his forgiving family – ordinary things like a meal shared with those we care about, or a meal for strangers, water for washing, a flag to stand under, a joining of hands.

How the relationship between the visible and ordinary and the invisible and extraordinary is understood varies with church tradition. At one extreme, for the Roman Catholic Church the sign becomes what it signifies; at the other extreme, the relationship is viewed as purely symbolic. All agree that the sacraments point the believer to Christ and his death and Resurrection.

2. The one true Sacrament

Christ has been described as the one, true, original Sacrament. 'He is the way by which men come to the Father and the way by which the grace of God comes to them, the indispensable way.'[9] He invites us to apprehend the ordinary events of his life – birth, baptism and temptation, shared meals and teaching – and his death and Resurrection, in the light of eternal and invisible grace.

3. A sacramental people

As his sacramental people, we find him living and at work in our own life-experiences. We celebrate the presence, the gift, the healing, the reconciliation, the joy in our own life by connecting it with the earthly life of Jesus.

We are a sacramental community because our life, our work, and our celebrations centre on Christ, the one true Sacrament. Our life together is sacramental because we live by faith in him and our everyday lives reveal and offer unexpected grace, his undeserved gift, again and again.

We also recognise that God uses human beings to bring grace to each other. In a similar way to the prophets and apostles, all believers are called to speak on behalf of God by their words and through their lifestyle. The call to holiness of life is a call to sacramental living – demonstrating the grace of God in the ordinary.

4. The Salvation Army and the Sacraments

The Salvation Army is a permanent witness to the Church as to the possibility, and practicability, of sanctification without formal sacraments. Through the experience of holiness, 'the believer has direct communion with God through the spiritual presence of Christ in the heart ... the real presence of Christ is mediated through sanctification to the believer apart from outward forms'.[10] This ongoing commitment to model the conviction that 'no particular outward observance is necessary to inward grace',[11] demonstrates obedience to a specific calling to a distinctive and prophetic role within the Church.

Early in our history, The Salvation Army was led of God not to observe specific sacraments, that is baptism and the Lord's Supper, or Holy Communion, as prescribed rituals. In this we remind ourselves and others of the danger of trusting in the external rather than the grace it signifies or points to, and are a witness to the evidence and availability of that grace in all of human life. Nevertheless, we would also guard against the possibility that non-observance of the sign may also lead to neglect of the reality that is represented.

We do identify with the historic Church through its confession of one faith, one Lord, one baptism of the Holy Spirit, one salvation and one Church universal. We confess one sacramental meal, not administered ritually, but presided over by Christ himself at any table where he is received and honoured.

We observe the sacraments, not by limiting them to two or three or seven, but by inviting Christ to suppers, love feasts, birth celebrations, parties, dedications, sick beds, weddings, anniversaries, commissionings, ordinations, retirements and other significant events and, where he is truly received, watching him give a grace beyond our understanding. We can see, smell, hear, touch and taste it. We joyfully affirm that in our presence is the one, true, original Sacrament – Jesus Christ. And we know that what we have experienced is reality.

◆ *'In certain parts of the world, according to culture, the Army's non-observance of the Sacraments of Holy Communion and water baptism is sometimes not understood. Lack of understanding of the Army's position produces hindrances to the Army's growth and effectiveness.'[12] Are there particular challenges in your own context? What can be done to address them?*

◆ My life must be Christ's broken bread,
My love his outpoured wine,
A cup o'erfilled, a table spread
Beneath his name and sign,
That other souls, refreshed and fed,
May share his life through mine.

My all is in the Master's hands
For him to bless and break;
Beyond the brook his winepress stands
And thence my way I take
Resolved, the whole of love's demands
To give, for his dear sake.

Lord, let me share that grace of thine
Wherewith thou dids't sustain
The burden of the fruitful vine,
The gift of buried grain.
Who dies with thee, O Word divine
Shall rise and live again.[13]

What does this mean for your life?

F. Issues for Salvationists

1. Individual Salvationists and the Body of Christ

Salvationists need to understand the corporate dimension of our faith, we must recognise our place in the Body of Christ and give attention to the role the Church – especially The Salvation Army – plays in our own nurture, spiritual formation, Christian education and spiritual gift development. In this overly-individualised, alienated world we need to demonstrate how redemption through Christ changes the way we live together in community and how the Body of Christ expresses the life of the Kingdom of God.

2. The Salvation Army in the Body of Christ
It is possible that some Salvationists approach Salvationist witness and mission in the world as activities that are separate from the life of the whole Body of Christ. A deeper understanding of our calling and our life together, with other churches, as the Body of Christ, would enhance witness and mission by the Salvationist community to the world. It would encourage understanding of our need to work as partners, supporting one another and sharing our gifts and resources.

3. Salvationists and other denominations
Salvationists have sometimes been tempted to judge other denominations harshly in the light of our own standards, particularly with reference to mission and care for the marginalised. Such superior attitudes are unacceptable and can be counteracted by a proper understanding of the Church and The Salvation Army's place within it. Conversely, some have felt that The Salvation Army has been judged as inferior by other denominations who cannot accept the Salvationist approach to the sacraments. This attitude too is unacceptable and should not be allowed to affect the self-worth or the practice of the Salvationist.

4. Salvationists and the sacraments
In some parts of the world where the Army ministers, there is pressure from other denominations, and sometimes from a few individuals within the Army, to consider re-instituting one or both of the Protestant sacraments, that is baptism and the Eucharist. The Army holds the view that as all of life is sacramental, so is all of worship. Salvationists have the liberty to explore all means by which grace can be received and celebrated.[14] It is helpful and illuminating to consider what truths and values we actually celebrate when we

come together in praise, worship and fellowship to discern the ways in which this might be described as 'sacramental' in its truest sense.

◆ *Identify and research the various expressions of Christian faith and belief in your local area. Reflect upon their distinctive contributions to the universal Christian Church. In what ways are they similar to, or different from, The Salvation Army? What can we learn from them and what could we teach them?*

◆ *Think of your corps as a human body. List the ways in which people in the fellowship enable the body to function. Who in the body has yet to find their role, and what part do you think they might be gifted to play? If possible compare your thoughts with someone else from your corps or community.*

◆ *Do Salvationists need to develop a clearer understanding of the nature and identity of the Church?*

◆ *Consider how your corps or worshipping community is nurturing good disciples of Christ. What might make this even more effective?*

---

[1] Bramwell Booth, 1926, *Echoes and Memories*. London: Hodder & Stoughton: 65

[2] John Calvin, *Institutes of the Christian Religion* Book 4: Chapter 1
http://www.godrules.net/library/calvin/calvin_iv_iv.htm

[3] George Scott Railton, 1887, *Heathen England*. The Salvation Army:145

[4] Bramwell Booth, 1926, *Echoes and Memories*. London: Hodder & Stoughton: 65

[5] Philip Needham, 1987 *Community in Mission: A Salvationist Ecclesiology*. London: International Headquarters :115

[6] First published in *The Salvation Army Year Book* 1994 London: The Salvation Army

[7] *The Salvation Army in the Body of Christ: An Ecclesiological Statement* London: Salvation Books, The Salvation Army International Headquarters: 10-11; Appendix 5

[8] Catechism of the Church of England.

[9] *Handbook of Doctrine* 1969 The Salvation Army: International Headquarters: 187

[10] R. David Rightmire, 1990 *Sacraments and The Salvation Army: Pneumatological Foundations*. Scarecrow Press :184

[11] Robert Street, 2008 *Called to be God's People.* London: Salvation Books:109
[12] Robert Street, 2008 *Called to be God's People.* London: Salvation Books:107
[13] Albert Orsborn, *The Song Book of the Salvation Army* 1986: 512
[14] Robert Street, 2008 *Called to be God's People.* London: Salvation Books: 115

Appendix 1

The Classical Creeds

The historic creeds are brief and comprehensive statements of Christian belief which date from the earliest days of Christianity. They have a twofold purpose. They are a confession of faith; a common testimony to the truth as received in Jesus Christ. They are also a defence of sound teaching; by defining agreed truth they guard against error.

Their beginnings lie in the definitions of Christian experience and faith contained in the New Testament. The earliest confessions of belief were short and simple: for example, 'Jesus is Lord' (1 Corinthians 12:3) or 'I believe that Jesus Christ is the Son of God' (Acts 8:37). They developed into more comprehensive statements which were recited by converts as baptismal confessions of faith when admitted to the fellowship of believers. Later, in the fourth century, the great ecumenical councils of the Church met to refute heresy and more accurately define orthodox faith by the development of commonly agreed statements of belief.

The Apostles' Creed has its foundations in the Old Roman Creed from the early third century, and represents a significant development of the simple trinitarian baptismal formula. While it is not apostolic in authorship, it is nevertheless apostolic in content. It describes the fundamental articles of the Christian faith. The Old Roman Creed was written in Latin but there was a more or less identical older Greek version. The Apostles Creed begins with 'I believe', which is different from some of the later creeds formulated by Church councils, which begin with 'we believe'.

The Nicene Creed was probably based on earlier creeds from Jerusalem and Antioch. Its purpose was to define the true faith and therefore to prove false the teaching of certain heretics. It expresses the faith of the first Ecumenical Council which was held in Nicea in 325 AD. The Creed was enlarged and approved by the Council of Constantinople in 381 AD and confirmed by the Council of Chalcedon in 451 AD. It affirms the unity of God, insists that the Son is God in every respect, and upholds the divinity of the Holy Spirit.

The Nicene Creed is the most ecumenical of the creeds, having acceptance in both the Eastern and Western churches. Even so, a difference of opinion relating to the statement about the Holy Spirit was the cause of a schism between the Eastern and Western churches in 1054 AD. The Latin form of the creed states that the Holy Spirit 'proceeds from the Father and the Son', while the Eastern church retains the original Greek version, 'proceeds from the Father'. This difference is still a difficulty (see Chapter 3).

The Athanasian Creed was formulated in the mid-5th century in Spain or France by an unknown author from the Augustinian tradition. It was written as a teaching resource. Later it was used in services as a credal hymn. It contains a clear and concise statement of the Trinity and the Incarnation of Christ. This creed is not as widespread in its use as the Apostles' Creed and the Nicene Creed.

We can have confidence in the teaching of the creeds, which bring the basic truths of Christianity to us from the proclamation of the Apostles and the life and teaching of the Lord Jesus Christ.

The Apostles' Creed

I believe in God the Father almighty, Maker of Heaven and earth:

And in Jesus Christ his only Son our Lord, who was conceived by the Holy Ghost, born of the Virgin Mary, suffered under Pontius Pilate, was crucified, dead and buried; he descended into Hell; the third day he rose again from the dead. He ascended into Heaven, and sitteth on the right hand of God the Father almighty; from thence he shall come to judge the quick and the dead.

I believe in the Holy Ghost, the holy catholic Church, the communion of saints, the forgiveness of sins, the resurrection of the body, and the life everlasting.

The Nicene Creed

We believe in one God the Father almighty, Maker of Heaven and earth, and of all things visible and invisible.

And in one Lord Jesus Christ, the only-begotten Son of God, begotten of his Father before all worlds, God of God, Light of Light, very God of very God, begotten, not made, being of one substance with the Father, by whom all things were made:

Who for us men and for our salvation came down from Heaven, and was incarnate by the Holy Ghost of the Virgin Mary, and was made man, and was crucified also for us under Pontius Pilate. He suffered and was buried, and the third day he rose again according to the Scriptures, and ascended into Heaven, and sitteth on the right hand of the Father. And he shall come again with glory to judge both the quick and the dead; whose Kingdom shall have no end.

And we believe in the Holy Ghost, Lord and Giver of life, who proceedeth from the Father and the Son, who with the Father and the Son together is worshipped and glorified, who spake by the prophets.

And we believe in one holy catholic and apostolic Church. We acknowledge one baptism for the remission of sins. And we look for the resurrection of the dead, and the life of the world to come.

The Athanasian Creed

Whosoever wills to be in a state of salvation, before all things it is necessary that he hold the catholic [apostolic/universal] faith, which except everyone shall have kept whole and undefiled without doubt he shall perish eternally.

Now the catholic faith is that we worship One God in Trinity and Trinity in Unity; neither confounding the Persons nor dividing the substance. For there is one Person of the Father, another of the Son, and another of the Holy Spirit. But the Godhead of the Father, of the Son and of the Holy Spirit, is One, the Glory equal, the Majesty co-eternal.

Such as the Father is, such is the Son, and such is the Holy Spirit, the Father uncreated, the Son uncreated, and the Holy Ghost uncreated; the Father infinite, the Son infinite, and the Holy Spirit infinite, the Father eternal, the Son eternal, and the Holy Spirit eternal. And yet not three eternals but one eternal, as also not three infinites, nor three uncreated, but one uncreated, and one infinite. So, likewise, the Father is almighty, the Son almighty, and the Holy Spirit almighty, and yet they are not three Almighties but one Almighty.

So the Father is God, the Son God, and the Holy Spirit God; and yet they are not three Gods but one God. So the Father is Lord, the Son Lord, and the Holy Spirit Lord; and yet not three Lords but one Lord. For like as we are compelled by the Christian truth to acknowledge every Person by himself to be God and Lord; so we are forbidden by the catholic religion to say, there be three Gods or three Lords.

The Father is made of none, neither created nor begotten. The Son is of the Father alone, not made nor created but begotten. The Holy Spirit is of the Father and the Son, not made nor created nor begotten but proceeding. So there is one Father not three Fathers, one Son not three Sons, and one Holy Spirit not three Holy Spirits. And in this Trinity there is nothing before or after, nothing greater or less, but the whole three Persons are co-eternal together and co-equal.

So that in all things, as is aforesaid, the Trinity in Unity and the Unity in Trinity is to be worshipped. He therefore who wills to be in a state of salvation, let him thus think of the Trinity.

But it is necessary to eternal salvation that he also believe faithfully the Incarnation of our Lord Jesus Christ. For the right faith therefore is that we believe and confess that our Lord Jesus Christ, the Son of God, is God and Man.

He is God of the substance of the Father begotten before the worlds, and he is man of the substance of his mother born in the world; perfect God, perfect man subsisting of a reasoning soul and human flesh; equal to the Father as touching his Godhead, and inferior to the Father as touching his Manhood.

Who although he be God and man yet he is not two but one Christ; one however not by conversion of the Godhead in the flesh, but by taking of the manhood in God; one altogether not by confusion of substance but by unity of Person. For as the reasoning soul and flesh is one man, so God and man is one Christ.

Who suffered for our salvation, descended into Hell, rose again from the dead, ascended into Heaven, sits on the right hand of the Father, from whence he shall come to judge the living and the dead. At whose coming all men shall rise again with their bodies and shall give account of their own works. And they that have done good shall go into life eternal, and they who indeed have done evil into eternal fire.

This is the catholic faith, which except a man shall have believed faithfully and firmly, he cannot be in a state of salvation.

Glory be to the Father, and to the Son, and to the Holy Spirit; as it was in the beginning, is now, and ever shall be: world without end. Amen.

Appendix 2

The Doctrines of the Methodist New Connexion (1838)

1. We believe that there is one God, who is infinitely perfect, The Creator, Preserver and Governor of all things.

2. We believe that the Scriptures of the Old and New Testaments are given by Divine Inspiration and form a complete rule of faith and practice.

3. We believe that three persons exist in the Godhead: the Father, the Son, and the Holy Ghost, undivided in essence, and co-equal in power and glory.

4. We believe that in the person of Jesus Christ the divine and human natures are united, so that he is truly and properly God, and truly and properly man.

5. We believe that man was created in righteousness and true holiness, but that by his disobedience, Adam lost the purity and happiness of his nature; and, in consequence, all his posterity are involved in depravity and guilt.

6. We believe that Jesus Christ has become the propitiation for the sins of the whole world, that he rose from the dead, and that he ever liveth to make intercession for us.

7. We believe that repentance toward God, and faith in our Lord Jesus Christ, are necessary to salvation.

8. We believe that justification is by grace, through faith, and that he that believeth hath the witness in himself: and that it is our privilege to be fully sanctified in the name of the Lord Jesus Christ, and by the spirit of our God.

9. We believe that man's salvation is of God, and that his damnation is of himself. We believe, also, that in the gospel plan of redemption, men are treated as rational, accountable creatures; that 'it is God that worketh in us to will and to do of his own good pleasure;' and that we are to 'work out our own salvation, with fear and trembling'.

10. We believe that it is possible for man to fall finally from grace.

11. We believe the soul to be immortal, and that after death it immediately enters upon a state of happiness or misery.

12. We believe in the resurrection of the body – in the general judgment at the last day – in the eternal happiness of the righteous – and in the endless punishment of the wicked.

Appendix 3

The Lausanne Covenant

The Lausanne Covenant was drafted by the Congress on World Evangelisation held in 1974 in Lausanne, Switzerland. Two thousand seven hundred participants from 150 nations praised God for his provision of salvation and rejoiced in the evangelical fellowship they discovered in obedience to the Great Commission of their Lord: 'Therefore go and make disciples of all nations, baptising them in the name of the Father and of the Son and of the Holy Spirit, and teaching them to obey everything I have commanded you' (Matthew 28:19, 20).

The adoption of the Lausanne Covenant marked a theological consensus among evangelicals on the basis and nature of evangelisation. Because the evangelical constituency which gathered on that occasion was so diverse in terms of nationality, culture, denomination, theological beliefs and programme priorities, the production of this document was a defining event for the 20th century evangelical community.

The Lausanne Covenant provided a foundation for subsequent meetings of evangelicals. In 1982, a further major consultation of 50 evangelical leaders from six continents was convened in Grand Rapids, Michigan to clarify the relationship between evangelism and social responsibility. That discussion focused on article five of the Lausanne Covenant, entitled 'Christian Social Responsibility'.

Another aspect of the Lausanne Covenant was developed at Lausanne II (1989) when more than 3,000 delegates from 170 countries met in Manila, The Philippines, with the theme, 'Calling the Whole Church to take the Whole Gospel to the Whole World'.

The Manila Manifesto which issued from this consultation, was endorsed by The Salvation Army as part of its Vision 2000 direction for the 1990s.

It may be too early to consider the Lausanne Covenant as a 'creed' in the classical sense of that term. It is included as an appendix of *The Handbook of Doctrine* as having relevance to Salvation Army belief and practice. It has the potential to provide the basis for an evangelical credal statement which unites believers and informs Christian life and mission in the contemporary world.

The Covenant
Let the earth hear his voice

Introduction
We, members of the Church of Jesus Christ, from more than 150 nations, participants in the International Congress on World Evangelisation at Lausanne, praise God for his great salvation and rejoice in the fellowship he has given us with himself and with each other. We are deeply stirred by what God is doing in our day, moved to penitence by our failures and challenged by the unfinished task of evangelisation. We believe the gospel is God's Good News for the whole world, and we are determined by his grace to obey Christ's commission to proclaim it to every person and to make disciples of every nation. We desire, therefore, to affirm our faith and our resolve, and to make public our covenant.

1. The purpose of God
We affirm our belief in the one eternal God, Creator and Lord of the world, Father, Son and Holy Spirit, who governs all things according to the purpose of his will. He has been calling out from the world a people for himself, and sending his people back into the world to be his servants and his witnesses, for the extension of his Kingdom, the building up of Christ's Body, and the glory of his name. We confess with shame that we have often denied our calling and failed in our mission, by becoming conformed to the world or by

withdrawing from it. Yet, we rejoice that even when borne by earthen vessels the gospel is still a precious treasure. To the task of making that treasure known in the power of the Holy Spirit we desire to dedicate ourselves anew.

2. The authority and power of the Bible

We affirm the divine inspiration, truthfulness and authority of both Old and New Testament Scriptures in their entirety as the only written word of God, without error in all that it affirms, and the only infallible rule of faith and practice. We also affirm the power of God's word to accomplish his purpose of salvation. The message of the Bible is addressed to all men and women. For God's revelation in Christ and in Scripture is unchangeable. Through it the Holy Spirit still speaks today. He illumines the minds of God's people in every culture to perceive its truth freshly through their own eyes and thus discloses to the whole Church ever more of the many-coloured wisdom of God.

3. The uniqueness and universality of Christ

We affirm that there is only one Saviour and only one gospel, although there is a wide diversity of evangelistic approaches. We recognise that everyone has some knowledge of God through his general revelation in nature. But we deny that this can save, for people suppress the truth by their unrighteousness. We also reject as derogatory to Christ and the gospel every kind of syncretism and dialogue which implies that Christ speaks equally through all religions and ideologies. Jesus Christ, being himself the only God-man, who gave himself as the only ransom for sinners, is the only mediator between God and people. There is no other name by which we must be saved. All men and women are perishing because of sin, but God loves everyone, not wishing that any should perish but that all should repent. Yet those who reject Christ repudiate the joy of salvation and condemn themselves to eternal separation from God. To proclaim Jesus as 'the Saviour of the world' is not to affirm that all people are either automatically or ultimately saved, still less to affirm that all religions offer salvation in Christ. Rather it is to proclaim God's love for a world of sinners and to invite everyone to respond to him as Saviour and Lord in the whole-hearted personal commitment of repentance and faith. Jesus Christ has been exalted above every other name; we long for the day when every knee shall bow to him and every tongue shall confess him Lord.

4. The nature of evangelism

To evangelise is to spread the Good News that Jesus Christ died for our sins and was raised from the dead according to the Scriptures, and that as the reigning Lord he now offers the forgiveness of sins and the liberating gift of the Spirit to all who repent and believe. Our Christian presence in the world is indispensable to evangelism, and so is that kind of dialogue whose purpose is to listen sensitively in order to understand. But evangelism itself is the proclamation of the historical, biblical Christ as Saviour and Lord, with a view to persuading people to come to him personally and so be reconciled to God. In issuing the gospel invitation we have no liberty to conceal the cost of discipleship. Jesus still calls all who would follow him to deny themselves, take up their cross, and identify themselves with his new community. The results of evangelism include obedience to Christ, incorporation into his Church and responsible service in the world.

5. Christian social responsibility

We affirm that God is both the Creator and the Judge of all. We, therefore, should share his concern for justice and reconciliation throughout human society and for the liberation of men and women from every kind of oppression. Because men and women are made in the image of God, every person, regardless of race, religion, colour, culture, class, sex or age, has intrinsic dignity because of which he or she should be respected and served, not exploited. Hereto we express penitence both for our neglect and for having sometimes regarded evangelism and social concern as mutually exclusive. Although reconciliation with other people is not reconciliation with God, nor is social action evangelism, nor is political liberation salvation, nevertheless we affirm that evangelism and socio-political involvement are both part of our Christian duty. For both are necessary expressions of our doctrines of God and man, our love for our neighbour and our obedience to Jesus Christ. The message of salvation implies also a message of judgment upon every form of alienation, oppression and discrimination, and we should not be afraid to denounce evil and injustice wherever they exist. When people receive Christ they are born again into his Kingdom and must seek not only to exhibit but also to spread its righteousness in the midst of an unrighteous world. The salvation we claim should be transforming us in the totality of our personal and social responsibilities. Faith without works is dead.

6. The Church and evangelism
We affirm that Christ sends his redeemed people into the world as the Father sent him, and that this calls for a similar deep and costly penetration of the world. We need to break out of our ecclesiastical ghettos and permeate non-Christian society. In the Church's mission of sacrificial service, evangelism is primary. World evangelisation requires the whole Church to take the whole gospel to the whole world. The Church is at the very centre of God's cosmic purpose and is his appointed means of spreading the gospel. But a Church which preaches the Cross must itself be marked by the Cross. It becomes a stumbling block to evangelism when it betrays the gospel or lacks a living faith in God, a genuine love for people, or scrupulous honesty in all things including promotion and finance. The Church is the community of God's people rather than an institution, and must not be identified with any particular culture, social or political system or human ideology.

7. Co-operation in evangelism
We affirm that the Church's visible unity in truth is God's purpose. Evangelism also summons us to unity, because our oneness

strengthens our witness, just as our disunity undermines our gospel of reconciliation. We recognise, however, that organisational unity may take many forms and does not necessarily forward evangelism. Yet we who share the same biblical faith should be closely united in fellowship, work and witness. We confess that our testimony has sometimes been marred by sinful individualism and needless duplication. We pledge ourselves to seek a deeper unity in truth, worship, holiness and mission. We urge the development of regional and functional cooperation for furtherance of the Church's mission, for strategic planning, for mutual encouragement and for the sharing of resources and experience.

8. Churches in evangelistic partnership

We rejoice that a new missionary era has dawned. The dominant role of western missions is fast disappearing. God is raising up from the younger churches a great new resource for world evangelisation and is thus demonstrating that the responsibility to evangelise belongs to the whole Body of Christ. All churches should therefore be asking God and themselves what they should be doing both to reach their own area and to send missionaries to other parts of the world. A re-evaluation of our missionary responsibility and role should be continuous. Thus a growing partnership of churches will develop and the universal character of Christ's Church will be more clearly exhibited. We also thank God for agencies which labour in Bible translation, theological education, the mass media, Christian literature, evangelism, missions, church renewal and other specialist fields. They, too, should engage in constant self-examination to evaluate their effectiveness as part of the Church's mission.

9. The urgency of the evangelistic task

More than 2,700 million people, which is more than two-thirds of all humanity, have yet to be evangelised. We are ashamed that so many have been neglected; it is a standing rebuke to us and to the whole Church. There is now, however, in many parts of the world an unprecedented receptivity to the Lord Jesus Christ. We are convinced that this is the time for churches and para-church agencies to pray earnestly for the salvation of the unreached and to launch new efforts to achieve world evangelisation. A reduction of foreign missionaries and money in an evangelised country may sometimes be necessary to facilitate the national church's growth in self-reliance and to release resources for unevangelised areas. Missionaries should flow ever more freely from and to all six continents in a spirit of humble service. The goal should be, by all available means and at the earliest possible time, that every person will have the opportunity to hear, understand and receive the Good News. We cannot hope to attain this goal without sacrifice. All of us are shocked by the poverty of millions and disturbed by the injustices which cause it. Those of us who live in affluent circumstances accept our duty to develop a simple lifestyle in order to contribute more generously to both relief and evangelism.

10. Evangelism and culture

The development of strategies for world evangelisation calls for imaginative pioneering methods. Under God, the result will be the rise of churches deeply rooted in Christ and closely related to their culture. Culture must always be tested and judged by Scripture. Because men and women are God's creatures, some of their culture is rich in beauty and goodness. Because they are fallen, all of it is tainted with sin and some of it is demonic. The gospel does not presuppose the superiority of any culture to another, but evaluates all cultures according to its own criteria of truth and righteousness and insists on moral absolutes in every culture. Missions have all too frequently exported with the gospel an alien culture and churches have sometimes been in bondage to culture rather than to Scripture. Christ's evangelists must humbly seek to empty themselves of all but their personal authenticity in order to become the servants of others, and churches must seek to transform and enrich culture, all for the glory of God.

11. Education and leadership

We confess that we have sometimes pursued church growth at the expense of church depth, and divorced evangelism from Christian nurture. We also acknowledge that some of our missions have been too slow to equip and encourage national leaders to assume their rightful responsibilities. Yet we are committed to indigenous principles and long that every church will have national leaders who manifest a Christian style of leadership in terms not of domination but of service. We recognise that there is a great need to improve theological education, especially for church leaders. In every nation and culture there should be an effective training programme for pastors and laity in doctrine, discipleship, evangelism, nurture and service. Such training programmes should not rely on any stereotyped methodology but should be developed by creative local initiatives according to biblical standards.

12. Spiritual conflict

We believe that we are engaged in constant spiritual warfare with the principalities and powers of evil, who are seeking to overthrow the Church and frustrate its task of world evangelisation. We know our need to equip ourselves with God's armour and to fight this battle with the spiritual weapons of truth and prayer. For we detect the activity of our enemy, not only in false ideologies outside the Church, but also inside it in false gospels which twist Scripture and put people in the place of God. We need both watchfulness and discernment to safeguard the biblical gospel. We acknowledge that we ourselves are not immune to worldliness of thought and action, that is to a surrender to secularism. For example, although careful studies of church growth, both numerical and spiritual, are right and valuable, we have sometimes neglected them. At other times, desirous to ensure a response to the gospel, we have compromised our message, manipulated our hearers through pressure techniques and become unduly preoccupied with statistics or even dishonest in our use of them. All this is worldly. The Church must be in the world; the world must not be in the Church.

291

13. Freedom and persecution

It is the God-appointed duty of every government to secure conditions of peace, justice and liberty in which the Church may obey God, serve the Lord Christ and preach the gospel without interference. We therefore pray for the leaders of the nations and call upon them to guarantee freedom of thought and conscience, and freedom to practise and propagate religion in accordance with the will of God and as set forth in the Universal Declaration of Human Rights. We also express our deep concern for all who have been unjustly imprisoned and especially for those who are suffering for their testimony to the Lord Jesus. We promise to pray and work for their freedom. At the same time we refuse to be intimidated by their fate. God helping us, we, too, will seek to stand against injustice and to remain faithful to the gospel, whatever the cost. We do not forget the warnings of Jesus that persecution is inevitable.

14. The power of the Holy Spirit

We believe in the power of the Holy Spirit. The Father sent his Spirit to bear witness to his Son; without his witness ours is futile. Conviction of sin, faith in Christ, new birth and Christian growth are all his work. Further, the Holy Spirit is a missionary spirit; thus evangelism should arise spontaneously from a Spirit-filled Church. A Church that is not a missionary Church is contradicting itself and quenching the Spirit. Worldwide evangelisation will become a realistic possibility only when the Spirit renews the Church in truth and wisdom, faith, holiness, love and power. We, therefore, call upon all Christians to pray for such a visitation of the sovereign Spirit of God that all his fruit may appear in all his people and that all his gifts may enrich the Body of Christ. Only then will the whole Church become a fit instrument in his hands, that the whole earth may hear his voice.

15. The return of Christ

We believe that Jesus Christ will return personally and visibly, in power and glory, to consummate his salvation and his judgment.

This promise of his coming is a further spur to our evangelism, for we remember his words that the gospel must first be preached to all nations. We believe that the interim period between Christ's Ascension and return is to be filled with the mission of the people of God, who have no liberty to stop before the end. We also remember his warning that false Christs and false prophets will arise as precursors of the final Antichrist. We, therefore, reject as a proud, self-confident dream the notion that people can ever build a utopia on earth. Our Christian confidence is that God will perfect his Kingdom, and we look forward with eager anticipation to that day, and to the new Heaven and earth in which righteousness will dwell and God will reign forever. Meanwhile we rededicate ourselves to the service of Christ and of people in joyful submission to his authority over the whole of our lives.

Conclusion

Therefore, in the light of this our faith and our resolve, we enter into a solemn covenant with God and with each other, to pray, to plan and to work together for the evangelisation of the whole world. We call upon others to join us. May God help us by his grace and for his glory to be faithful to this our covenant! Amen, Allelujah!

(International Congress on World Evangelisation, Lausanne, Switzerland, July 1974, copyright Lausanne Committee for World Evangelisation, used by permission)

Appendix 4

The report of the International Spiritual Life Commission

The Salvation Army has a God-given freedom in Christ which, if used to the full, could enrich the Army's spiritual life and total ministry in ways far beyond those already enjoyed.

This freedom should never be underestimated, undervalued or neglected, but be warmly embraced and positively engaged to the glory of God and for the extension of his Kingdom. It is firmly rooted in the Army's tradition, has always been at the heart of its most inspiring and effective initiatives and points the way ahead for what God has planned for his people.

This is the conviction of the International Spiritual Life Commission, convened by the General to examine and identify aspects of the Army's life which are essential or integral to the spiritual growth of individual Salvationists and the movement itself.

In its five week-long meetings the Commission became increasingly aware both of the rich cultural diversity possessed by the Army (in 2009 at work in 118 countries), and of the unifying power found in its shared universal beliefs and practices.

The commission also took note of the correspondence, papers, suggestions and support given by fellow Salvationists who took up the worldwide opportunity to share in this challenging and exciting task.

Among aspects Salvationists confirmed as integral to the Army's life were its ministry to the unchurched, the priesthood of all believers (total mobilisation), personal salvation, holiness of life, the use of the mercy seat, and social ministry (unreservedly given).

It was when giving consideration to practices of other churches that the value of the Army's freedom in Christ was particularly evident. The setting of fixed forms of words or acts is not part of Salvationist tradition, though the value placed upon them by some other denominations is recognised.

A great deal of time, prayer and consultation was given to examining the value of introducing or reintroducing a form of holy communion. In addition to considering the large amount of correspondence on the subject, the Commission held a number of Bible studies, gave time to further prayer and also arranged for the visit of a former chairman of the Church of England's Doctrine Commission. Many points of view of various persuasions and convictions were considered, and the members of the Commission itself helpfully reflected those differences. Although such differences still exist, the Commission has been able to present its recommendations in a spirit of unity and harmony, recognising the vast potential for innovative worship and ministry within the freedom which the Army already enjoys in Christ.

Sacraments

It was recognised that the forms of worship used by Christians of the early Church (including the common meal) were not known as sacraments, yet the importance of keeping Christ's atoning sacrifice at the centre of its corporate worship has always been vital to the spiritual life of the Army. Recognising the freedom to celebrate Christ's real presence at all meals and in all meetings, the Commission's statement on Holy Communion encourages Salvationists to use the opportunity to explore together the significance of the simple meals shared by Jesus and his friends, and by the first Christians. It also encourages the development of resources for such events, which would vary according to culture, without ritualising particular words or actions.

The Army's long-held beliefs that no particular outward observance is necessary to inward grace, and that God's grace is freely and readily accessible to all people at all times and in all places were unanimously reaffirmed, as was every Salvationist's freedom to share in communion services conducted in other Christian gatherings.

When considering the subject of baptism the Commission recognised the scriptural truth that there is one body and one Spirit ... 'one Lord, one faith, one baptism; one God and Father of all, who is over all and through all and in all' (Ephesians 4:5, 6). All who are in Christ are baptised into the one body by the Holy Spirit (1 Corinthians 12:12, 13).

Swearing-in

There are many ways in which Christians publicly witness to having been baptised into Christ's body. Water baptism is one of them, but the ceremony, like that of the swearing-in of a Salvation Army soldier, is essentially a witness to the life-changing encounter with Christ which has already happened. The ceremony itself is not the encounter and should not be confused with the act of becoming a Christian. Bearing this in mind, the Commission recommends that the Soldier's Covenant, signed by new soldiers, should incorporate reference to each soldier's baptism into Christ by the Holy Spirit at the moment of conversion.

Specific recommendations made by the Commission to the General highlight ways in which preaching and teaching of the word of God should be given prominence. They encourage cultural expressions of worship and give special emphasis to Bible study, education and training. The importance of Salvationists being better informed and more adequately educated on matters of faith was frequently highlighted in the Commission's deliberations.

There is also a strong recommendation that Army leadership at every level should conform to the biblical model of servant leadership. To assist with this, a re-evaluation of structures, ranks and systems is urged, as is the need to make spirituality an essential quality and qualification for leadership in the movement. Training and development of officers and local officers to assist their spiritual development is also regarded as a priority.

Study

In addition to making recommendations at the General's request for his consideration (together with the Army's international leaders), the Commission makes a Call to Salvationists worldwide to recognise that any outward movement of love for the world requires first of all an inward movement from each Christian towards God. The vitality of our spiritual life as a movement will be seen and tested in our turning to the world in evangelism and service, but the springs of our spiritual life are to be found in our turning to God in worship, in the disciplines of life in the Spirit, and in the study of God's word. Twelve specific calls are made, together with complementary affirmations.

In the Call, the Commission expresses its belief that each Salvationist's equipping for spiritual warfare must come from God and be rooted in the conviction of the triumph of Christ. The living out of the Christian life in all its dimensions, personal, relational, social and political, can only be achieved by embracing Christ's lordship and the Holy Spirit's enabling.

The Commission has recognised the impossibility of providing (and the foolishness of attempting to provide) guidelines and strategies that would suit all countries and cultures in which the Army operates. One of the Army's greatest strengths is its diversity of culture, methods and resources.

Nevertheless, the Commission saw again how integral the Army's internationalism and unity are to achieving the world mission given to it by God. The Commission also indicated its readiness to assist with relevant resourcing by providing material that can be used for teaching, clarifying and supporting fellow Salvationists. The teaching aid *Holiness Unwrapped* (with its accompanying DVD) is a recent example. The Commission's work is ongoing in the same way that commitment to God and one another has always been at the heart of the Army. May coming days bring a deeper and revitalised recognition of what God can do in and through his Army by his Spirit and in the freedom which Christ gives.

A Statement on Baptism

After full and careful consideration of The Salvation Army's understanding of, and approach to, the sacrament of water baptism, the International Spiritual Life Commission sets out the following points regarding the relationship between our soldier enrolment and water baptism.

1. Only those who confess Jesus Christ as Saviour and Lord may be considered for soldiership in The Salvation Army.

2. Such a confession is confirmed by the gracious presence of God the Holy Spirit in the life of the believer and includes the call to discipleship.

3. In accepting the call to discipleship Salvationists promise to continue to be responsive to the Holy Spirit and to seek to grow in grace.

4. They also express publicly their desire to fulfil membership of Christ's Church on earth as soldiers of The Salvation Army.

5. The Salvation Army rejoices in the truth that all who are in Christ are baptised into the one body by the Holy Spirit (1 Corinthians 12:13).

6. It believes, in accordance with Scripture, that there 'is one body and one Spirit ... one Lord, one faith, one baptism; one God and Father of all, who is over all and through all and in all' (Ephesians 4:5, 6).

7. The swearing-in of a soldier of The Salvation Army beneath the trinitarian sign of the Army's flag acknowledges this truth.

8. It is a public response and witness to a life-changing encounter with Christ which has already taken place, as is the water baptism practised by some other Christians.

9. The Salvation Army acknowledges that there are many worthy ways of publicly witnessing to having been baptised into Christ's body by the Holy Spirit and expressing a desire to be his disciple.

10. The swearing-in of a soldier should be followed by a lifetime of continued obedient faith in Christ.

A Statement on Holy Communion

After full and careful consideration of The Salvation Army's understanding of, and approach to, the sacrament of Holy Communion*, the International Spiritual Life Commission sets out the following points:

1. God's grace is freely and readily accessible to all people at all times and in all places.

2. No particular outward observance is necessary to inward grace.

3. The Salvation Army believes that unity of the Spirit exists within diversity and rejoices in the freedom of the Spirit in expressions of worship.

4. When Salvationists attend other Christian gatherings in which a form of Holy Communion is included, they may partake if they choose to do so and if the host Church allows.

5. Christ is the one true Sacrament, and sacramental living – Christ living in us and through us – is at the heart of Christian holiness and discipleship.

6. Throughout its history The Salvation Army has kept Christ's atoning sacrifice at the centre of its corporate worship.

7. The Salvation Army rejoices in its freedom to celebrate Christ's real presence at all meals and in all meetings, and in its opportunity to explore in life together the significance of the simple meals shared by Jesus and his friends and by the first Christians.

8. Salvationists are encouraged to use the love feast and develop creative means of hallowing meals in home and corps with remembrance of the Lord's sacrificial love.

9. The Salvation Army encourages the development of resources for fellowship meals, which will vary according to culture, without ritualising particular words or actions.

10. In accordance with normal Salvation Army practice, such remembrances and celebrations, where observed, will not become established rituals, nor will frequency be prescribed.

Terminology varies according to culture and denomination, and is not always interchangeable.

A Call to Salvationists

1. We call Salvationists worldwide to worship and proclaim the living God, and to seek in every meeting a vital encounter with the Lord of life, using relevant cultural forms and languages.

2. We call Salvationists worldwide to a renewed and relevant proclamation of and close attention to the word of God, and to a quick and steady obedience to the radical demands of the word upon Salvationists personally, and upon our movement corporately.

3. We call Salvationists worldwide to recognise the wide understanding of the mercy seat that God has given to the Army; to rejoice that Christ uses this means of grace to confirm his presence; and to ensure that its spiritual benefits are fully explored in every corps and Army centre.

4. We call Salvationists worldwide to rejoice in our freedom to celebrate Christ's real presence at all our meals and in all our meetings, and to seize the opportunity to explore in our life together the significance of the simple meals shared by Jesus and his friends and by the first Christians.

5. We call Salvationists worldwide to recognise that the swearing-in of soldiers is a public witness to Christ's command to make disciples and that soldiership demands ongoing radical obedience.

6. We call Salvationists worldwide to enter the new millennium with a renewal of faithful, disciplined and persistent prayer; to study God's word consistently and to seek God's will earnestly; to deny self and to live a lifestyle of simplicity in a spirit of trust and thankfulness.

7. We call Salvationists worldwide to rejoice in their unique fellowship; to be open to support, guidance, nurture, affirmation and challenge from each other as members together of the body of Christ; and to participate actively and regularly in the life, membership and mission of a particular corps.

8. We call Salvationists worldwide to commit themselves and their gifts to the salvation of the world, and to embrace servanthood, expressing it through the joy of self-giving and the discipline of Christ-like living.

9. We call Salvationists worldwide to explore new ways to recruit and train people who are both spiritually mature and educationally competent; to develop learning programmes and events that are biblically informed, culturally relevant, and educationally sound; and to create learning environments which encourage exploration, creativity, and diversity.

10. We call Salvationists worldwide to restate and live out the doctrine of holiness in all its dimensions – personal, relational, social and political – in the context of our cultures and in the idioms of our day while allowing for and indeed prizing such diversity of experience and expression as is in accord with the Scriptures.

11. We call Salvationists worldwide to join in the spiritual battle on the grounds of a sober reading of Scripture, a conviction of the triumph of Christ, the inviolable freedom and dignity of persons, and a commitment to the redemption of the world in all its dimensions – physical, spiritual, social, economic and political.

12. We call Salvationists worldwide to restore the family to its central position in passing on the faith, to generate resources to help parents grow together in faithful love and to lead their

children into wholeness, with hearts on fire for God and his mission.

The Founders of The Salvation Army declared their belief that God raised up our movement to enter partnership with him in his great business of saving the world. We call upon Salvationists worldwide to reaffirm our shared calling to this great purpose, as signified in our name.

Salvation begins with conversion to Christ, but it does not end there. The transformation of an individual leads to a transformation of relationships, of families, of communities, of nations. We long for and anticipate with joy the new creation of all things in Christ.

Our mission is God's mission. God in love reaches out through his people to a suffering and needy world, a world that he loves. In mission we express in word and deed and through the totality of our lives the compassion of God for the lost.

Our identification with God in this outward movement of love for the world requires a corresponding inward movement from ourselves towards God. Christ says 'come to me' before he says 'go into the world'. These two movements are in relation to each other like breathing in and breathing out. To engage in one movement to the exclusion of the other is the way of death. To engage in both is the way of life.

The vitality of our spiritual life as a movement will be seen and tested in our turning to the world in evangelism and service, but the springs of our spiritual life are to be found in our turning to God in worship, in the disciplines of life in the Spirit, and in the study of God's word.

Affirmations

Worship

1. The meeting
We affirm that God invites us to a meeting in which God is present, God speaks, and God acts. In our meetings we celebrate and experience the promised presence of Christ with his people. Christ crucified, risen and glorified is the focal point, the epicentre of our worship. We offer worship to the Father, through the Son, in the Spirit, in our own words, in acts which engage our whole being: body, soul and mind. We sing the ancient song of creation to its Creator, we sing the new song of the redeemed to their Redeemer. We hear proclaimed the word of redemption, the call to mission and the promise of life in the Spirit.

2. Preaching
We affirm that when the gospel is preached God speaks. The Bible is the written word of God. Preaching is that same word opened, read, proclaimed and explained. When in our human weakness and foolishness we faithfully proclaim and explain the word, the world may hear and see a new thing; God speaks and God acts. To respond in obedient faith results in a decisive encounter with God. We affirm that God speaks profound truth in simple words, common language and potent metaphor, and we confess that at times our words, too often shallow, obscure, archaic or irrelevant, have veiled, not revealed, our God.

3. The mercy seat
We affirm that the mercy seat in our meetings symbolises God's unremitting call to his people to meet with him. It is not only a place for repentance and forgiveness, but also a place for communion and commitment. Here we may experience a deep awareness of God's abundant grace and claim his boundless salvation. The mercy seat may be used by anyone, at any time, and particularly in Army

meetings when, in response to the proclaimed word, all are invited to share loving and humble communion with the Lord.

4. The hallowing of meals

We affirm that the Lord Jesus Christ is the one true sacrament of God. His incarnation and continuing gracious presence with his people by means of the indwelling Holy Spirit is the mystery at the heart of our faith. We hear our Lord's command to remember his broken body and his outpoured blood as in our families and in our faith communities we eat and drink together. We affirm that our meals and love feasts are an anticipation of the feasts of eternity, and a participation in that fellowship which is the Body of Christ on earth.

5. Soldiership

We affirm that Jesus Christ still calls men and women to take up their cross and follow him. This wholehearted and absolute acceptance of Christ as Lord is a costly discipleship. We hear our Lord's command to make disciples, baptising them in the name of the Father, the Son and the Holy Spirit. We believe that soldiership is discipleship and that the public swearing-in of a soldier of The Salvation Army beneath the Army's trinitarian flag fulfills this command. It is a public response and witness to the life-changing encounter with Christ which has already taken place, as is the believer's water baptism practised by some other Christians.

The disciplines of life in the Spirit

6. The disciplines of the inner life

We affirm that the consistent cultivation of the inner life is essential for our faith-life and for our fighting fitness. The disciplines of the inner life include solitude, prayer and meditation, study, and self-denial. Practising solitude, spending time alone with God, we discover the importance of silence, learn to listen to God and discover our true selves. Praying, we engage in a unique dialogue that encompasses adoration and confession, petition and intercession. As we meditate we attend to God's transforming word. As we study we train our minds towards Christlikeness, allowing the word of God to shape our thinking. Practising self-denial, we focus on God and grow in spiritual perception. We expose how our appetites can control us, and draw closer in experience, empathy and action to those who live with deprivation and scarcity.

7. The disciplines of our life together

We affirm the unique fellowship of Salvationists worldwide. Our unity in the Holy Spirit is characterised by our shared vision, mission and joyful service. In our life together we share responsibility for one another's spiritual well-being. The vitality of our spiritual life is also enhanced by our accountability to one another, and when we practise the discipline of accountability our spiritual vision becomes objective, our decisions more balanced, and we gain the wisdom of the fellowship and the means to clarify and test our own thinking. Such spiritual direction may be provided effectively through a group or by an individual. Mutual accountability also provides the opportunity to confess failure or sin and receive the assurance of forgiveness and hope in Christ.

8. The disciplines of our life in the world

We affirm that commitment to Christ requires the offering of our lives in simplicity, submission and service. Practising simplicity we become people whose witness to the world is expressed by the values we live by, as well as by the message we proclaim. This leads to service which is a self-giving for the salvation and healing of a hurting world, as well as a prophetic witness in the face of social injustice.

Training in God's Word

9. Cultivating faith

We affirm that our mission demands the formation of a soldiery which is maturing, and is being equipped for faithful life and ministry in the world. In strategic and supportive partnership with the family, the Christian community has a duty to provide opportunities for growth into maturity by means of preaching and teaching, through worship and fellowship, and by healing and helping.

10. Teaching holiness

We affirm that God continues to desire and to command that his people be holy. For this Christ died, for this Christ rose again, for this the Spirit was given. We therefore determine to claim as God's gracious gift that holiness which is ours in Christ. We confess that at times we have failed to realise the practical consequences of the call to holiness within our relationships, within our communities and within our movement. We resolve to make every effort to embrace holiness of life, knowing that this is only possible by means of the power of the Holy Spirit producing his fruit in us.

11. Equipping for war

We affirm that Christ our Lord calls us to join him in holy war against evil in all its forms and against every power that stands against the reign of God. We fight in the power of the Spirit in the assurance of ultimate and absolute victory through Christ's redemptive work. We reject extreme attitudes towards the demonic: on the one hand, denial; on the other, obsession. We affirm that the Body of Christ is equipped for warfare and service through the gifts of the Spirit. By these we are strengthened and empowered. We heed the injunction of Scripture to value all God's gifts and rejoice in their diversity.

12. Helping the family

We affirm that the family plays a central role in passing on the faith. We also recognise that families everywhere are subject to dysfunction and disintegration in an increasingly urbanised world in which depersonalisation, insignificance, loneliness and alienation are widespread. We believe that in the home where Christ's Lordship is acknowledged and the family is trained in God's word a spiritually enriching and strengthening environment is provided.

Fellowship meals

Recognising that every meal may be hallowed, whether in the home or with a congregation, there are strategic occasions when the planning of a fellowship meal may especially enrich corporate spiritual life. Such occasions could include the following:

- In preparation for and during the Easter period.

- At the beginning of a mission or spiritual campaign.

- At a corps celebration such as an anniversary, a New Year's Eve watchnight service, or the opening of a new building.

- At a soldiers' meeting.

- For the census board or corps council, particularly when important decisions need to be made.
- For the launching of the Annual Appeal when the significance of work/service being undertaken in Christ's name could be emphasised.

- Harvest thanksgiving.

- Between meetings when a meal is required and members of the congregation are unable to travel home to eat because of distance.

- When there has been a breakdown in relationships and healing is sought by reflecting on Christ's great act of reconciliation through the Cross.

- Whenever it is thought that such a gathering would strengthen the spiritual life and wider fellowship of the corps or centre.

- Small group meetings, especially house groups, mid-week meetings or (for example) at the conclusion of a recruits' preparation for soldiership course.

- Corps camps, fellowship weekends or retreats.

Two features of the common fellowship meal in the early New Testament Church were the scope for spontaneity and the element of charity, with the poor being included. These elements are also worth noting.

Appendix 5

The Salvation Army in the Body of Christ

An Ecclesiological Statement

A statement issued by the International Headquarters of The Salvation Army in 2008 by authority of the General, in consultation with the International Doctrine Council and the International Management Council

Summary Statement

1. The Body of Christ on earth (also referred to in this paper as the Church Universal) comprises all believers in Jesus Christ as Saviour and Lord.

2. Believers stand in a spiritual relationship to one another, which is not dependent upon any particular church structure.

3. The Salvation Army, under the one Triune God, belongs to and is an expression of the Body of Christ on earth, the Church Universal, and is a Christian denomination in permanent mission to the unconverted, called into and sustained in being by God.

4. Denominational diversity is not self-evidently contrary to God's will for his people.

5. Inter-denominational harmony and co-operation are to be actively pursued for they are valuable for the enriching of the

life and witness of the Body of Christ in the world and therefore of each denomination.

6. The Salvation Army welcomes involvement with other Christians in the many lands where the Army is privileged to witness and serve.

Amplified Statement

The Body of Christ on Earth

1. WE BELIEVE that the Church, the Body of Christ on earth, often referred to in the New Testament as 'the saints' (*hoi hagioi* – Ephesians 1:23), comprises all who are born not of natural descent, nor of human decision, or a husband's will, but born of God (John 1:13). The Church Universal includes all who believe in the Lord Jesus Christ, confessing him as Saviour and Lord, and witnessing to that sacred commitment through loving mutual submission (Matthew 18:15-20; John 13:34, 35; Ephesians 5:21) and sacrificial service (Mark 8:34; Matthew 20:25-28; John 13:1-17).

   WE DO NOT BELIEVE that the Church Universal depends for its existence or validity upon any particular ecclesiastical structure, any particular form of worship, or any particular observance of ritual.

2. WE BELIEVE that the Church Universal is the whole of the worshipping, witnessing Christian community throughout the centuries comprised of whatever groupings, large or small, accepted or persecuted, wealthy or poor, into which her members may have been gathered in the past or in the present.

   WE DO NOT BELIEVE that an adequate definition of the Body of Christ on earth, the Church Universal, can be confined in terms of ecclesiastical structure, but must rather be stated in terms of a spiritual relationship of grace that must find expression in all ecclesiastical structures. Members of the Body are those who are incorporate in Christ Jesus (Ephesians 1:1) and therefore reconciled to God through his Son. All such are in a spiritual relationship one with the other, which begins and continues regardless of externals, according to the prayer of Jesus that those who are his may be one (John 17:23). These words of Jesus ask for a oneness as is found in the oneness of Father, Son and Holy Spirit. This oneness is spiritual, not organisational.

3. WE BELIEVE that The Salvation Army belongs to, and is a particular communion of, the Church Universal and a representative of the Body of Christ. Christ is the True Vine (John 15:1) and all believers are his living, fruit-bearing branches, exhorted by Scripture to live in Christlike unity (1 Corinthians 12:12).

   WE DO NOT BELIEVE that any community made up of true followers of Christ can rightly be regarded as outside the Church Universal, whatever their history, customs or practices when compared with those of other Christian communities. God alone knows those who are truly his (2 Timothy 2:19).

Denominational variety

4. WE BELIEVE that God's dealings with his people are perfect according to his will, but that human responses are imperfect and prone to error. It may be God's dealings or fallible human responses to those dealings which have brought about the rich and varied denominational tapestry discernible today.

   WE DO NOT BELIEVE that denominational or organisational variety can automatically and in every case be said to be contrary to God's will for his people.

5. WE BELIEVE that God raised up The Salvation Army according to his purposes for his glory and for the proclamation and demonstration of the gospel.

WE DO NOT BELIEVE that The Salvation Army's existence as an independent and distinctive Christian church, having no formal, structural ties with other Christian churches, is an affront to the gospel of Jesus Christ or self-evidently contrary to God's will for the whole of his Body on earth.

6. WE BELIEVE that the practices of The Salvation Army have much in common with the practices of other churches, but that being raised up by God for a distinctive work, the Army has been led of God to adopt the following combination of characteristics:

a) its emphasis upon personal religion and individual spiritual regeneration through faith in Christ leading in turn to a commitment in mission to seek to win others to Christ;

b) its commitment to the unceasing proclamation of the gospel and its insistence that this gospel is for the whosoever;

c) its teaching concerning sanctification and holy living;

d) its teaching that the receiving of inward spiritual grace is not dependent upon any particular outward observance;

e) its worldwide tradition of service (arising out of the compassionate love of Christ for all persons) without discrimination or preconditions, to the distressed, needy and marginalised, together with appropriate advocacy in the public domain on matters of social justice;

f) its willingness to obey the 'great commission' of Jesus Christ, under the guidance of the Holy Spirit, by ongoing expansion of Salvationist witness and service into new countries, with a consequential celebration, with thanksgiving to God, of its internationalism;

g) its preference for non-liturgical and flexible forms of worship, seeking to encourage spontaneity, for example in prayer and in spoken personal witness and testimony;

h) its tradition of inviting public response to the presentation of the gospel message, and its use of the mercy seat for this and other spiritual purposes;

i) its focus, in self-expression, on the biblical military metaphor of living in the world and of serving God as soldiers of Jesus Christ (2 Timothy 2:3; Ephesians 6:11-17);

j) its requirement that adults and children wishing to become full members (soldiers and junior soldiers), and thereby wishing to make a commitment to formal membership of the Body of Christ on earth, should publicly confess their faith in Jesus Christ as Saviour and Lord, the children making a simple statement of faith with promises as to lifestyle and the primary spiritual disciplines, and the adults entering into formal doctrinal and ethical commitments, the latter focusing on the sacredness of human relationships, but including also the personal disciplines of abstention from alcohol, tobacco, and non-medical use of addictive drugs;

k) its wearing of distinctive uniforms as a witness to belonging to Christ and as a signal of availability to others;

l) its encouragement into Salvation Army fellowship of those who do not wish to enter into the full commitment of soldiership (see j above), but are willing to become adherent members as a step in the journey of faith;

m) its recognition of the equal place within the Body of Christ of men and women in all aspects of Christian service, ministry and leadership including the holding of ecclesiological authority;

n) its readiness to use all forms of musical expression in worship and evangelism, and its encouragement in many cultures of the indigenisation of worship expressions and styles.

WE DO NOT BELIEVE it to be self-evidently God's will for his people in the Army that they cast aside in haste the leadings of God or the blessings of the years, but rather, in humility, to value them, learn from them, and harness and adapt them for ongoing relevance in future witness and service.

The local church

7. WE BELIEVE that just as the true Church Universal comprises all who believe on the Lord Jesus Christ, so each denominational church comprises a community of believers who have in common the way the Lord, through the Holy Spirit, has dealt with them as a community. In turn, each denominational church comprises local congregations regularly meeting together for worship, fellowship and service in a relatively confined geographical location.

WE DO NOT BELIEVE that the validity of a denomination or its local congregations depends upon any particular ecclesiastical tradition, structure, hierarchy, form of worship, or ritual. Where even two or three gather in Christ's name there he is present (Matthew 18:20) with a presence no less real than that discerned in larger, more formal, ceremonial or liturgical settings.

The Army's identity

8. WE BELIEVE that The Salvation Army is an international Christian church in permanent mission to the unconverted, and is an integral part of the Body of Christ like other Christian churches, and that the Army's local corps are local congregations like the local congregations of other Christian churches. The Army springs from the Methodist Revival and has remained unassimilated by any other denomination. Like other reformers before him, William Booth did not intentionally set out to found a new denomination. However, through the years Salvationism has moved on in its emerging self-perception, and in the perceptions of others, from being a para-church evangelistic revival movement (at first known as The Christian Mission) to being a Christian church with a permanent mission to the unsaved and the marginalised. Salvationists remain comfortable in being known simply as 'the Army', or a 'mission', or a 'movement', or for certain purposes as a 'charity'. All of these descriptors can be used alongside 'church'. With this multi-faceted identity the Army is welcomed to, and takes its place at, the ecumenical table at local, national and international levels.

WE DO NOT BELIEVE that The Salvation Army's history, structures, practices or beliefs permit it to be understood as anything other than a distinct Christian denomination with a purpose to fulfil and a calling to discharge under God. Similarly, its local corps cannot properly be understood unless seen primarily as local church congregations meeting regularly by grace and in Christ's name for worship, fellowship and service. Typically a local Army congregation will offer an integrated and holistic ministry, with both spiritual and social service dimensions, to the local population. Commissioned officers (both men and women) of The Salvation Army are duly ordained Christian leaders and ministers of the Christian gospel, called by God and empowered by the Holy Spirit to preach and teach biblical, apostolic truth (Acts 2:42), and to serve others in the name of Christ and for his sake.

The Army and other churches

9. WE BELIEVE that it is God's will that harmonious relations are built up and sustained, by divine grace, between Christians everywhere and between all Christian denominations including their local congregations. The Army's numerous and widespread contacts with other Christian communities around the world serve to enrich the Army and to enhance its understanding of the work of the Holy Spirit. For this reason the Army welcomes such contacts and seeks cordially to extend and deepen them.

   WE DO NOT BELIEVE that narrowness or exclusiveness are consistent with God's will for his people, or that God has nothing to teach us by our sharing and co-operating with his people in other denominations. As in humility we learn from others, also we come to the ecumenical table ready to share whatever God in his wisdom has graciously bestowed upon the Army.

10. WE BELIEVE that every visible expression of the Church Universal is endowed with its own blessings and strengths as gifts from God. We respect and admire those strengths, recognising too that because of human frailty every such expression, including The Salvation Army, has its imperfections.

    WE DO NOT BELIEVE it is our task to comment negatively upon, or to undermine, the traditions of other denominations, and certainly not in relation to the sacraments (on which our distinctive, though not unique, position sees the whole of life as a sacrament with a calling from God to Salvationists to witness to a life of sanctity without formal sacraments). It is contrary to our practices to offer adverse comment upon the life of any denomination or local congregation. We seek to be careful not to belittle the doctrines or practices of any other Christian group. The Army places emphasis in its teaching not upon externals but upon the need for each believer personally to experience that inward spiritual grace to which an external observance testifies. We maintain that no external observance can rightly be said to be essential to salvation or to the receiving of divine grace and that the biblical truth is that we can meet with God and receive his grace anywhere at any time through faith. We recognise that external observances such as baptism and eucharist are used in many denominations as a means of grace. We believe that our calling into sanctity without sacraments is not a contradiction of the ways of other churches, but is something beautiful for Christ, to be held in creative tension with the equally beautiful, but very different, practices of other denominations. In the overall economy of God there are no inherent contradictions, but there are creative paradoxes.

11. WE BELIEVE that The Salvation Army was called into being by the will of God, is sustained in being by God's grace, and is empowered for obedience by the Holy Spirit. Its overriding purpose as encapsulated in the name God has given us – The Salvation Army – is therefore to strive to lead men and women and boys and girls into saving faith in Jesus Christ, working tirelessly and for Christ's sake, to develop them in holy living, that they might better serve suffering humanity while remaining unpolluted by the world (James 1:26, 27).

WE DO NOT BELIEVE that we alone are called to these sacred and awesome tasks, and therefore we rejoice exceedingly because in other Christian churches we find co-workers for God.

Appendix 6

Salvation Army Covenants

Junior Soldier's Promise

Having asked God for forgiveness, I will be his loving and obedient child. Because Jesus is my Saviour from sin, I will trust him to keep me good, and will try to help others to follow him. I promise to pray, to read my Bible and, by his help, to lead a life that is clean in thought, word and deed. I will not smoke, take harmful drugs or drink alcoholic drinks.

Soldier's Covenant

Promises made when becoming a soldier in The Salvation Army

HAVING accepted Jesus Christ as my Saviour and Lord, and desiring to fulfil my membership of his Church on earth as a soldier of The Salvation Army, I now by God's grace enter into a sacred covenant.

I believe and will live by the truths of the word of God expressed in The Salvation Army's eleven articles of faith:

We believe that the Scriptures of the Old and New Testaments were given by inspiration of God: and that they only constitute the Divine rule of Christian faith and practice.

We believe that there is only one God, who is infinitely perfect, the Creator. Preserver, and Governor of all things, and who is the only proper object of religious worship.

We believe that there are three persons in the Godhead – the Father, the Son and the Holy Ghost, undivided in essence and co-equal in power and glory.

We believe that in the person of Jesus Christ the Divine and human natures are united, so that he is truly and properly God and truly and properly man.

We believe that our first parents were created in a state of innocency, but by their disobedience they lost their purity and happiness; and that in consequence of their fall all men have become sinners, totally depraved. and as such are justly exposed to the wrath of God.

We believe that the Lord Jesus Christ has, by his suffering and death, made an atonement for the whole world so that whosoever will may be saved.

We believe that repentance towards God, faith in our Lord Jesus Christ and regeneration by the Holy Spirit are necessary to salvation.

We believe that we are justified by grace, through faith in our Lord Jesus Christ; and that he that believeth hath the witness in himself.

We believe that continuance in a state of salvation depends upon continued obedient faith in Christ.

We believe that it is the privilege of all believers to be wholly sanctified, and that their whole spirit and soul and body may be preserved blameless unto the coming of our Lord Jesus Christ.

We believe in the immortality of the soul; in the resurrection of the body; in the general judgment at the end of the world; in the eternal happiness of the righteous; and in the endless punishment of the wicked.

Therefore

I will be responsive to the Holy Spirit's work and obedient to his leading in my life, growing in grace through worship, prayer, service and the reading of the Bible.

I will make the values of the Kingdom of God and not the values of the world the standard for my life.

I will uphold Christian integrity in every area of my life, allowing nothing in thought, word or deed that is unworthy, unclean, untrue, profane, dishonest or immoral.

I will maintain Christian ideals in all my relationships with others: my family and neighbours, my colleagues and fellow Salvationists, those to whom and for whom I am responsible, and the wider community.

I will uphold the sanctity of marriage and of family life.

I will be a faithful steward of my time and gifts, my money and possessions, my body, my mind and my spirit, knowing that I am accountable to God.

I will abstain from alcoholic drink, tobacco, the non-medical use of addictive drugs, gambling, pornography, the occult, and all else that could enslave the body or spirit.

I will be faithful to the purposes for which God raised up The Salvation Army, sharing the good news of Jesus Christ, endeavouring to win others to him, and in his name caring for the needy and the disadvantaged.

I will be actively involved, as I am able, in the life, work, worship and witness of the corps, giving as large a proportion of my income as possible to support its ministries and the worldwide work of the Army.

I will be true to the principles and practices of The Salvation Army, loyal to its leaders, and I will show the spirit of Salvationism whether in times of popularity or persecution.

I now call upon all present to witness that I enter into this covenant and sign these articles of war of my own free will, convinced that the love of Christ, who died and now lives to save me, requires from me this devotion of my life to his service for the salvation of the whole world; and therefore do here declare my full determination, by God's help, to be a true soldier of The Salvation Army.

Officer's covenant

My Covenant
Called by God to proclaim the gospel of our Lord and Saviour Jesus Christ as an officer of The Salvation Army, I bind myself to him in this solemn covenant: to love and serve him supremely all my days, to live to win souls and make their salvation the first purpose of my life, to care for the poor, feed the hungry, clothe the naked, love the unlovable, and befriend those who have no friends, to maintain the doctrines and principles of The Salvation Army, and, by God's grace, to prove myself a worthy officer.

Done in the strength of my Lord and Saviour, and in the presence of [the following wording to be adapted to local circumstances] the Territorial Commander, training college officers and fellow cadets.

How to use the *Handbook of Doctrine*

The Handbook of Doctrine provides an exposition of the Salvation Army Articles of Faith and a source of study material for use by individuals and groups. It can help us to understand our faith better and challenges us to discern the ways in which what we believe provides the foundation for our daily living as Salvationists.

The beginning of each chapter provides the formal and officially approved Salvation Army exegesis of the doctrine. This is the starting point for our study and reflection. It offers an expanded explanation of the meaning of the doctrine in the context of Scripture, including biblical references at relevant points. It will be best understood if the biblical references are read and considered alongside the text of the Handbook.

The second part of each chapter, entitled 'For further exploration' offers relevant study materials related to the doctrine and, in some instances, a brief introduction to associated theological topics. It shows how Salvation Army doctrine is connected to, and grows from, the historic faith of the Christian Church through the centuries. It raises issues for Salvationists to consider in our personal spiritual life, in our corps life, in our life as a denomination, and in our life in the world.

At regular intervals there are suggested activities, ideas for reflection and topics for discussion. It is not envisaged that any individual or group will do all of these, or that all will be relevant in every context, but they are offered as possible ways of grounding the study in our individual and corporate lives.

The book can be used in a number of ways by individuals and groups for study and spiritual development. These include:

- Bible studies relating to individual doctrines, or a series. Look carefully at the Bible references given. How are they enlarging your understanding of God, his dealings with humanity and your place in the Kingdom of God?

- Use the 'for further exploration' sections as a study guide to add to your theological knowledge. This can be done either as an individual or in a group. Regularly review what you are learning and consider how it is enhancing your faith.

- Begin from one of the discussion questions which relates to your own context eg Chapter 2, For further exploration A 'There is only one God. What opportunities and challenges does this belief bring in your cultural context?' Explore the issues that are relevant. What specifically is significant for you – secularism? other faiths? How does this affect your congregation or the people among whom you are working? Read the exposition of the doctrine. How can this help to shape your mission or your teaching?

- Invite a group or an individual to work through some of the creative activities, and to devise some of their own which are inspired by particular doctrines. Hold an exhibition at which they display their work and describe the theological significance.

- Link a discussion group to a series of meetings which take individual doctrines as their theme. Either use the suggested topics or devise questions related to your particular situation.

- Use the Salvation Army Lectionary (Appendix 8) as the basis of a planned preaching programme.

- Use your Salvation Army songbook to provide poetry on which you reflect and from which you gain inspiration. Some options are offered, but there are many others which can offer insight.

- Take individual paragraphs and, having explored and reflected on their meaning, use them as a starting point for prayer, for example Chapter 2D2 'Caring for God's World'. This could then lead to discussion of the practical things you can do as stewards of God's world.

- Convene a discussion group that looks at current social and political issues in the light of our faith. Reflect upon a news item – local, national or international – how can the *Handbook of Doctrine* help to inform our response as Salvationists? What do we know about the nature of God, humanity and redemption that might enable us to assess and analyse the situation? Use the reflections as a basis for prayer and any practical action that might be appropriate.

- Select a theme and follow it through the whole Handbook. Examples include God's character – Chapters 2B, 6A E, 7C D, 8C, 10, 11: Humanity and our response to God – Chapters 3C 5, 6 C D E, 7 A B, 8 A B , 9 B C, 10, 11C: God's mission in the world – Chapters 2F, 4E 5F, 6F, 7 D4, 10B4, 11D; A Salvationist understanding of the Church.

Other ways of using the book will be relevant in particular situations. Studying and reflecting on Salvation Army doctrine can be enjoyable, life enhancing, a source of spiritual enrichment and of personal development. Care must be taken that it does not become a theoretical issue, divorced from the reality of Christian living in the

21st century. Doctrine arises from the development of Christian beliefs which have been formed in the life of the Church as it has struggled with the challenges of its time. It is the elucidation of the Word that is the 'light for our path' (Psalm119:105) and is relevant to the present and the future as we 'explore boldly the mysteries of a new time, by the light of ancient truth, confident that the light will not fail.'[1]

---

[1] Morris West 1990 *Lazarus* London: Mandarin: 178

Appendix 8

A Salvation Army Lectionary

Based on *The Handbook of Doctrine*

The following is a lectionary which allows the *Handbook of Doctrine* to be covered within approximately one year.

Each Sunday or Church/Army festival is assigned a portion or text which will provide a theme for the day. The Scripture portions suggested in the *Handbook of Doctrine* will provide inspiration for a variety of approaches to the subject in question. The lectionary selects particular themes for major festivals and then provides suggestions for Sunday themes throughout the year. Although part B works systematically through the chapters, there is no reason why it cannot be rearranged thematically, to support and develop the themes of the festivals, or simply to give variety through the year. Anyone following the lectionary will find that the main themes of the Christian faith are covered and this will provide a balanced programme of teaching to nourish and nurture disciples. Discerning preachers and teachers will best know their own people's needs.

The lectionary lists:

A.   Major festivals of the Church and of the Salvation Army year

B.   Sunday themes for the rest of the year

Where there are no preaching opportunities on a weekday festival, the chosen portion could be used on a Sunday either before or after the date.

A. Major festivals of the Church and of the Salvation Army year

328

B. Sunday themes for the rest of the year

330

331

332

333

Appendix 9

People and events from Church history

Abelard, Peter (1079-1142 AD)
Abelard was a French theologian, academic and philosopher who spent time as both a monk and a hermit. He contributed to the understanding of the Atonement, particularly by developing Augustinian ideas that the Incarnation of Jesus was a demonstration of the extent of God's love which therefore evokes a response of love from humanity.

Alexander of Alexandria (d. c 326AD)
Alexander was Bishop of Alexandria and was the leader of the opposition to Arianism at the Council of Nicea (325 AD), although his deacon Athanasius, who would later succeed Alexander, was the spokesperson.

Anselm of Canterbury (c1033-1109 AD)
Anselm was a Benedictine monk who was Archbishop of Canterbury 1093-1109 AD. He is famous as the originator of the ontological argument for the existence of God.

Apollinarius (c310-390 AD)
Known as Apollinarius of Laodicea, Apollinarius was an enthusiastic supporter of Athanasius, but his views led him to extreme conclusions. His position was condemned by the Council of Constantinople.

Aquinas, Thomas (1225-1274 AD)

Thomas Aquinas was an Italian priest and theologian who was also a monk in the Dominican order. He is regarded as the greatest theologian of his age and his work has been key to the development of theology, particularly in Roman Catholic circles. His work draws on Augustine and the philosopher Aristotle, and is sometimes described as Thomist theology. He is known and quoted variously as Aquinas, St Thomas or Thomas, as well as by his full name.

Arius (c250-c336 AD)

An Egyptian priest who believed that Jesus was the first created being, Arius was opposed by Athanasius. He was excommunicated by his Bishop, Alexander of Alexandria, and his works destroyed.

Arminius, Jacobus (1560-1609 AD)

Arminius is famous as the leading opponent to the five points of Calvinism, hence the subsequent development of the Arminian theology which was influential in Wesley's theology and subsequently in the development of Salvation Army doctrine. Arminius was a Dutch theologian and pastor.

Athanasius (c296-c373 AD)

Athanasius was an Egyptian priest who is best known for his conflict with Arius at the Council of Nicea (Chapter 4). He later became Bishop of Alexandria.

Augustine of Hippo (354-430 AD)

One of the most influential Christian thinkers in the history of the Church, Augustine became Bishop of Hippo in North Africa in 395 AD. He is one of the founders of systematic theology, with his most significant contributions concerning the doctrines of the Church, grace and the Trinity.

Barth, Karl (1886-1968 AD)

Barth was a Swiss Reformed theologian who is considered to be one of the most influential theological thinkers of the 20th century. For

Barth, theology seeks to keep the proclamation of the Church faithful to its foundation in Jesus Christ, as revealed in the Bible.

Basil of Caesarea (c330-379 AD)

One of the Cappadocian Fathers, with Gregory of Nazianus and Gregory of Nyssa, Basil was a theologian and a monastic. He supported the Nicene Creed, opposing the viewpoints of both Arianism and Apollinarnism.

Bohler, Peter (1712-1775 AD)

A German-born Moravian missionary, Peter Bohler was influential in the Americas and England during the 18th century. He was a significant influence in John Wesley's spiritual development.

Bonhoeffer, Dietrich (1906-1945 AD)

Bonhoeffer was a Gerrman Lutheran pastor and theologian who was involved in the German Resistance movement in opposition to Hitler. This led to his arrest and execution just before the end of the Second World War. His work has been a significant factor in the development of theological thinking throughout the second half of the 20th century.

Booth, Bramwell (1856-1929 AD)

The son of William and Catherine Booth, Bramwell Booth was the second General of The Salvation Army. From 1881 until 1912, when he became General on the promotion to Glory of William Booth, Bramwell was the Chief of the Staff and was responsible for many of the developments in the organisation and governance of the movement. Bramwell was also known as a teacher of the doctrine of holiness.

Booth, Catherine (1829-1890 AD)

Known as the 'Army Mother' and co-founder of The Salvation Army, Catherine Booth was vital to the formulation of Salvation Army doctrine and practice. Although particularly known for her defence of women's ministry, she was a significant voice in all aspects of

Salvation Army development, including the focus upon holiness teaching and the decision to discontinue the sacraments of Baptism and The Lord's Supper.

Booth, William (1829-1912 AD)
William Booth was a minister in the Methodist New Connexion who by calling and conviction was an evangelist. His itinerant ministry eventually led to the development of The Christian Mission from which The Salvation Army grew and developed. Alongside the need for personal conversion, Booth was convinced of the need for the developing life of holiness in the Christian believer. Booth came to believe that genuine Christian religion also includes the relief of human suffering.

Brengle, Samuel Logan (1860-1936 AD)
Brengle was an American Salvation Army officer whose writing on holiness shaped much of the understanding of the doctrine in The Salvation Army in the first half of the 20th century. He believed in a 'second work of grace' that would lead to a state of 'perfect love'. The work of Brengle continues to inform the holiness teaching of The Salvation Army and other holiness movements.

Calvin, John (1509-64 AD)
Calvin was a French theologian and pastor during the Protestant Reformation who was influenced by the Augustinian tradition. His theology, known as Calvinism, includes the doctrine of predestination and the absolute sovereignty of God in salvation. 'Calvinism' is sometimes used to refer to the theology of people or religious bodies, such as the Reformed church, which were deeply influenced by Calvin's work.

Cappadocian Fathers
This term is used to describe three major Greek-speaking theologians of the patristic period: Basil of Caesarea and Gregory of Nyssa, who were brothers, and Gregory of Nazianus. Cappadocia is the area in Asia Minor (now Turkey) where they lived and worked.

Cerinthus (c100 AD)

Cerinthus was an Egyptian gnostic heretic who may have been Jewish. The exact dates of his birth and death are unknown. He founded a school and gathered disciples, teaching a mixture of Gnosticism, Judaism and Ebionitism.

Council of Chalcedon/ Caledonian Definition (451 AD)

The Council of Chalcedon was an ecumenical church council which focused particularly on the divine and human natures of Jesus Christ and which led to the formulation of the Chalcedonian definition (for further exploration 4C2c).

Council of Nicea/Nicene Creed (325 AD)

This is believed to have been the first truly ecumenical council of the Christian Church which resulted in the Nicene Creed, a statement which was significant in defining the Church's understanding of the relationship between God the Father and Jesus Christ.

Cyril of Alexandria (375-444 AD)

Cyril, the Pope of Alexandria, was influential in the 5th-century Church, especially on Christological issues, emphasising the unity of the divinity and humanity of Christ.

Cyril of Jerusalem (c315-386 AD)

Cyril became Bishop of Jerusalem, probably in late 350AD. Although by nature inclined to conciliation and compromise, in the Nicene controversy he supported Athanasius, which led to difficulties with his Arian supporting superiors and therefore to periods of exile.

Edwards, Jonathan (1703-1758 AD)

Edwards was an American Calvinist preacher, theologian and missionary to native Americans. He was an influential figure in the American revival known as the Great Awakening, and in the early development of the holiness movement.

Erasmus of Rotterdam (c1466-1536 AD)
Erasmus was a Dutch priest and scholar whose work was foundational to the Protestant Reformation, although he was not a Protestant. He believed that the future vitality of Christianity would be determined by the laity rather than the clergy, and was responsible for the first printed text of the Greek New Testament.

Eusebius of Caesarea (c263-c339 AD)
Eusebius became Bishop of Caesarea c 314. He is often described as the father of Church history because of his work in recording the history of the Early Church.

Eutyches (c380-c456 AD)
Eutyches was a priest at Constantinople who challenged the work of Nestorius. However, his belief in Christ as a third kind of being led to his condemnation for heresy at the Council of Chalcedon.

Gregory of Nazianzus (c329-389 AD)
Gregory was influential in the development of Trinitarian theology, particularly regarding the relationship between the Father, Son and Holy Spirit. He was one of the Cappadocian fathers.

Gregory of Nyssa (c330-395 AD)
A priest and bishop, Gregory was one of the Cappadoican fathers. He defended the Nicene Creed against Arianism at the Council of Constantinople in 381 AD. He was the younger brother of Basil of Caesarea.

Irenaeus (c130- c200 AD)
One of the earliest theologians, Irenaeus eventually became Bishop of Lyons. He was a defender of Christian orthodoxy in the face of heresy, especially Gnosticism.

Joachim of Fiore (1132-1202 AD)
Joachim was a mystic and theologian who was the founder of the monastic order of San Giovanni.

Josephus, Flavius (c37-100 AD)

Josephus was a Jewish historian who eventually became a Roman citizen. His work provides insight into Jewish history, religion and culture in biblical times. He is quoted as an extra-biblical source for the historical existence of Jesus.

Luther, Martin (1483-1546 AD)

Luther initiated the Protestant Reformation in 1517 by claiming that salvation could not be bought either by works or with money. He taught that salvation is a free gift of God, that justification can only be received by grace, through faith in Jesus Christ (Chapter 7) and that all Christians belong to the priesthood of all believers (Study notes: The Church). Luther also translated the Bible into the language of the people (German), thus making the biblical text more accessible.

Marcion (c85-c160 AD)

Marcion was the first Christian leader to propose a definitive list of texts for Christianity, a canon of the New Testament. However, his theology was judged to be seriously flawed by other Church leaders and he was excommunicated as a heretic. This may have contributed to the idea that the Church must be the guardian of sound, or orthodox, Christian teachings.

Moltmann, Jurgen (1926-)

Moltmann is a German Protestant theologian whose theology of the crucified God challenged the idea that God cannot suffer. His theology of the suffering God has shaped some strands of theological thinking regarding the problem of evil and suffering.

Nestorius (c386-451 AD)

Nestorius was Archbishop of Constantinople from 428-431 AD, when he was removed from office and declared a heretic by the Council of Ephesus.

Origen of Alexandria (c185-c254 AD)

Origen developed the idea of the allegorical interpretation of Scripture, which he claimed would give a deeper spiritual meaning than other forms of biblical interpretation. He also believed in distinguishing between the full divinity of the Father and the lesser divinity of the Son. This may have influenced the thinking of Arius (Chapter 3).

Patristic Period

Derived from the Latin *pater* (father), this covers the broad period from the end of the New Testament writing until the Council of Chalcedon (451 AD). Many theological ideas which have shaped the development of Christian belief were formed during this period.

Pelagius (c354-c420 AD)

Pelagius denied the doctrine of original sin. His emphasis upon free will and human responsibility is known as Pelagianism. It is contrasted with Augustine's emphasis on the power of original sin to negate, or severely hamper, human freedom. He was excommunicated at the Council of Carthage.

Pliny the Younger (62-113 AD)

Pliny was a Roman official whose writings give insight into life in the first century AD. His work contains a brief reference to Jesus.

Protestant Reformation

A term describing the 16th century movement which criticised the practices and theology of the Roman Catholic Church. It is derived from the Latin *protestari* which means to witness. Initially conceived as a reforming movement within the Church, it eventually evolved into a new group of churches with varying emphases and distinctive theology.

Railton, George Scott (1849-1913AD)

An early pioneer in The Salvation Army, Railton worked with William, Catherine and Bramwell Booth in shaping the fledging movement. Intelligent, articulate and with strong convictions, Railton was instrumental in establishing the work of The Salvation Army in a number of countries including the United States of America, Germany and West Africa.

Second Vatican Council (1962-65)
The Council was convened by Pope John XXIII in order to review the theology and practices of the Roman Catholic Church. It became a landmark event which shaped Roman Catholic theology and traditions in the second half of the 20th century, including liturgy, ecclesiology and understanding of the role of Scripture in the Church. Significant reforms to Roman Catholic Church practice and policy resulted from the Council's deliberations and report.

Spener, Philip Jacob (1635-1705 AD)
A German theologian, Spener is known as the father of pietism through the influence of his book *Pia Desideria* (1675) which addressed the need for the revitalisation of the Church.

Suetonius (c69-c140 AD)
Suetonius was a Roman historian whose most significant surviving work was a history of the battles of the 12 Roman Emperors from Julius Caesar to Domitian. He makes one reference to Jewish disturbances in Rome 'at the instigation of one Chrestus'.

Tacitus (c55 – after 117 AD)
A Senator and historian of the Roman Empire, Tacitus makes a brief reference to Jesus as 'suffering the extreme penalty during the reign of Tiberius'.

Tertullian (c160-c225 AD)
Influential in the development of the doctrine of the Trinity, Tertullian may have been the first to use the term. He believed in the sufficiency of Scripture – that no reference to secular philosophy is necessary to give a true knowledge of God.

Tyndale, William (c1494-1536 AD)
Between 1525 and 1535 William Tyndale translated the New Testament and half of the Old Testament into English. Hostility to his work forced him to work in Europe, smuggling the Bibles back into England. Copies of the translations were hunted out and destroyed by the established church. He was martyred as a heretic near Brussels in 1536.

von Zinzendorf, Nicolas Ludwig Graf (1700-1760 AD)
The Imperial Count of Zinzendorf and Pottendorf, Zinzendorf was a German religious and social reformer and the founder of the Moravians.

Waldo, Peter (c1140-1218 AD)
Waldo was the founder of a spiritual movement of the Middle Ages, known as the Waldensians. He advocated voluntary poverty, lay preaching and the translation of the Bible into the language of the people.

Wesley, John (1703-1791 AD)
John Wesley was an Anglican clergyman and theologian whose open-air preaching, Arminian theology and emphasis upon personal experience and developing discipleship eventually led to the founding of the Methodist Church. Wesley's theology, including his emphasis upon the possibility of salvation for all people and growth towards holiness, were vital in the development of Salvation Army doctrine.

Whitefield, George (1714-1770 AD)
Whitefield was an Anglican minister who was a gifted and effective evangelist in both the United Kingdom and the United States of America. He is credited with suggesting the idea of open-air preaching to John Wesley. In contrast with Wesley's Arminian beliefs, Whitefield was a Calvinist.

Glossary of theological terms

abba:
a common Aramaic word from the time of Jesus meaning 'father', expressing the closest possible father-child relationship

adoptionism:
belief that Jesus was only human and was chosen to be Son of God during his lifetime

Anabaptist:
the term is derived from the Greek word for re-baptiser. The Anabaptists were the most radical group of the 16th century reformers who viewed the Church as an alternative society, an 'assembly of the righteous'

Apocrypha:
'hidden writings' – ancient writings whose place in Scripture is disputed

apostolic:
with the authority, from the time, or in the tradition of the apostles

Arianism:
an early heresy that essentially denied the full divinity of Jesus Christ

assurance:
confidence in the reality of personal salvation, made possible by the work of the Holy Spirit

atonement:
literally, 'at-one-ment', restoration of a right relationship with God

canon:
(canonical)
literally, 'a rod or measuring stick', the universally accepted list of books belonging within the Bible

catholic:
from a Greek word meaning 'universal' and referring to the Church as a whole, not a particular denomination

Christology:
theology which explores the identity of Jesus Christ, particularly in relation to his divine and human nature

conversion:
the act of turning to Christ, including both repentance and saving faith

344

covenant: (covenantal)	a binding agreement between two parties; in Scripture, the agreement offered to humanity by God of loving faithfulness in return for complete devotion
creed:	a corporate statement of belief, used to (credal) express commitment to the faith
deism:	a belief that God exists, while denying that he actively reveals himself or intervenes in the world in any way
demonic:	pertaining to the devil or evil supernatural powers
depravity: (total)	the corrupted, perverted nature of humanity under the power of original sin
docetism:	a heresy which essentially denied the full humanity of Jesus Christ
dualism: (dualistic)	the belief that there are two co-equal eternal realities, one good and the other evil
Ebionitism:	an early heresy that regarded Jesus as a purely human figure, though specially gifted by God
Eschatology:	theology which deals with 'last things'
Evangelical:	a term used to denote theological groups and churches which place specific emphasis on the atoning death of Christ, the authority of Scripture and personal faith
faith:	confident, obedient trust in the living God
feminist theology:	movement which looks at theology, church practices, traditions and the biblical text from the perspective of women
grace:	the persistent, loving favour of God towards undeserving humanity
heresy: (heretical)	belief which is contrary to Christian doctrine

humanism: (humanist)	a belief that humanity in itself is capable of improving the world by moral development and education
immortality:	life untouched by decay and death, never-ending, eternal life
inbred sin:	the corrupted, perverted nature of humanity under the power of original sin
Incarnation: (incarnate)	the act of becoming flesh, as God took on full humanity for our salvation and became a man in Jesus of Nazareth
inspiration:	literally 'in-breathing', the stimulation of the mind, spirit or creative abilities by the aid of the Holy Spirit
justification:	God's act of declaring people to be righteous before him, accepting them despite their past sins
liberation theology:	type of theology which seeks to bring justice for the marginalised and oppressed
millennialism:	beliefs connected with the end times, especially that the Kingdom of God will flourish for a thousand years on earth
modalism:	a doctrine of God which denies that there are three distinct persons in the Godhead; each person is seen as one aspect, or mode, of God's existence
monotheism:	the belief that there is only one God
mythology: (mythologies)	traditional narratives which express world views and truths, and explain moral codes and religious rituals
ontological argument:	argument for the existence of God based upon the necessity of divine existence
original sin:	the inclination to sin which arises from the Fall, and is basic to fallen human nature
orthodoxy:	literally 'right teaching', belief consistent with Christian truth

pantheism:	the belief that all living things are divine, and so the objects of worship
parousia:	the return of Christ in glory, often referred to as the Second Coming
Pentecost:	the name for the Jewish Feast of Weeks, associated by Christians with the first, great outpouring of the Holy Spirit and the beginning of the Christian Church
pluralism: (pluralist)	the existence of many ethnic and religious groups in society or the belief that all religious views are equally valid
polytheism:	belief in and worship of more than one god
predestination:	a belief of some Christians that God has already determined who will be saved
prevenient grace:	literally 'grace' which 'comes before', the action by which God prepares and helps the hearer to seek him and find salvation
Protestant:	term referring to the churches arising from the work of the 16th century reformers in Europe. Now used widely as a term to denote churches which are neither Orthodox nor Roman Catholic
regeneration:	literally 're-birth', the renewal by the Holy Spirit which comes with the acceptance of God's grace
reincarnation:	the belief that all souls are immortal and live many succeeding lives on earth
repentance:	change of direction; the action of turning away from sin and towards God
revelation:	God's action in making himself known to the world
righteousness: (righteous)	being in a right relationship with God and people

sacrament: (sacramental)	an action or ceremony used in Christian worship which is an outward sign and has an inner meaning
sanctification:	the crisis and process by which the Christian's life and character become Christlike, through the work of the Holy Spirit
subordinationism:	a belief that God the Son and God the Holy Spirit are inferior to God the Father
syncretism:	an attempt to combine distinct and different religious teaching, a mixture of religious ideas from many sources
transcendence:	God's nature which extends beyond the limitations of his creation
Trinity: (triune, trinitarianism)	belief in one God who is at the same time Father, Son and Holy Spirit
tritheism:	belief that the Trinity is not one God but three
vicarious:	something borne or done on behalf of another, used especially of the sacrifice of Christ on the Cross
wrath:	God's active opposition to evil in all its forms, the other side of his love

Glossary of English usage

accountability: responsibility, to others or to God

allegiance: loyalty to authorities or to God

awe: reverential fear or wonder in the presence of God

beguile: cheat, seduce, divert attention

community: body of people with shared identity, goals and relationships

consensus: agreement by reaching common ground

consummation: completion; reaching the desired end; fulfilment

corporate: having to do with a body of people rather than an individual

cosmos: the universe as an ordered whole

deity: divine status; divinity

destiny: final goal or purpose of existence

dilemma: having to choose between difficult alternatives

empower: to give authority with support; to enable
(empowerment)

essence: basic nature or quality

faulty: imperfect, untrue

foreshadow: to give a prior sign with characteristics of what is to come

foretaste: prospect; advance enjoyment

foundational: basic

guarantee: pledge; security; token of commitment

hallmark: mark used by goldsmiths to confirm a standard

hierarchy:	organised, graded status
inaugurate:	begin, initiate
indifferent:	uninterested, uncaring
integral:	necessary to the whole; essential
investment:	something used or given to produce growth
jealous:	pained by unfaithfulness
luminous:	giving off light
lurking:	hidden; watching without being seen, usually with evil intent
malevolent: (malevolence)	desiring evil to others
manifestation:	revelation, clear evidence or proof
mar:	ruin or spoil
mysticism:	the practice of contemplating mysteries and/or seeking union with the divine
neo-paganism:	new versions of pagan beliefs
overwhelming:	overpowering
pervasive:	spread throughout
philosophy:	love of knowledge or truth
precursor:	forerunner; something that goes before
potency:	power; might; strength
radical:	springing from its root and returning to basic principles
ransom:	sum of money or value paid for release
reconciliation:	coming together following separation, the healing of broken relationships

remorse:	deep regret for wrong done
resuscitate:	revive, restore to life
simultaneous:	occurring or operating at the same time
spiritism:	communication with departed spirits
substitute:	someone who fills a place for another
tangible:	what can be touched or clearly grasped
thwart:	frustrate, prevent
traumatic:	involving deep emotional upheaval
travesty:	an unworthy, unrealistic imitation
unique:	unmatched, unequalled
validity:	soundness; truth

Index

K